Building Natural Language Generation Systems

This book explains how to build Natural Language Generation (NLG) systems – computer software systems which use techniques from artificial intelligence and computational linguistics to automatically generate understandable texts in English or other human languages, either in isolation or as part of multimedia documents, Web pages, and speech output systems. Typically starting from some nonlinguistic representation of information as input, NLG systems use knowledge about language and the application domain to automatically produce documents, reports, explanations, help messages, and other kinds of texts.

The book covers the algorithms and representations needed to perform the core tasks of document planning, microplanning, and surface realization, using a case study to show how these components fit together. It also discusses engineering issues such as system architecture, requirements analysis, and the integration of text generation into multimedia and speech output systems.

It is essential reading for researchers interested in NLP, AI, and HCI, and for developers interested in advanced document-creation technology.

Ehud Reiter is a lecturer in Computing Science at the University of Aberdeen. He previously worked at the University of Edinburgh and at CoGenTex, a small company that specialises in building NLG systems. He completed his Ph.D. at Harvard University in 1990. He is currently secretary of SIGGEN, the ACL Special Interest Group on (Natural Language) Generation.

Robert Dale is director of the Microsoft Research Institute at Macquarie University in Sydney, Australia; he also leads the Institute's Language Technology Group. He previously lectured at the University of Edinburgh, where he completed his Ph.D. in 1988. He has authored and edited three previous books on NLG topics.

T0279670

Studies in Natural Language Processing

Building Natural Language Generation Systems

Ehud Reiter
University of Aberdeen

Robert Dale
Macquarie University

CAMBRIDGE
UNIVERSITY PRESS

CAMBRIDGE UNIVERSITY PRESS
Cambridge, New York, Melbourne, Madrid, Cape Town, Singapore, São Paulo

Cambridge University Press
The Edinburgh Building, Cambridge CB2 2RU, UK

Published in the United States of America by Cambridge University Press, New York

www.cambridge.org
Information on this title: www.cambridge.org/9780521620369

© Cambridge University Press 2000

This publication is in copyright. Subject to statutory exception
and to the provisions of relevant collective licensing agreements,
no reproduction of any part may take place without
the written permission of Cambridge University Press.

First published 2000
This digitally printed first paperback version 2006

A catalogue record for this publication is available from the British Library

Library of Congress Cataloguing in Publication data
Reiter, Ehud, 1960–
Building natural language generation systems / Ehud Reiter, Robert
Dale.
p.   cm. – (Studies in natural language processing)
ISBN 0-521-62036-8
1. Natural language processing (Computer science)   I. Dale,
Robert, 1959– .   II. Title.   III. Series.
QA76.9.N38R45   1999
006.3′5 – dc21   99-14937
                                                        CIP

ISBN-13 978-0-521-62036-9 hardback
ISBN-10 0-521-62036-8 hardback

ISBN-13 978-0-521-02451-8 paperback
ISBN-10 0-521-02451-X paperback

Contents

List of Figures

Preface

The Purpose of This Book

This book describes NATURAL LANGUAGE GENERATION (NLG), which is a subfield of artificial intelligence and computational linguistics that is concerned with building computer software systems that can produce meaningful texts in English or other human languages from some underlying nonlinguistic representation of information. NLG systems use knowledge about language and the application domain to automatically produce documents, reports, help messages, and other kinds of texts.

As we enter the new millennium, work in natural language processing, and in particular natural language generation, is at an exciting stage in its development. The mid- to late 1990s have seen the emergence of the first fielded NLG applications, and the first software houses specialising in the development of NLG technology. At the time of writing, only a handful of systems are in everyday use, but many more are under development and should be fielded within the next few years. The growing interest in applications of the technology has also changed the nature of academic research in the field. More attention is now being paid to software engineering issues, and to using NLG within a wider document generation process that incorporates graphical elements and other realities of the Web-based information age such as hypertext links.

However, despite the growing interest in NLG in general and applied NLG in particular, it is often difficult for people who are not already knowledgeable in the field to obtain a comprehensive overview of what is involved in building a natural language generation system. There are no existing textbooks on NLG; most books in the area are either revised doctoral dissertations or edited collections derived from workshops and conferences. Textbooks in the broader area of natural language processing as a whole typically devote a single chapter to natural language generation. There are some very good review articles which provide overviews of work in NLG, but most of these concentrate on theoretical issues; and in any case, it is difficult to give a comprehensive overview of a field as rich as NLG in twenty or thirty pages.

The goals of this book are to fill this void and to provide a resource which describes NLG from the perspective of what is involved in building complete NLG systems. The book is intended to serve a number of audiences. We hope to meet the needs of the following communities:

Students should be able to use our book as a textbook for a postgraduate course in NLG, as supplemental reading in general courses on natural language processing, and as a general resource for learning about NLG in institutions where formal courses on the subject are not available.

We know of many students who are interested in NLG but are discouraged by the fact that it is difficult to learn about the field; we hope that our book will encourage more students to pursue their interests in the area.

Academics working in related areas – such as natural language analysis, writing-support tools, and advanced hypertext technologies – can use our book to understand the goals, underlying theories, representations, and algorithms of NLG and how these relate to their own fields.

We hope this will encourage more interaction and cross-fertilisation between NLG and these related areas.

Software developers working on applications which need to produce linguistic output, such as software that generates letters and reports, can use our book to understand what NLG has to offer in building such systems and how to incorporate the relevant aspects of NLG into these systems. We believe that one of the major impediments to the use of NLG in real systems is the difficulty of learning about the technology. A major goal for our book is to help remove this barrier.

Last but not least, we hope that the synthesis of NLG work presented here will help define a framework within which new and existing work in NLG can be discussed. It is often difficult to compare or combine results from the work of different researchers, because their work often is based on different assumptions about the inputs, outputs, and expected functionalities of the various components of an NLG system. The problems in reconciling these differences are sometimes exacerbated by a lack of relevant detail in the published research literature. In this book we present an NLG system architecture which embodies one particular set of assumptions about inputs, outputs, and the modularisation of functionality within an NLG system. Our aim is to provide a model that is sufficiently well specified that it can be used as a basis for comparison of alternatives.

The Approach Taken in This Book

The approach we take to NLG in this book is oriented towards the construction of NLG systems. We discuss theoretical issues and models, but we generally keep these discussions short and rely on the primary sources for further detail unless we can relate these issues quite directly to the construction of NLG systems.

For example, we spend some pages discussing Rhetorical Structure Theory (RST) and Systemic Functional Grammar (SFG), because a good understanding of RST is very useful in the context of document structuring, and similarly a good understanding of SFG is very useful when using popular realisation packages such as SURGE and KPML. Our discussion of speech act theory is very brief, however, and we say nothing about psychological models of word meanings; although these are interesting topics in their own right, it is less obvious that they have a significant impact on building NLG systems.

Because of this approach, we also discuss engineering issues of importance to those building systems but of less interest perhaps to those pursuing theoretical issues. So, for example, we spend time discussing topics such as requirements analysis, domain modelling, and knowledge acquisition. We also give some engineering-oriented evaluations of when competing NLG techniques should be used – for example when comparing schemas with bottom-up approaches to document structuring and when comparing different approaches to linguistic realisation.

Throughout the book we illustrate the points we make with examples from NLG systems. When possible we use examples from systems with which we have had some personal involvement, such as IDAS, PEBA, MODELEXPLAINER, and STOP; but where appropriate we also use examples from other well-known applied NLG systems, such as FOG. Citations to work that provides descriptions of these systems are provided in the body of the text at appropriate places.

We also make extensive use of a design study for a hypothetical NLG system called WEATHERREPORTER. This system is intended to produce summaries of past weather conditions on the basis of automatically collected meteorological data; we describe how corpus analysis is used to analyse the requirements for WEATHERREPORTER and to construct a domain model and message definitions, and we illustrate various implementation options with regard to algorithms and data structures using examples from the WEATHERREPORTER domain. We have implemented several prototype versions of the component parts of WEATHERREPORTER as a means of exploring the different algorithms and data structures discussed in the book; however, at the time of writing there is no complete implementation of WEATHERREPORTER with the maturity and robustness of systems such as IDAS, PEBA, and FOG.

Our book is based on one particular architectural decomposition of the NLG task which consists of three modules: document planning, microplanning, and surface realisation. DOCUMENT PLANNING is our name for what is often called 'text planning', and includes subtasks we refer to as CONTENT DETERMINATION and DOCUMENT STRUCTURING. MICROPLANNING includes AGGREGATION, REFERRING EXPRESSION GENERATION, and some aspects of LEXICALISATION. SURFACE REALISATION includes LINGUISTIC REALISATION and STRUCTURE REALISATION. All of these concepts are explored in detail in the book.

In terms of intermediate representations, the output of the document planner in our model is a DOCUMENT SPECIFICATION. This is a tree made up of information-bearing units called MESSAGES, often with DISCOURSE RELATIONS specified between parts of the tree. The output of the microplanner is a TEXT SPECIFICATION. This is a tree whose leaf nodes specify PHRASE SPECIFICATION (our category-neutral term for what are often called SENTENCE PLANS in the literature) which can be processed by realisers (such as KPML, SURGE, and REALPRO); and whose internal nodes specify the logical structure of the document in terms of paragraphs, sections, and so forth.

Broad support for an architectural decomposition along these lines can be found in the literature; as argued in Reiter (1994), something similar to this architecture is adopted by most extant NLG systems.

Using the Book

We end this preface by offering some suggestions on how the book can be used.

All readers should read Chapter 1 (Introduction) and Chapter 3 (Architecture). The description in Chapter 3 of the NLG system architecture we propose, along with its intermediate representations, is essential to understanding subsequent chapters.

Chapter 2 (NLG in Practice) is important for those interested in building systems but can be skipped by readers with primarily theoretical interests.

Chapter 4 (Document Planning), Chapter 5 (Microplanning), and Chapter 6 (Surface Realisation) are the heart of the book and describe techniques for performing specific NLG tasks. Students should read all three of these chapters in depth. System builders and academics with specialised interests may find it appropriate to initially skim through these chapters, identify relevant sections, and read these in depth.

Chapter 7 (Beyond Text Generation) can be skipped by readers whose primary interest is in generating pure texts; but it is important for readers who are interested in generating documents which include typography, hypertext links, graphics, and/or speech.

In terms of prerequisite knowledge, we assume throughout the book that the reader has some background in computer science and artificial intelligence and has at least been exposed to the basic concepts in linguistics and natural language processing. Pointers to introductory material in these and other areas related to NLG are given in Section 1.6.

Acknowledgements

When we started writing this book, we naïvely hoped that it would largely be a matter of selecting from and consolidating the vast body of work in the field.

This was not to be so. The research literature embodies a great variety of differing views and assumptions, and we often had to go back to the source literature again and again to see how various ideas could be combined. In many cases we had to create algorithms and representations to fill the gaps that appeared when we tried to bring together well-established ideas in the field. If the end result has anything like the coherence we aimed for, this is in no small part due to the helpful comments of the many people who carefully read drafts of various chapters of the book. We would particularly like to thank each of the following, all of whom provided useful insights and comments without which this book would be less than it is: Elisabeth André, John Bateman, Sarah Boyd, Stephan Busemann, Alison Cawsey, José Coch, Phil Collier, Maria Milosavljevic, Daniel Paiva, James Shaw, Peter Spyns, Elke Teich, Michael White, and Sandra Williams. Of course, even with these inputs, the result of our labours over the last three years still contains errors and omissions. Some of these we know about, and others we will no doubt be alerted to by readers; we remain solely responsible for these imperfections.

Many other people played a role in this book finally seeing the light of day. We would like to thank, in particular, David Bradshaw, who provided considerable help in assisting with the WEATHERREPORTER design study, and in implementing a number of the WEATHERREPORTER prototype systems; and Alan Harvey at Cambridge University Press, who was constantly helpful in providing prompt responses to our queries regarding the logistics of publishing the book. Elisabeth André, Norbert Driedgar, John Levine, Benoit Lavoie and Maria Milosavljevic very kindly provided figures demonstrating, respectively, the WIP, FOG, IDAS, MODELEXPLAINER and PEBA systems; and John Bateman, Michael Elhadad, and Owen Rambow entered into extensive email discussions that much enhanced our understanding of, respectively, the KPML, FUF, and REALPRO systems. Of course, our thinking on the topic of natural language generation has been influenced in innumerable ways by the colleagues and students with whom we have interacted over the years in a variety of fora; there are too many names here to mention without the risk of inadvertently omitting some.

Finally, we offer our very grateful thanks for the support given us by the Computing Science Department of the University of Aberdeen and the Microsoft Research Institute at Macquarie University.

1   Introduction

NATURAL LANGUAGE GENERATION (NLG) is the subfield of artificial intelligence and computational linguistics that focuses on computer systems that can produce understandable texts in English or other human languages. Typically starting from some nonlinguistic representation of information as input, NLG systems use knowledge about language and the application domain to automatically produce documents, reports, explanations, help messages, and other kinds of texts.

NLG is both a fascinating area of research and an emerging technology with many real-world applications. As a research area, NLG brings a unique perspective on fundamental issues in artificial intelligence, cognitive science, and human–computer interaction. These include questions such as how linguistic and domain knowledge should be represented and reasoned with, what it means for a text to be well written, and how information is best communicated between machine and human. From a practical perspective, NLG technology is capable of partially automating routine document creation, removing much of the drudgery associated with such tasks. It is also being used in the research laboratory, and we expect soon in real applications, to present and explain complex information to people who do not have the background or time required to understand the raw data. In the longer term, NLG is also likely to play an important role in human–computer interfaces and will allow much richer interaction with machines than is possible today.

The goal of this book is to explain the central ideas in NLG both to the advanced student who is interested in learning about NLG as a research area and to the software developer who is building sophisticated document generation or information presentation systems and wants to learn about new technologies developed by the NLG community. We hope that students will be as fascinated as we are by the intellectual problems and insights of NLG and that developers will be able to exploit the techniques we describe to improve the systems they build.

1.1   The Research Perspective

From a research perspective, NLG is a subfield of natural language processing (NLP), which in turn can be seen as a subfield of both computer science and cognitive science. The relation between NLG and other aspects of NLP is further discussed below. From the broader perspective of computer science and cognitive science as a whole, NLG provides an important and unique perspective on many fundamental problems and questions, including the following:

- How should computers interact with people? What is the best way for a machine to communicate information to a human? What kind of linguistic behaviour does a person expect of a computer he or she is communicating with, and how can this behaviour be implemented? These are basic questions in human–computer interaction, an area of computer science which is becoming increasingly important as the quality of computer software is judged more and more by its usability.
- What constitutes 'readable' or 'appropriate' language in a given communicative situation? How can the appropriate pragmatic, semantic, syntactic, and psycholinguistic constraints be formalised? What role does context in its many aspects play in the choice of appropriate language? These issues are basic questions in linguistics, and also important in philosophy and psychology; as such they are core issues in cognitive science.
- How can typical computer representations of information – large amounts of low-level (often numeric) data – be converted into appropriate representations for humans, typically a small number of high-level symbolic concepts? What types of domain and world models and associated reasoning are required to 'translate' information from computer representations to natural language, with its human-oriented vocabulary and structure? These questions are aspects of the larger question of how humanlike intelligence can be modelled and simulated on a computer, which is one of the main goals of artificial intelligence (AI).

Although work in natural language generation can provide insights in these related fields, it also draws on these fields for ideas. For example, many NLG systems use ideas developed within artificial intelligence, such as planning techniques and production rules, to determine the information content of a text; and most NLG systems use formal linguistic models of syntax to ensure that their output text is grammatically correct.

1.1.1   *Differences between NL Generation and NL Understanding*

Natural language generation is of course closely related to natural language understanding, which is the study of computer systems that understand English and other human languages. Both NL understanding and NL generation are concerned with computational models of language and its use; they share many of the same theoretical foundations and are often used together in application programs. Together, natural language understanding and natural language generation form the field of natural language processing (NLP).

At a rather abstract level, one can think of the process of natural language generation as being the inverse of the process of natural language understanding. Natural language generation is the process of mapping internal computer representations of information into human language, whereas natural language understanding is the process of mapping human language into internal computer representations. Thus, at least in general terms the two processes have the same end points, and their difference lies in the fact that they are concerned with navigating between these end points in opposite directions.

But the internal operations of these processes are quite different in character. Most fundamentally, as has been observed by McDonald (1992), the process of natural language understanding is best characterised as one of HYPOTHESIS MANAGEMENT: Given some input, which of the multiple possible interpretations at any given stage of processing is the appropriate one? Natural language generation is best characterised as a process of CHOICE: Given the different means that are available to achieve some desired end, which should be used?

1.1.2   *Sharing Knowledge between Generation and Understanding*

Some research in the area has attempted to construct 'reversible' components which can be used in both NLG and NLU systems. This idea has been explored in particular for the mapping between semantic representations and the surface-form sentences that correspond to those representations: a BIDIRECTIONAL GRAMMAR uses a single declarative representation of a language's grammar to perform both parsing in NLU systems (that is, mapping sentences into internal semantic representations) and linguistic realisation in NLG systems (that is, mapping semantic representations into surface sentences). Bidirectional grammars are discussed in Section 6.8.

Unfortunately, despite the elegance and intuitive appeal of the idea, it is difficult to build effective bidirectional systems in practice. This is largely because many important NLU problems are not issues in NLG and vice versa. For example, a major problem in building real NLU systems is the need to be able to handle grammatically incorrect or ill-formed input, which is not a problem in NLG, whereas a major problem in NLG is ensuring that generated text is easily comprehensible by humans, which is not a problem in NLU. A related problem for bidirectional systems is that the internal representations used by NLG and NLU systems are very different. For example, the representations which most NLU parsers produce as output are quite different from the input representations required by most NLG realisers. This basic incompatibility makes it difficult to build a system that does both parsing and realisation.

Bidirectional grammars have been used in machine translation systems, where the input representations are often already in sentence-sized pieces, but they have not been widely used in NLG systems, which generate text from some underlying nonlinguistic representation of information, which is our focus in this book. Of course, this may change in the future, as our understanding of both NLG and NLU grows; it seems intuitively plausible that the same representations of knowledge about language should be used for both generation and analysis. However, it is unlikely that we will ever view NLG as NLU 'in reverse'. Given our current understanding of the processes involved in using language, many of the fundamental tasks of NL generation, such as deciding what information should be communicated in a text, have no clear analogue in NL understanding.

An important difference between NLG and NLU comes from a rather pragmatic aspect of work in the two areas. In very general terms, much of NL understanding is driven by the need to be able to handle the large variety of complex linguistic structures that make up any natural language. This aspect of coverage is of somewhat less importance in NL generation, and indeed the texts produced by most NL generation systems are much simpler in linguistic terms than the texts that NL understanding systems aspire to process. For work in NLG, it is often good enough to have one way of saying something, whereas any experiment in NLU has to take account of the fact that many different inputs may be used to express much the same thing. This again emphasises the difference in characterisation of process we described earlier: Work in NLU is often concerned with clearing away what are thought of as 'superficial differences', so that, for example, *John ate the biscuit* and *The biscuit was eaten by John* receive the same interpretation. Work in NLG is instead often concerned with choosing between such utterances in a principled way.

1.2   The Applications Perspective

From an applications perspective, most current NLG systems are used either to present information to users, or to (partially) automate the production of routine documentation. Information presentation is important because the internal representations used by computer systems often require considerable expertise to interpret. Representations such as airline schedule databases, accounting spreadsheets, expert system knowledge bases, grid-based simulations of physical systems, and so forth are straightforward for a computer to manipulate but not always easy for a person to interpret. This means that there is often a need for systems which can present such data, or summaries of the most important aspects of the data, in an understandable form for nonexpert users. When the best presentation of the data is in English, Spanish, Chinese, or some other human language, NLG technology can be used to construct the presentation system.

Automating document production is important because many people spend large proportions of their time producing documents, often in situations where they do not see document production as their main responsibility. A doctor, for example, may spend a significant part of his or her day writing referral letters, discharge summaries, and other routine documents. Similarly, a computer programmer may spend as much time writing text (code documentation, program logic descriptions, code walkthrough reviews, progress reports, and so on) as writing code. Tools which help such people quickly produce good documents may considerably enhance both productivity and morale.

When we build a complete NLG system, a major design decision that has to be taken is whether that system will operate in standalone mode, generating texts without any human information, or whether it will operate by producing what are in effect drafts of texts that are subsequently modified by a human author. This distinction is essentially the same as that found more broadly in work in expert systems, where it is often deemed appropriate to maintain the presence of a 'human in the loop', especially in contexts where a mistake on the part of the system could be life-threatening or disastrous in some other way. In the case of NLG, the reasons for including a human in the authoring process are generally less dramatic. Put simply, in many contexts it is simply not possible to create texts of the appropriate quality or with the required content without human intervention.

1.2.1   Computer as Authoring Aid

In practice, current NLG technology and the limitations of the information available in host systems mean that it is often not possible for the system to create the final product; instead, the NLG system is used to produce an initial draft of a document which can then be further elaborated or edited by a human author. A variant of this approach is for the NLG system to focus on producing routine factual sections of a document (which human authors often find monotonous to write), leaving analytical and explanatory sections to the human author.

Examples of NLG systems used as authoring assistants are the following:

- FOG (Goldberg, Driedger, and Kittredge, 1994), which helps meteorologists compose weather forecasts; see Section 1.3.2.
- PLANDOC (McKeown, Kukich, and Shaw, 1994), which helps telephone network engineers document the results of simulations of proposed network changes.
- ALETHGEN (Coch, 1996a), which helps customer-service representatives write response letters to customers.
- DRAFTER (Paris et al., 1995), which helps technical authors write software manuals.

This list is indicative only, and by no means complete; numerous other authoring-assistant systems have been described in the NLG literature.

A significant measure of success in technology transfer is the extent to which an idea or system has been actively deployed in the field. As of mid-1998, FOG and PLANDOC are fielded and in everyday use. ALETHGEN has passed the sponsor's acceptance tests but has not yet been deployed. DRAFTER's developers have applied for a patent and intend to commercialise the system once the patent is granted.

1.2.2   *Computer as Author*

As indicated above, it is probably true to say that most practical systems are required to operate in the 'computer as authoring aid' mode, sometimes for legal or contractual reasons. However, many experimental NLG systems have been developed with the aim of operating as standalone systems that require no human intervention when creating texts. Some such systems are as follows:

- MODELEXPLAINER (Lavoie, Rambow, and Reiter, 1997), which generates textual descriptions of classes in an object-oriented software system, using information extracted from a computer-aided software engineering database; see Section 1.3.4.
- KNIGHT (Lester and Porter, 1997), which explains information extracted from an artificial intelligence knowledge base.
- LFS (Iordanskaja et al., 1992), which summarises statistical data for the general public.
- PIGLET (Cawsey, Binstead, and Jones, 1995), which gives hospital patients explanations of information in their patient records.

Again this list is indicative only, and by no means exhaustive.

None of the systems listed above have been fielded yet (as of mid-1998). Given the current state of NLG technology, systems which work in collaboration with a human author are more practical, allowing a symbiotic approach where the machine produces the more routine aspects of documents and leaves the more difficult-to-automate aspects to the human. However, advances in NLG technology should make it possible in the near future to build fieldable standalone systems in some domains, just as mail-merge systems are used to customise letters to individual recipients without a perceived need for each letter to be checked by a human.[1]

1.2.3   *Uses of NLG Technology*

When developers build a complete NLG system, they do so with a certain application context in mind. The system serves some purpose. Currently, most NLG systems

---

[1] Of course, stories of such systems generating meaningless letters to deceased persons or other inappropriate categories of recipients abound. The difficulty of predetermining all the relevant circumstances is one very good reason for maintaining the role of a human overseer in systems of any complexity.

are built with the purpose of presenting information to the user in a straightforward and unbiased manner. However, some experimental systems have explored other uses of NLG technology, including the following:

Teaching. The ICICLE system (McCoy, Pennington, and Suri, 1996) helps deaf people learn the syntax of written English.

Marketing. The DYD system (van Deemter and Odijk, 1997) generates descriptions of a music CD which are intended to increase interest in and sales of that CD.

Behaviour Change. The STOP system (Reiter, Robertson, and Osman, 1997) generates personalised letters which encourage people to stop smoking; see Section 1.3.6.

Entertainment. The JAPE system (Binstead and Ritchie, 1997) generates jokes (more specifically, punning riddles).

All of the aforementioned systems are research prototypes. To be really successful in their domains of application, systems such as these need to embody models of how to teach effectively, how to persuade people to buy things, how people break addictive habits, and what people find amusing. Currently we do not have precise computational models in any of these areas, which means that building effective systems is partially a research project in the computational modelling of teaching, persuasion, and so forth, as well as in language generation.

It is perhaps unfortunate that the popular media pay far more attention to systems which generate fictional forms such as jokes, novels, or poetry than to any other kind of NLG system. For example, the JAPE system mentioned above has been reported upon in the UK in both the tabloid and the more serious press, and in radio and television broadcasts. In contrast, most of the NLG systems we describe in this book have never been mentioned in the popular media at all. There is no doubt that 'What happens if you cross a comic with a computer'[2] is a more appealing headline than 'Computer helps telephone engineer document simulation results'; nevertheless, the media's bias may tend to give the lay population the mistaken impression that NLG is mostly concerned with producing fictional material whose purpose is to entertain readers. This is certainly an interesting potential use of NLG technology, but, as should be clear by now, it is by no means the only, or even the primary, use of NLG.

1.3   Some Example NLG Systems

To make our discussion more concrete, in this section we introduce the WEATHER-REPORTER design study and also give brief descriptions of several implemented NLG systems: FOG, IDAS, MODELEXPLAINER, PEBA, and STOP. We will use these

---

[2] *Sunday Telegraph*, 29 August 1994.

systems throughout the book to illustrate technical points and discussions. We also occasionally use examples from other systems, but we try when possible to base examples on one of the systems described in this section. References for and very brief descriptions of all the NLG systems mentioned in this book are given in Appendix A.

Particular emphasis is placed in the book on the WEATHERREPORTER design study, which is intended to serve as a unifying case study for the book. It is impossible to illustrate all aspects of NLG by means of a single case study, and hence we discuss and draw examples from many other systems as well; but by focusing on a specific system, we hope to give an idea of how the different aspects of NLG fit together.

1.3.1   WeatherReporter

The WEATHERREPORTER design study is used throughout this book as a central case study to illustrate the process of developing an NLG system. We have implemented several prototype versions of various WEATHERREPORTER components using a variety of algorithms and data structures. However, these implementations are early prototypes lacking the maturity and robustness of systems such as FOG, IDAS, MODELEXPLAINER, and PEBA. We describe how corpus analysis is used to analyse the requirements of WEATHERREPORTER and to construct a domain model and message definitions. We also illustrate various implementation options with regard to algorithms and data structures using examples from the WEATHERREPORTER domain.

The purpose of WEATHERREPORTER is to provide retrospective reports of the weather over periods whose duration is one calendar month. It does this by taking as input a large set of numerical data collected automatically by meteorological devices, from which it produces short texts of one or two paragraphs in length. The application is quite simple in many regards, thus allowing us to demonstrate how the techniques presented in this book can be used while avoiding the relative complexity of more sophisticated systems.

Figure 1.1 shows an example text that might be produced by WEATHERRE-PORTER. This is fairly typical of the kinds of texts required. It provides information on temperature and rainfall for the month as a whole, and it provides descriptions of spells of weather that are noteworthy for one reason or another. Some of the texts can be quite different from this general form, depending on the nature of the data to be reported; these variations are explored in more detail later in the book.

> The month was cooler and drier than average, with the average
> number of rain days. The total rain for the year so far is well below
> average. There was rain on every day for eight days from the 11th
> to the 18th.

Figure 1.1   The Macquarie weather summary for February 1995.

Figure 1.2 shows a fragment of the data that WEATHERREPORTER uses as input. Each line represents one data record, these being collected at 15-minute intervals by an automatic weather station.

Retrospective weather reports similar to the one shown in Figure 1.1 are currently written manually for the staff newsletter of Macquarie University, where one of us (Dale) works, and the data shown in Figure 1.2 is real data collected automatically by meteorological data gathering equipment on the university campus. The WEATHERREPORTER design study is thus based on real input data and a real corpus of human-written texts, and our description of WEATHERREPORTER in this book shows how humanlike texts can be generated from real input data using NLG techniques.

1.3.2   FOG

The FOG system (Goldberg et al., 1994) generates textual weather forecasts from numerical weather simulations produced by a supercomputer and annotated by a human forecaster. More precisely, it takes as input a numerical prediction of how wind speeds, precipitation type and intensity, and other meteorological phenomena vary over a given region in a specified time interval, and produces as output a textual summary of this information. An example of a graphical rendition of some of FOG's input is shown in Figure 1.3, which depicts the predicted weather system over Northern Canada at 0600 GMT on 14 August 1998. An example of FOG's output is shown in Figure 1.4; this is a marine forecast issued at 04:25 EDT (09:25 GMT) on 13 August 1998, which describes the predicted weather over various points in Northern Canada. Because it is a marine forecast, it emphasises wind and precipitation information and says nothing about temperature; other types of forecasts would emphasise different information.

The texts produced by FOG are not very exciting, but they are useful and more difficult to generate than might at first seem to be the case. One complexity in FOG that may not be immediately apparent is that it must decide how detailed the information it provides should be. In the example in Figure 1.4, for instance, FOG has decided to produce a single summary forecast that covers both East Brevoort and East Davis but a separate forecast for East Clyde. Also, FOG needs to decide when it can use inexact temporal terms like *late this evening* or *early Friday evening* and when it should use a more precise phrase such as *at midnight*.

Another technically interesting aspect of FOG is that it can produce forecast texts in both English and French; in other words, it is a MULTILINGUAL system. Internally, FOG first produces a language-independent abstract representation of the forecast text and then maps this into each output language using appropriate grammatical and lexical resources.

The FOG system was developed by CoGenTex, a specialist NLG software house, for Environment Canada (the Canadian weather service). It has been in everyday use since 1993.

96,122,1,5,2.00,200,-14.41,-3.668,-1.431,.345,1023,15.41,15.82,20.07,-11.1,-2.878,104.2,.28,153.6,53.19,0,16.26
96,122,1,5,2.25,215,-10.72,-3.241,-1.35,.152,1023,15.3,15.78,20.07,-11.42,-2.762,105,.208,98.2,822,0,17.05
96,122,1,5,2.50,230,-8.37,-1.282,-.904,2.15,1022,15.3,15.71,20.05,-11.66,-3.206,104.4,.2,141.6,42.96,0,17.7
96,122,1,5,2.75,245,-12.81,-2.11,-1.067,2.119,1022,15.33,15.79,19.99,-11.15,-3.093,104.8,.2,186.5,11.32,0,17.81
96,122,1,5,3.00,300,-13.68,-3,-1.35,1.075,1022,15.36,15.79,19.96,-10.63,-3.005,104.6,.402,285.8,61.45,0,18.47
96,122,1,5,3.25,315,-10.2,-2.457,-1.13,-.73,1022,15.32,15.66,19.92,-11.17,-3.263,103.6,.304,354.7,36.29,0,19.03
96,122,1,5,3.50,330,-9.33,-1.353,-.942,.902,1022,15.21,15.62,19.9,-10.95,-2.903,104.3,.313,302.2,34.69,0,19.16
96,122,1,5,3.75,345,-7.29,-.285,-.76,2.048,1022,15.24,15.63,19.87,-10.68,-3.27,104,.252,313,29.7,0,19.61
96,122,1,5,4.00,400,-6.822,-.365,-.653,1.531,1022,15.25,15.63,19.83,-9.93,-3.316,104,.331,274.2,52.98,0,20.42
96,122,1,5,4.25,415,-8.78,-.65,-.747,1.602,1023,15.35,15.66,19.79,-9.77,-2.656,103.3,.253,247.7,10.99,0,21.08
96,122,1,5,4.50,430,-8.73,-.641,-.741,1.785,1023,15.46,15.81,19.75,-9.16,-2.782,103.7,.2,295.29,15.0,21.3
96,122,1,5,4.75,445,-11.45,-2.671,-1.03,-.456,1022,15.46,15.82,19.74,-8.81,-2.464,103.7,.2,355.3,23.98,0,21.65
96,122,1,5,5.00,500,-13.12,-4.3,-1.306,-1.359,1022,15.42,15.75,19.76,-9.39,-2.49,103.4,.2,20.67,.188,0,21.83
96,122,1,5,5.25,515,-13.62,-4.621,-1.344,.842,1022,15.32,15.67,19.81,-9.47,-2.703,103.7,.2,20.65,.183,0,21.98
96,122,1,5,5.50,530,-13.8,-3.534,-1.325,.943,1022,15.23,15.61,19.86,-10.92,-3.384,103.9,.2,20.65,.183,0,22.14
96,122,1,5,5.75,545,-14.7,-3.748,-1.419,.385,1022,15.06,15.47,19.9,-11.62,-2.868,104.4,.2,341.6,18.6,0,22.36
96,122,1,5,6.00,600,-13.61,-2.315,-1.287,2.038,1022,14.98,15.42,19.9,-12.37,-3.092,104.7,.2,298.6,5.173,0,22.54
96,122,1,5,6.25,615,-14,-2.894,-1.293,.669,1022,14.92,15.36,19.88,-12.48,-3.808,104.7,.591,320.3,21.07,0,22.87

The 22 data values in each record are as follows: the year; the day of the year as a value between 1 and 365; the month of the year; the day of the month; the time in 24 hour notation; the time in hours and minutes; four radiation readings; the barometric pressure; the temperature, referred to as 'dry bulb temperature'; the wet bulb temperature, which is used to calculate humidity; the soil temperature; the soil heat flux at two depths; relative humidity; average wind speed; wind direction; the standard deviation of wind direction; precipitation within the 15 minute period; and amount of sunlight.

Figure 1.2 Data input for the WEATHERREPORTER system.

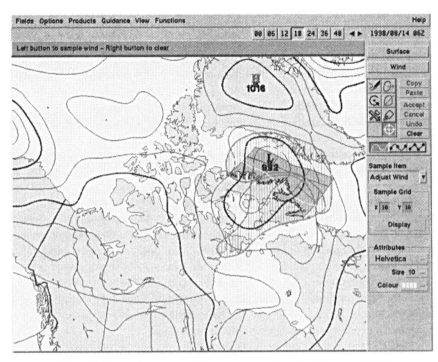

Figure 1.3 FOG input: a weather system over Canada. (Courtesy of Environment Canada.)

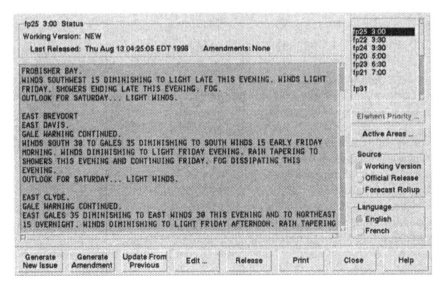

Figure 1.4 Some example forecasts from FOG. (Courtesy of Environment Canada.)

1.3.3   IDAS

The IDAS system (Reiter, Mellish, and Levine, 1995) produces on-line hypertext help messages for users of complex machinery, using information stored in a knowledge base that describes that machinery. Figure 1.5 shows a series of texts produced by IDAS in response to user queries; in this case the machine being described is a bicycle. All underlined words in the system's responses are hypertext links which can be clicked on; each click results in a new text being produced.[3] For example, if the user clicks on *front gear mechanism* in the *What are the parts of the gearing system* box (in the top-left corner of Figure 1.5), she will see a pop-up menu which lists a number of questions she can ask about this device, including *What is its purpose*. Selecting this question results in the system producing a text on *What is the purpose of the front gear mechanism*; this box is shown in the middle of the top row of boxes in Figure 1.5. The bold font words at the bottom of each box enable further questions to be asked about the same component. For example, clicking on USE in the *What is the purpose of the front gear mechanism* box results in a text on *How do I use the front gear mechanism*; this box is shown in the top-right corner of Figure 1.5. IDAS is a DYNAMIC HYPERTEXT system, in that all texts are generated dynamically from the knowledge base at run-time. The links are not pointers to static files, but rather requests to run a program (IDAS) to generate an appropriate response in the current context.

IDAS can vary the REFERRING EXPRESSIONS it uses to refer to objects according to context. For example, consider the response text for *How do I use the front gear mechanism* (top-right box in Figure 1.5):

(1.1)   Pull the left gear lever backwards to shift to a higher gear. Push it forwards to shift to a lower gear.

In the second sentence of this example, IDAS has used the pronoun *it* to refer to the left gear lever of the bicycle; this is possible because this object was introduced in the first sentence of this text.

From a technical perspective, IDAS is interesting for its use of hypertext, and for the way it selects appropriate referring expressions. With some knowledge bases (but not the bicycle KB used to produce Figure 1.5, which is relatively simple), it can also vary response texts according to a user model which describes the user's expertise and task.

The IDAS system was developed as a research prototype at the University of Edinburgh in the early 1990s. It was never put into everyday use, but many of the ideas developed in IDAS have influenced later NLG systems.

---

[3] The hypertext interface used in IDAS is somewhat primitive, since the system predates the World Wide Web and its associated hypertext browsers.

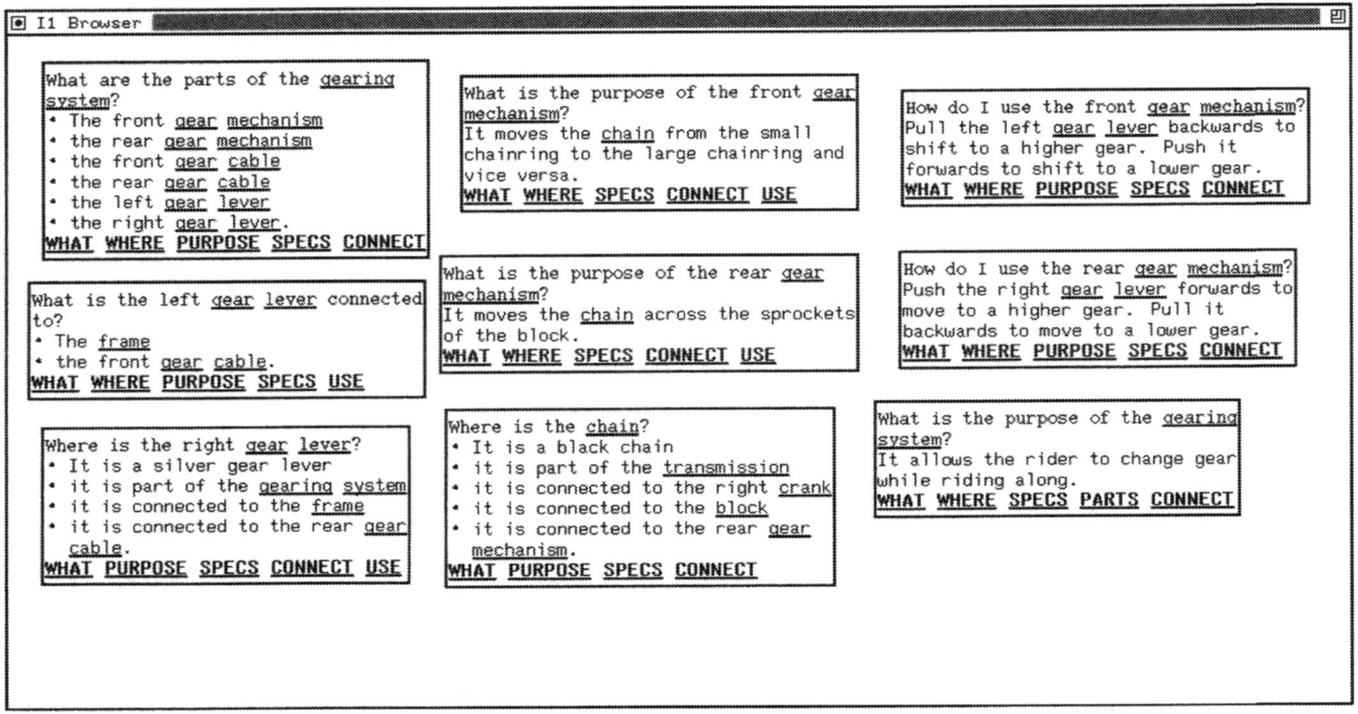

Figure 1.5 Some example texts from IDAS. (Courtesy of John Levine.)

☐ I1 Browser ▯

What are the parts of the gearing
system?
• The front gear mechanism
• the rear gear mechanism
• the front gear cable
• the rear gear cable
• the left gear lever
• the right gear lever.
WHAT WHERE PURPOSE SPECS CONNECT

What is the purpose of the front gear
mechanism?
It moves the chain from the small
chainring to the large chainring and
vice versa.
WHAT WHERE SPECS CONNECT USE

How do I use the front gear mechanism?
Pull the left gear lever backwards to
shift to a higher gear. Push it
forwards to shift to a lower gear.
WHAT WHERE PURPOSE SPECS CONNECT

What is the left gear lever connected
to?
• The frame
• the front gear cable.
WHAT WHERE PURPOSE SPECS USE

What is the purpose of the rear gear
mechanism?
It moves the chain across the sprockets
of the block.
WHAT WHERE SPECS CONNECT USE

How do I use the rear gear mechanism?
Push the right gear lever forwards to
move to a higher gear. Pull it
backwards to move to a lower gear.
WHAT WHERE PURPOSE SPECS CONNECT

Where is the right gear lever?
• It is a silver gear lever
• it is part of the gearing system
• it is connected to the frame
• it is connected to the rear gear
  cable.
WHAT PURPOSE SPECS CONNECT USE

Where is the chain?
• It is a black chain
• It is part of the transmission
• it is connected to the right crank
• it is connected to the block
• it is connected to the rear gear
  mechanism.
WHAT PURPOSE SPECS CONNECT

What is the purpose of the gearing
system?
It allows the rider to change gear
while riding along.
WHAT WHERE SPECS PARTS CONNECT

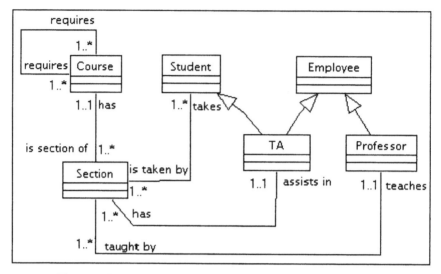

Figure 1.6 An example MODELEXPLAINER input: an object-oriented class model. (Courtesy of CoGenTex, Inc.)

1.3.4   ModelExplainer

The MODELEXPLAINER system (Lavoie et al., 1997) generates textual descriptions of information in models of object-oriented (O-O) software. More specifically, it takes as input a specification of an object-oriented class model and produces as output a text describing the model or portions of it. An example of MODELEXPLAINER's output is shown in Figure 1.7; this describes the class Section in the O-O model which is graphically shown in Figure 1.6.

O-O models are usually depicted graphically, and MODELEXPLAINER is intended to be used as a supplement to, rather than as a replacement for, graphical depictions; this is useful because certain kinds of information are better communicated textually. For example, the text in Figure 1.7 makes it clear to the reader that a Section must be taught by exactly one Professor; this is perhaps less immediately obvious in the graphical depiction of this object model, especially for people who are not familiar with the notation used in the graphical depiction.

MODELEXPLAINER is a highly customisable system. Whereas most NLG systems can be modified only by their developers, MODELEXPLAINER also allows users (or system administrators at user organisations) to modify the content of its descriptions. Like IDAS, it makes extensive use of hypertext; all underlined words in the output text shown are hypertext links on which the user can click.

From a technical perspective, among the many interesting aspects of MODELEXPLAINER are the AGGREGATION processes it performs in order to produce sentences which contain several clauses. An example of this is the first sentence in the

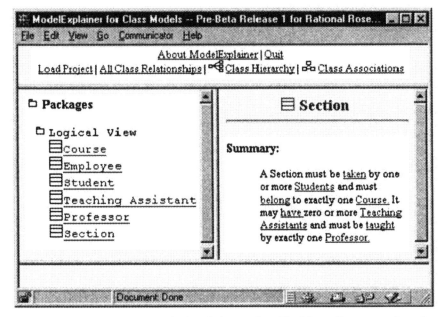

Figure 1.7   An example description produced by MODELEXPLAINER from the model in Figure 1.6. (Courtesy of CoGenTex, Inc.)

Summary section of Figure 1.7, which was produced by aggregating the information that might otherwise have been presented in the separate sentences *A Section must be taken by one or more students* and *A Section must belong to exactly one Course*. Another interesting aspect of MODELEXPLAINER is that it must express relations from the object model (such as Teaches) in a variety of linguistic contexts; for example, *a Professor teaches a course*, *a Section must be taught by a Professor*, and *Professor Smith does not teach any Sections*.

MODELEXPLAINER was developed by CoGenTex, the same company which developed the FOG system.

1.3.5   PEBA

PEBA (Milosavljevic and Dale, 1996) is a natural language generation system which interactively describes entities in a taxonomic knowledge base via the dynamic generation of hypertext documents, presented as World Wide Web pages.

In PEBA, the information provided to the user varies depending upon the context of use: The system produces different texts for novice and expert users and varies the content of the text presented depending on what material the user has seen before. Figure 1.8 shows a Web page generated by PEBA; this provides a comparison of two objects in the knowledge base, as requested by the user. The

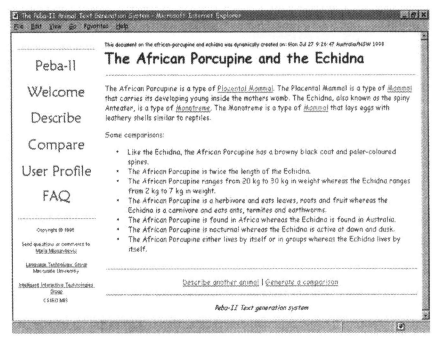

Figure 1.8   A www page generated by PEBA. (Courtesy of Maria Milosavljsevic.)

underlying knowledge base contains information about individual objects – here, this is a representation of a fragment of the Linnaean taxonomy of animals – expressed in a simple knowledge representation formalism that permits the system to automatically construct descriptive texts. The system was developed to explore what the next generation of intelligent encyclopaedias might look like. By taking into account some characterisation of the user's background knowledge, and also by maintaining a record of the information already presented to the user, the system can tailor texts appropriately; this means that a description of an object may be different for different people, and may vary depending on the path they have taken through the hypertext system. The ability to automatically generate arbitrary comparisons of pairs of entities on demand means that the system can generate many more individualised texts than it would be feasible to write by hand.

The PEBA system can be accessed on the Web at http://www.mri.mq.edu.au/peba.

1.3.6   STOP

STOP (Reiter et al., 1999) is a natural language generation system which produces personalised smoking-cessation letters. Personalisation is based on an 'Attitudes

Towards Smoking' questionnaire which smokers fill out; this includes questions about topics such as health problems, previous attempts to quit, and what the person likes and dislikes about smoking.

STOP was still under development at the time this book was written. Figure 1.9 shows a page generated by a prototype version of STOP.[4] This letter was generated for a smoker who does not currently intend to quit but who would quit if quitting were an easy process – in short, someone who would like to quit but doesn't feel she will be able to, and hence is not planning to try. In this case, STOP gently encourages the smoker to consider making another attempt to quit, by

- pointing out to her that she dislikes many more things about smoking than she likes, using information about likes and dislikes extracted from the questionnaire;
- emphasising that she can quit if she really wants to, even if she has failed in the past;
- giving some practical advice about addiction, which is a special concern to this smoker (this includes an additional nontailored 'back page', not shown in Figure 1.9, on nicotine patches); and
- pointing her towards further sources of advice and help.

STOP deliberately does not hector or argue, since this may cause some people to 'switch off'. Instead, it adopts a positive tone, stressing benefits of quitting, encouraging people who lack confidence, addressing problems or concerns the smoker may have (for example, addiction, or fear of gaining weight after quitting), and giving practical advice.

From a technical perspective, perhaps the most interesting aspect of STOP is the knowledge acquisition techniques that the developers used to interact with the domain experts. Based on techniques developed by researchers on expert systems, these included protocol analysis, sorting, and role playing. STOP is also interesting for its use of typographic and multimodal elements such as different typefaces, itemised lists, and embedded graphics.

STOP will be evaluated in a controlled clinical study begun in late 1998; this will measure how many recipients of STOP letters quit as compared to control groups who received a nonpersonalised letter or no letter at all (but who did fill out a questionnaire).

---

[4] In fact, STOP generates four pages of output, not two: an initial page which contains various logos, a salutation, and an introductory paragraph; two pages which contain personalised text; and a final 'back' page which is selected from one of a dozen possible back pages but not otherwise personalised. To simplify the exposition, we show here only the personalised text produced by STOP in Figure 1.3.6; we have omitted the introductory logos and back page and have presented the salutation and introductory paragraph on the same pages as the rest of the personalised text.

Smoking Information for Jane Smith

Dear Mrs Smith

Thank you for taking the trouble to return the smoking questionnaire that we sent you. It appears from your answers that although you do not intend to stop smoking in the near future, you would like to stop if it was easy. You think it would be difficult to stop because you think you are too addicted to the nicotine in cigarettes, you find it difficult to resist the craving for cigarettes, and you don't have the willpower. However, you have reasons to be confident of success if you did try to stop, and there are ways of coping with the difficulties.

You have good reasons to stop...

People stop smoking when they really want to stop. It is encouraging that you have many good reasons for stopping. The scales are tipped in your favour.

THINGS YOU LIKE

it stops stress

THINGS YOU DISLIKE
it's expensive
it makes you less fit
it's bad for you
it's a bad example for kids
it's unpleasant for others
you're addicted
it's a smelly habit
other people disapprove

You could do it...

Although you do not feel confident that you would be able to stop if you were to try, you have several things in your favour.

- Your partner doesn't smoke.
- You have stopped before for over three months.
- You expect support from your partner, your family, and your friends.
- You are a light smoker.
- You have good reasons for stopping smoking.

We know that all of these make it more likely that you will be able to stop. Most people who stop smoking for good have more than one attempt. You can learn from the times you tried before and be more prepared if you try again.

Overcoming the hurdles...

You said in your questionnaire that you might find it difficult to stop because you are *addicted to cigarettes*. If you were to stop smoking it might take a while for your body to get used to not having nicotine. While this is happening you might experience unpleasant side effects, but they will go away. Although you did not find nicotine patches useful last time it might be worth trying them again. They help to reduce the withdrawal symptoms while you break the habit of smoking. You can find more information about nicotine patches on the back page of this leaflet.

For more advice and support...

If you decide to stop smoking in the future and would like any advice or support you could get this from your GP or practice nurse. You could also phone Smokeline (telephone: 0800 84 84 84). Calls are free and there is someone to talk to from 12 midday to 12 midnight.

We hope this letter will help you to feel more confident that you could stop smoking if you really want to. Think about the reasons why you would like to stop smoking for a few minutes each day. We're sure you wouldn't regret stopping.

With best wishes,

Aberdeen Health Centre.

Figure 1.9 A letter generated by the prototype STOP system.

1.4   A Short History of NLG

NLG is still a young research field. A small amount of work on what we now call language generation was carried out in the 1950s and 1960s in the context of machine translation projects. However, that work focused on the needs of translation systems and was thus principally concerned with mapping representations which were often quite close to the surface into sentences of the target language. The 1960s also saw the first attempts at using natural language grammars as a means of randomly generating well-formed sentences.

As we emphasised earlier in this chapter, current work in NLG is concerned with much more than mapping the predetermined content of a sentence into a surface realisation of that content. The first work on NLG which adopted this modern emphasis upon the generation of texts to communicate or explain nonlinguistic information appeared in the 1970s. This included the first Ph.D. theses devoted to NLG: in particular, Goldman's (1975) research on choosing appropriate words to express abstract conceptual content and Davey's (1979) work on generating appropriate textual structures and referring expressions in descriptions of tic-tac-toe games. These pioneering efforts helped to establish some of the main issues in NLG and made it clear that language generation was not simply language understanding in reverse. It became apparent very early on that there were important questions to be answered in natural language generation that had no obvious corollaries in the concerns of natural language understanding research.

This realisation drove much of the research carried out in the 1980s, a decade in which NLG really came into its own. A number of significant and influential Ph.D. theses appeared in the early 1980s, including McKeown's work on schemas (McKeown, 1985) and Appelt's work on reference (Appelt, 1985). These pieces of work have had an enduring impact on the field and implicitly set agendas which have been pursued in a great deal of subsequent research. It would be inappropriate to say that the field matured at this stage – it might be better to think of this period as the onset of adolescence – but a number of quite significant developments occurred during this decade. In general terms, as a better appreciation of the different issues to be addressed in NLG developed, the most significant trend was a move away from building large, monolithic systems that attempted to perform all aspects of the generation task, towards analysing specific NLG problems, such as syntactic realisation, lexical choice, and text planning. Many of the basic ideas and techniques presented in this book originated in this 1980s research. The NLG research community also acquired more of a distinct identity by holding dedicated NLG workshops; the first International Workshop on Natural Language Generation was held in 1983. By the end of the 1980s a significant number of new researchers had moved into the area, and two traditions developed. Following on from much of the early work in the field, a considerable amount of research came from an AI perspective; at the same time, there grew up a body of work whose motivations came more from linguistics and computational linguistics.

NLG has continued to grow as a research field in the 1990s, with many more papers, Ph.D. theses, workshops, and available research software. Work in the field is now very diverse, and it can be difficult to grasp the nature of the field as a whole. This was one of our motivations for writing this book. Of perhaps equal importance to this tremendous growth in activity is the emergence in the 1990s of fielded real-world application systems that use NLG technology, including the pioneering FOG system (see Section 1.3.2), which was the first NLG system to enter everyday use. In parallel with the emergence of applications there has been an increased interest in the research community in applied issues such as comparing the engineering costs and benefits of different NLG techniques, and a concern with the evaluation of systems.

We are too close to work in the 1990s to be able to characterise the significant trends of the decade; such a perspective only comes with hindsight. However, some key themes are evident. Interest is growing in combining text generation with graphics generation; this is a realism borne of the observation that most real-world documents contain diagrams and pictures as well as text, and analysing how text compares to graphics as a communication medium raises many fundamental questions in cognitive science. There is also more interest in multilingual generation and in finding architectures and techniques that can easily produce equivalent texts in several languages. But whether these trends persist or are just passing fads is something that only future authors will be able to say with confidence.

1.5   The Structure of This Book

The remainder of this book is structured as follows.

In Chapter 2, we discuss requirements analysis issues, including when NLG technology is an appropriate way to build a system and how corpus analysis can be used to determine the desired functionality of a system. The focus in this chapter is very much on issues surrounding the application of the technology; readers who are primarily interested in the internals of NLG system construction may wish to skip it.

In Chapter 3 we introduce an architecture for NLG systems which we will assume throughout the rest of the book. It consists of a three-stage pipeline with separate stages for what we call document planning, microplanning, and surface realisation. This architecture is by no means the only way of building an NLG system, but it is broadly compatible with many existing applied NLG systems; and we take the view that we can only satisfactorily discuss algorithms for specific NLG tasks and processes if we have an architecture in place which specifies how different tasks and processes are integrated into a complete system.

In Chapter 4, we discuss document planning in detail and introduce specific techniques that can be used for the tasks of content determination (deciding what information should be present in the generated text) and document structuring (organising this information into a rhetorically coherent structure).

In Chapter 5, we discuss microplanning and describe techniques that can be used to perform the tasks of aggregation (chunking information into sentences and paragraphs), lexicalisation (choosing words to communicate domain concepts), and referring expression generation (producing noun phrases that describe and identify entities in the domain).

In Chapter 6, we discuss surface realisation. The bulk of this chapter is devoted to describing syntactic realisation, with an emphasis on the use of existing software packages that address this task. We also discuss other aspects of realising the various elements of a text.

Finally, in Chapter 7, we look beyond the generation of disembodied fragments of text and consider how NLG ideas can be incorporated into systems that generate documents which make use of typographic devices and contain graphics and hypertext as well as text; we also discuss the problem of generating spoken as opposed to written output.

Appendix A provides brief summary descriptions, with appropriate pointers to the literature, of every NLG system mentioned in this book.

1.6   Further Reading

As far as we are aware, this is the first book intended as a general introduction to the topic of natural language generation. Several shorter, article-length surveys and introductions to the field are available: see, in particular, Kempen (1989) and McDonald (1992). For some observations on the special character of NLG as a field of research, see Mann (1987).

Most texts on natural language processing contain a chapter on natural language generation. Good introductory sources on the field of NLP as a whole are Gazdar and Mellish (1989) and Allen (1995). A range of seminal papers, including several pioneering NLG articles from the early 1980s, are reprinted in Grosz, Jones, and Webber (1986).

Looking more broadly, there are a wide variety of introductory textbooks on artificial intelligence, cognitive science, and human–computer interaction. Russell and Norvig (1995) is a currently popular introduction to artificial intelligence; Pinker (1994) provides a very readable introduction to language from a cognitive science perspective; and Dix (1993) provides an introduction to the area of human–computer interaction. Collins and Smith (1988) and Baecker and Buxton (1987) collect together important papers in the areas of cognitive science and human–computer interaction, respectively.

These materials tend to have little to say about NLG, however. From the mid-1980s on, the best way to find out about the historical evolution of research in NLG is by consulting the now considerable number of volumes of collected papers in the field, many of which are publications following from the European and International Natural Language Generation Workshops (see Kempen (1987),

McDonald and Bolc (1988); Zock and Sabah (1988a,b); Dale, Mellish, and Zock (1990); Paris, Swartout, and Mann (1991); Pattabhiraman and Cercone (1991); Dale et al. (1992); Horacek and Zock (1993); Adorni and Zock (1996); and Dale, Eugenio, and Scott (1998). Papers on NLG also appear in the proceedings of the conferences of the Association for Computational Linguistics, the American Association for Artificial Intelligence, and the International Joint Conference on Artificial Intelligence.

For pointers to the specific systems described in this chapter, see Appendix A. Hutchins (1986) gives a history of the field of machine translation and includes some discussion of the earliest work on NLG (sometimes referred to as 'synthesis'). A more recent introduction to machine translation is provided by Arnold et al. (1994). Although Kay, Gawron, and Norvig (1994) describe one particular machine translation exercise, their book contains a wealth of relevant background information.

Pointers to further reading on each of the specific aspects of NLG covered in this book are provided at the end of each chapter.

2   Natural Language Generation in Practice

Before commencing our exploration of the technical content of work in natural language generation, in this chapter we take a step back and consider questions that arise when we look at putting NLG technology to work. We consider alternatives to NLG, and we discuss the circumstances under which it is appropriate to use NLG technology. We also look at requirements analysis and the evaluation and fielding of NLG systems. These topics are rarely discussed in the research literature but are of major significance when we are concerned with the construction of an operational natural language generation system.

2.1   Introduction

Research activity in natural language generation is sometimes carried out with relatively little attention being paid to how the fruits of the research might be transferred into a working environment. This approach may be entirely appropriate for work that focuses on research issues where even the questions to be asked are unclear; it can often be useful to abstract away from situations of use to clarify the underlying issues.

In this book, however, we also are concerned with how NLG technology can be used to build real working systems that are intended to be put into everyday use. This means that we have to think about issues such as the specification of system requirements and the problems that can arise in fielding systems. These are problems to be faced in any software engineering exercise; the aim of this chapter is to explore how they impact upon the construction of NLG systems in particular.

The success of an implemented natural language generation system depends not just on the technology itself but also on how well the system fulfills the user's needs and on how much 'value added' the use of NLG techniques provides over alternative ways of meeting the user's needs. REQUIREMENTS ANALYSIS is the name generally given to the task of understanding the user's problems and desires, and of specifying the functionality of a system which addresses these problems and desires. Requirements analysis is absolutely essential to the success of any system-building project whose goal is to solve a real-world problem.

The software engineering discipline has developed a range of general techniques for requirements analysis, many of which can be applied to building NLG systems. We will not review these techniques here; the interested reader is encouraged to consult any standard textbook on software engineering (see, for example, Pressman (1997)). Instead, we concentrate in this chapter on some specific issues which apply to analysing requirements for NLG systems.

More specifically, in Section 2.2, we discuss some of the alternatives to NLG that can serve to meet a user's document generation or information presentation needs, and consider the advantages and disadvantages of NLG compared to these other approaches. There is no point in building an NLG system when the user's needs would be better met by a different approach, such as the development of a system which communicates information via other modalities or a system which uses mail-merge techniques to customise documents. The first question any developer considering the use of NLG techniques needs to ask, then, is whether this is indeed the most appropriate technology for the application.

The following may appear obvious but still bears restating: When implementing a natural language generation system, a key element in determining the user's requirements is the careful identification of the kinds of texts that are to be generated. In Section 2.3, we discuss a corpus-based approach to this question which can be of use in many situations. In particular, we discuss how this technique can be used to locate areas where the user is asking for the impossible by requiring the system to communicate information it does not have access to – a fairly common problem in the initial stages of requirements analysis in the context of NLG. The method outlined here is based on the identification of an agreed-upon corpus of representative target texts which demonstrate by example the range of outputs that can be expected of the system to be constructed.

We conclude this chapter with brief discussions of how NLG systems can be evaluated (Section 2.4), and some of the issues and problems that arise in getting people to use an NLG system, even if it is effective and meets its requirements (Section 2.5). These sections are brief not because they are unimportant but because relatively little is known about the underlying issues. Finally, Section 2.6 provides some pointers to further reading on the topics discussed in this chapter.

2.2   When Are NLG Techniques Appropriate?

Developing a system based on NLG techniques is not always the best way to fulfil a user's needs. In some cases, it may be better to present the information that needs to be delivered in a graphical form rather than in a textual form. In other cases text is the best mode of presentation, but solutions based on the simple mail-merge facilities found in most word processors may be adequate as a means of delivering the results, and there may be no need to use more complex NLG techniques. In still other cases, the best solution is to hire a person to write documents or to explain things to users. Which approach is most appropriate in any given circumstance depends on a number of factors, including the type of information being communicated, the quality of text required, and the volume of text to be produced.

It is important to recognise that very few end-users explicitly perceive a need for a system based on NLG technology. It is much more common for people to perceive a need for a system which generates documents or presents information. NLG technology is one possible means to meeting such needs, and is only appropriate if it provides the cheapest or most effective solution to their document-generation or information-presentation requirements.

In the rest of this section, we discuss how the costs and benefits of NLG techniques compare to the costs and benefits of some other techniques for generating documents or presenting information. This discussion is primarily in qualitative terms because the technology is not yet well enough understood to give good quantitative rules for comparing the costs and benefits of different approaches.

2.2.1 Text versus Graphics

A Chinese proverb says that one picture is worth more than ten thousand words. There are many situations where pictures, schematic diagrams, maps, charts, and plots can be used to communicate information more effectively or more efficiently than would be the case if text were used. Anyone developing a system for information presentation therefore needs to consider whether text, graphics, or some mixture of the two is the best way to fulfil the user's requirements.

There are no hard and fast principles for deciding when information should be presented textually and when it should be presented graphically. One criterion that appears to affect this decision is the type of information being communicated. For example, the textual descriptions of component locations produced in the IDAS system described in Section 1.3.3 were sometimes difficult to interpret; in such cases, a picture of the machine with the component in question highlighted would probably have been more effective. In general, information about physical location may be better conveyed by an annotated picture than by words. However, it can be difficult to convey abstract concepts such as causality by graphical means, while this is straightforwardly achievable in text.

Another issue that may have an impact on which mode of presentation is best is the expertise of the users who will be consuming the texts produced. In particular, although graphics is sometimes presented as an 'easy-to-understand' way of presenting information which is suitable for novices, research in psychology (for example, Peter (1995)) shows that in many cases a considerable amount of expertise and background knowledge is needed to interpret a graphic correctly, and novices may be better off with a textual presentation of the information. This is in part due to the fact that textual presentations can exploit the tremendous store of shared conventions which the users of a language typically have, regardless of whether they are novices or experts in a particular domain – a vocabulary of tens of thousands of words, along with a rich set of syntactic, semantic, and pragmatic rules for combining and interpreting these elements. In the world of graphical depiction, however, while experts in a particular domain may have a rich domain-specific set of shared graphical conventions, these may not be known to novices in the domain; and domain-independent graphical conventions which are known to the general public, and can therefore be reliably assumed in presentations aimed at novices, are relatively few in number.

These issues and the ways they can be accommodated in sophisticated NLG systems are further discussed in Chapter 7. We discuss there how the generation of text and graphics can be combined to produce software that generates MULTIMODAL documents.

From a practical perspective, a good way to determine whether text or graphics should be used is to examine existing documents which present the information in question. This is not foolproof, of course, because there is no guarantee that the way things happen to be done now is the best way possible. However, in many areas the task of information presentation has become a well-developed art, and so it is worth seeking out best practice in the area. In some cases, the choice is dictated not by which medium is most effective but, rather, by legal requirements, convention, or distribution constraints. For example, the use of graphics will not be an option if the material is to be delivered via teletext, a slow Internet link, or down a telephone line as speech.

2.2.2   *Natural Language Generation versus Mail Merge*

Natural language generation techniques are not the only way to generate text on a computer. Many operational software systems that generate textual documents do so with the kind of mail-merge technology found in Microsoft Word and other popular document creation packages. While the simplest uses of mail-merge systems just involve the insertion of input data into predefined slots in a template document, the underlying functionalities provided by these systems often mean that they are essentially programming languages which allow the output text to vary in arbitrary ways depending on the input data.

From a theoretical perspective, there is no difference in the functionality that can be implemented with NLG techniques and with complex mail-merge systems; both are Turing-equivalent computational systems. Indeed, it can be argued that mail-merge systems are a kind of NLG technology, being just one point on a scale of complexity and sophistication, with full-blown NLG techniques lying at the other end of the scale.

From a practical perspective, the implementation effort required for a particular system may vary considerably depending on which kind of technology is used. Unfortunately, we still have a very limited understanding of when NLG techniques are and are not needed. Mail-merge systems can be very inexpensive and easy to develop, but NLG techniques can make it easier to generate more varied and potentially higher-quality texts than can be achieved straightforwardly using mail-merge techniques, and the compartmentalising of different types of knowledge that is common in NLG systems may make them easier to update and maintain.

Coch (1996a) carried out a detailed study of the extent to which the different technologies impacted on the quality of machine-generated texts. In this study, a panel of experts judged the relative quality of three sets of output data:

- business letters produced by a mail-merge system which was in regular use in a company;
- a set of letters produced by an NLG system which was a potential replacement for the mail-merge system; and
- a set of letters individually written by human authors.

Judging was blind, so that the judges did not know the origin of individual letters. The results showed that while the human-authored letters were perceived to be the best, the NLG system produced significantly better letters than the mail-merge system. The mail-merge system sometimes produced letters that were incomprehensible or grammatically incorrect, which the NLG system never did; and even when the mail-merge system did produce comprehensible and correct letters, the judges evaluated the NLG letters as being much better in terms of flow, personalisation, precise use of terminology, and other measures of quality.

Of course, Coch's study compared a specific NLG system to a specific mail-merge system, so we need to be cautious about generalising his findings to other situations. But the study does provide some suggestive evidence that NLG systems can produce better texts than mail-merge systems.

Another potential advantage of NLG systems over systems based on mail-merge technology is maintainability. At least in principle, NLG systems should be easier to update as requirements and user needs change, because they use general-purpose algorithms and models of language. For example, one factor in how well a text 'flows' is the use of appropriate referring expressions – linguistic elements such as pronouns, proper names, and descriptions (see Section 5.4). In mail-merge systems, the problem of referring expression generation is usually handled (if it is handled at all) by creating separate code fragments for each place where a referring expression is needed. Updating the text may require rewriting many of these code fragments, which is very time consuming and prone to the introduction of inconsistency. NLG systems, in contrast, can use general-purpose referring expression generation algorithms and formally-specified discourse models to generate appropriate references. Because the necessary contextual information for referring expression generation (such as what objects have been mentioned previously in the text) is captured in the discourse model, there is no need to update each slot-filling code fragment individually when the text content or structure is changed.

Nonetheless, there is very little data available on the maintainability advantages of NLG systems, in large part because there are, at the time of writing, so few NLG systems which are actually used on a regular basis. Maintainability cannot be properly evaluated until a system has been in use for a considerable period of time. The NLG system which has been in everyday use for the longest amount of time is FOG, which was described in Section 1.3.2. Goldberg et al. (1994) state that maintainability was indeed one of the main motivations for the development of FOG; prior attempts to use mail-merge-like techniques to produce weather reports resulted in systems which were difficult to adapt as requirements changed and which also could not easily support regional variations in weather forecasts. However, even in the case of FOG we do not yet have significant data on the relative expense of modifying an NLG-based system as compared to alternative systems based on mail-merge technology.

For interactive systems, an important consideration in choosing an appropriate technology is response time. Users of interactive systems generally expect to get a response within a few seconds (Shneiderman, 1998); in such contexts, this means that an NLG system which requires an excessive amount of computation time may not be acceptable, and a simpler approach may be required.

2.2.3   *Natural Language Generation versus Human Authoring*

Software systems are expensive to build, and developers need to demonstrate that developing an NLG system to produce documents or present information is a better solution than hiring and training someone to manually write the documents or present the information. A large part of this decision is based on economics: Is it cheaper to hire and train a person, or to create and maintain the software? The economic decision will usually depend largely on the volume of text produced. An NLG system which produces millions of pages of text per year will be easier to justify as cost-effective than a system which produces only hundreds of pages of text per year.

Producing a good costing for a software project and carrying out a cost–benefit analysis are major tasks in themselves. However, a quick order-of-magnitude calculation is instructive. Suppose it costs on the order of $1 million to construct, deploy, and maintain a sophisticated NLG system. Unless the system is simply an adaptation of existing software, this estimate is not unrealistic given the kinds of technologies currently used in NLG. Suppose the cost of manual document production is on the order of $20 per page. Again, apart from those circumstances where the texts can be produced by a quick copy-and-edit of a previously written text, this amount is not implausible and for many kinds of texts represents a gross underestimate. This suggests that the NLG system must generate at least ten thousand pages per year – twenty-five to thirty pages per day, every day of the year – in order to recoup the initial investment over a five-year period.

If we assume that the numbers used here are of the right order of magnitude, an NLG system which produces a hundred or even a thousand pages of text per year is unlikely to be economically justifiable, while a system which produces a hundred thousand or (better yet) a million pages of text a year is much more likely to be worth building.

Of course, cost is not the only factor in deciding whether to automate a document production task, and indeed in many cases it is not even the dominant factor. Other reasons for using NLG technology include:

- **Consistency.** Consistency may be required between texts and the input data. Because NLG systems generate text directly from the input data, they will always (provided the software works correctly) accurately communicate that data. Human authors, in contrast, may make mistakes as a result of carelessness, boredom, or fatigue. Such mistakes can be caught by a quality-assurance check, but this is expensive and may not detect all mistakes.

- **Conformance to standards.** In many cases, documents are required to conform to strict writing and content standards. For example, AECMA Simplified English (AECMA, 1986), from the European Association of Aerospace Industries, is used in the airline industry to ensure that maintenance manuals meet these kinds of requirements. Human authors can find it difficult always to write according to a prescribed standard, but an NLG system can be programmed to obey such a standard by giving it the necessary rules of grammar, style, and contents.

- **Speed of document production.** For example, Environment Canada is investigating the use of FOG to rapidly produce updated forecasts in severe weather conditions such as tornadoes and hurricanes. The advantage of adopting a software solution in this case is that it can produce a forecast in seconds, whereas a human forecaster will require several minutes to write the same forecast. In any case, in a severe weather situation, the human forecaster's time may be better spent on analysis than on writing forecast texts.

- **Generating documents in multiple languages.** Some NLG systems, such as FOG, can produce versions of a text in several languages. This allows users to produce documents in a language they do not know, without needing to involve a human translator. This is only useful, of course, if the quality of the generated texts is predictable enough to remove any need for expensive human checking of the results.

- **Staffing issues.** If a particular type of document is very boring to write, it may be difficult to employ or retain staff who are willing to write it. Computer systems do not get bored and indeed work best on exactly the kinds of monotonous tasks that people dislike.

Of course, there are also many reasons for preferring human writers to the use of NLG techniques. For example, if using an NLG system requires people to change the way they work (for instance, if it means they have to learn how to use a computer) or requires an organisation to change its processes (for instance, how it deals with handling complaints about products), then the system may not be adopted unless its perceived benefits are very high. Organisations have a limited capacity for change, and in many cases they have a large backlog of desirable changes they would like to make but have not yet been able to implement. If using an NLG system requires an organisation to change, then the system will not be adopted unless its benefits are larger than (or at least comparable to) the benefits of the other changes the organisation is contemplating.

Another issue that can discourage people from using computer-based text-generation systems is the question of responsibility for the generated texts. In particular, in many cases, a human expert may be deemed responsible for any mistakes in a document produced using NLG techniques. For example, if a doctor uses the STOP system described in Section 1.3.6 to produce customised letters for his patients, and these letters turn out to contain some incorrect information, then the patients may hold the doctor at least morally responsible. Many people do not like being responsible for documents they have not actually written themselves; we should thus not be surprised if some doctors are reluctant to use documents produced by NLG systems. There are also more general legal problems here not unlike those discussed within the expert systems community, where the issue of who is liable for machine-generated mistakes or incorrect advice is a serious concern.

There are, ultimately, many social, political, and economic factors that can play a role in determining the acceptability of an NLG system. These issues are ignored at the developer's peril; we return to this question in Section 2.5.

2.3   Using a Corpus to Determine User Requirements

Suppose we have determined that the use of NLG techniques is indeed an appropriate means whereby the user's document production needs can be met. We now require some way of determining rather more precisely just what is expected of the system to be constructed.

A requirements analysis process will identify many aspects of the system to be constructed, including performance characteristics such as speed and desirable properties of the human–computer interface and the wider operating environment. Requirements like these are relevant for many kinds of system development. Here, however, we focus on those requirements which are unique to NLG systems.

A key element of the requirements analysis task for an NLG system is the determination of the inputs the system will be provided with, the output texts it is expected to produce, and whether the output texts only communicate information which is available in the system's inputs. For example, in the context of the

WEATHERREPORTER case study introduced in Section 1.3.1, we cannot expect the system to produce output texts that explain that a particular dry spell is part of a worldwide drought if the system does not have access to information about the weather in other parts of the world and does not embody the reasoning abilities that would be required to determine this. No NLG system, no matter how sophisticated, can generate texts that communicate information that is not in some way available to the system.

Unfortunately, it is not uncommon for the initial specification of an NLG system to request exactly this kind of output. This is perhaps because people are accustomed to the behaviour of human document writers, who can insert into documents extra information based on general knowledge acquired from a wide variety of sources (such as the newspaper that the writer read over breakfast yesterday). Unfortunately, computer systems, at least in the late 1990s, cannot tap general information sources in the same way as humans; hence, they necessarily often produce more limited documents than human writers. The NLG developer needs to work with those who wish the system built to define a functionality which is both implementable and useful.

In the rest of this section, we describe an approach to analysing the inputs and outputs of an NLG system which is based on a collection of example inputs and associated output texts. In our view, it is generally easier to discuss functionality with users by showing such examples than by discussing NLG in a more abstract way, especially since many users have no previous experience with NLG technology. We call this collection of input and output data a CORPUS, and this approach a CORPUS-BASED APPROACH. A good corpus is also a very useful resource for designing specific NLG components, as will be discussed in subsequent chapters of this book.

The use of a corpus, and the notion of a corpus-based approach, is now quite common in many natural language analysis projects. However, in the context of natural language analysis, a corpus typically consists solely of a collection of example input texts to be analysed. In the context of natural language generation, to be maximally useful a corpus needs to contain examples of system inputs as well as examples of the corresponding output texts to be generated.

2.3.1   Assembling an Initial Corpus of Output Texts

The first step in carrying out a corpus-based requirements analysis is to create an INITIAL CORPUS of human-authored texts and their associated inputs. In the simplest case, the initial corpus can be created by using archived examples of human-authored texts. A business letter corpus can be based on real letters sent out in the past, for example, while a weather report corpus can be based on real previously-written reports. As far as possible, the corpus should cover the full range of texts expected to be produced by the NLG system. In particular, it should include boundary and unusual cases as well as typical cases. Of course, this is rather a

Summary:
The month was rather dry with only three days of rain in the middle
of the month. The total for the year so far is very depleted again,
after almost catching up during March. Mars Creek dried up again
on 30th April at the waterfall, but resumed on 1st May after a light
rain. This is the fourth time it dried up this year.

Figure 2.1   An example human-authored text in the WEATHERREPORTER domain.

difficult requirement to satisfy. A major reason for using NLG in the first place may
be to handle previously unseen variations in input data, so it can be difficult to
determine just what the full range of generated texts will be. Ultimately, exactly
what counts as a representative corpus is open to debate and must be mutually
agreed upon by developer and users.

Figure 2.1 shows a human-authored weather summary from WEATHERRE-
PORTER's initial corpus; this is the text provided by the meteorologist for the
month of April 1996. The raw input data underlying this text is of the general
form shown in Figure 1.2 in Chapter 1. Since these data records represent sets
of readings made every 15 minutes, there are 2,976 data records underlying the
text shown in Figure 2.1; in practice, we collate and simplify this data into DAILY
WEATHER RECORDS to make it easier to manage. An example data weather record
is shown in Figure 2.2. We will henceforth take this to be the input to the system,
but it should be borne in mind that some processing effort is required to create these
inputs from the raw data, and other packagings of the information are possible.

Of course, it is not always the case that human-authored examples of the required
output texts will already exist. In some cases, the reason NLG techniques may be
being considered is precisely because they enable the production of documents
that it is not viable to produce by hand; in such cases, there will be no preexisting
target texts. Often, the best strategy is to ask domain experts to write examples of
appropriate output texts. This is the approach taken in the development of the STOP

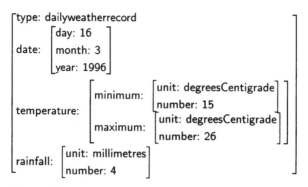

Figure 2.2   An example daily weather record.

system. Doctors and other health-care professionals were asked to write examples of appropriate letters for a group of patients who smoked. If this approach is used, it can be useful for subsequent analysis to record the experts 'thinking aloud' while writing some of the texts, if they agree to this; this can provide useful data to assist in subsequent analysis of the corpus.

2.3.2 Analysing the Information Content of Corpus Texts

Once an initial text corpus has been created, a proper analysis of the requirements for the NLG system can begin. The key goal is to determine the information content of the texts in the initial corpus. In particular, the developer needs to identify any parts of the human-authored corpus texts that convey information which is not available to the NLG system. As we will see in Chapter 4, we can analyse the content of texts in terms of informational elements which correspond to the predication of properties to objects or the identification of values of variables in the domain. These predications and identifications are expressed linguistically by means of a variety of grammatical constructs, most typically sentences and clauses.[1] Information content analysis thus requires classifying each sentence, clause, or other appropriate grammatical constituent of a corpus text into one of the following categories:

> **Unchanging text.** A textual constituent that is always present in the output texts. An example in Figure 2.1 is the initial title *Summary:*, which is present in every text in the corpus.
>
> **Directly-available Data.** Text that presents information which is available directly in the input data or an associated database or knowledge base. An example might be the reporting of the amount of rainfall on the wettest day in a given month; this information is straightforwardly derivable from a collection of data records like that shown in Figure 2.2.
>
> **Computable data.** Text that presents information which can be derived from the input data via some computation or reasoning involving other data sources. An example in Figure 2.1 is the sentence *The total for the year so far is very depleted again, after almost catching up during March.* The first clause in this sentence requires computing total rainfall in the year-to-date and comparing it to historical information, which is reasonably straightforward. The second clause, *after almost catching up during March*, is more complex and requires the system to look for interesting patterns in the data across several months.

---

[1] As explained later, a variety of other grammatical constructs can be used to express informational elements. We will use the term TEXTUAL CONSTITUENT to refer to any of these constructs.

Unavailable data. Text that presents information which is not present in or derivable from the input data. An example in Figure 2.1 is the pair of sentences about Mars Creek; there is no data in the input database or associated knowledge sources that would permit us to generate these sentences.

Unchanging textual constituents are of course the easiest kind to generate; they can simply be inserted in the output text as fixed strings. Textual constituents that present directly-available data pose no problems from the perspective of access to information, although of course they may present other difficulties for the NLG system with regard to the selection and expression of that information. For textual constituents that present computable data, a decision has to be made as to whether the results are worth the cost involved or whether the results fall into the category of unjustified 'bells and whistles'. In the example above, for instance, the developer may decide that it is reasonable to generate *The total for the year so far is very depleted*, but that it is not appropriate to construct the computational machinery required to generate the expression *after almost catching up during March*. The latter clause requires a considerable amount of sophisticated pattern matching within the source data and may not be valuable enough to users of the texts to warrant this effort.

Textual constituents that present unavailable data are, by definition, impossible to generate. No matter how sophisticated an NLG system is, it cannot include information in its output that is not present in its input. Unfortunately, textual constituents of this kind are fairly common in human-authored texts. There are a number of solutions in principle to the problem of unavailable data:

- Make more information available to the NLG system. For example, we could add to the input a database that records the status of local creeks. This kind of data provision could be expensive, however. For example, if there are no appropriate data sensors in Mars Creek, then either sensors must be installed or a human must manually enter the data into the database; both of these options are costly.
- Change the output text to eliminate constituents that express unavailable data. For example, we could specify that WEATHERREPORTER is expected to generate only the first two sentences shown in Figure 2.1 and not the two sentences about Mars Creek. Whether this is acceptable depends on how important the omitted sentences are to the users.
- Expect a human to write and incorporate textual constituents which communicate unavailable data. This is usually possible only if the NLG system is used as an authoring assistant, as described in Section 1.2.1. It will not be possible if the NLG system is expected to produce final versions of texts automatically, with no human contribution.

Which of the preceding solutions is best of course depends on the application in question. In the case of WEATHERREPORTER, we adopt the second approach; that is, output texts are changed to remove problematic clauses and sentences. In contrast, the IDAS system adopted the first approach: When it was determined that the texts to be generated required additional information, the IDAS knowledge base was updated to include this information. This was possible because IDAS was a research prototype and was based on a relatively small knowledge base; it would have been more difficult to continually update the knowledge base in this fashion in a system with a larger core knowledge base.

An example of a system where the developers took the third approach above is the MODELEXPLAINER system described in Section 1.3.4. The system can be run as a fully-automatic NLG system, which is useful for some validation tasks. However, MODELEXPLAINER is also used for generating archival documentation, and this documentation requires information (such as the purpose of a class) is not available in MODELEXPLAINER's input. Hence, when MODELEXPLAINER is used as a document production system, it is used as an authoring assistant and the human user is expected to write text portions which communicate information not available to the system.

2.3.3   Creating a Target Text Corpus

If, as outlined above, we take the approach of removing from the initial corpus those textual fragments that present data that is unavailable to the NLG system, it is clear that our target texts are no longer the same as originally specified. The developer and the users must therefore agree on a final target text corpus that incorporates these changes and any others that are required. In addition to this case, there are a number of other reasons why the initial corpus may need to be modified:

- We may remove textual constituents that correspond to those computable data elements which provide insufficient benefit to justify the cost of generating them. As discussed above, an example might be the clause *after almost catching up in March* in Figure 2.1.
- We may wish to improve the readability of the target texts. In some cases, someone considered to be a good source of advice on effective writing may suggest changes to the texts which will result in improvements over the originals. Caution is appropriate, however, since source texts which are apparently less than optimal are sometimes a consequence of domain-specific writing constraints or conventions that should not be violated.
- There may be mistakes in the initial text corpus that require correction. If the corpus is derived from an existing base of human-produced texts, it is not unusual to find grammatical errors and spelling mistakes. In some cases, close analysis may also reveal mistakes in content, perhaps due

to a misinterpretation or misreading of the input data on the part of the human author.

- There may be conflicts and inconsistencies amongst texts generated by different experts. In some cases, different experts may suggest substantially different texts corresponding to the same input data. If such a conflict is detected, it is sensible to draw it to the attention of the experts, and ask them as a group to discuss under what circumstances each text should be used.

In order to finalise a corpus of target texts, all of the above changes should of course be discussed with and approved by the system's expected users. Although some such changes may not even be noticed by the end-users, it is always possible that a change may seriously reduce the usefulness of the NLG system.

The result of all these changes is a set of texts which characterises the output that will be generated by the NLG system; we will refer to this as the TARGET TEXT CORPUS. Figure 2.3 shows the target text which corresponds to the initial text shown in Figure 2.1.

It is not uncommon for the final target texts to be quite different from the initial human-authored texts. In particular, target texts may be much shorter than the human-written texts, if the human authors used a lot of information not available to the NLG system; this is why, for example, the target text in Figure 2.3 is so much shorter than the initial text in Figure 2.1. This reflects the realities of the available data sources; in some situations, of course, the outcome of this process may be that the users decide that NLG technology is not appropriate for their application.

Because target texts can differ substantially from initial texts, some NLG projects do not use initial texts written by domain experts at all; rather, they directly produce a proposed target text corpus, based on the developer's intuition as to what texts are appropriate in the application. However, whenever possible it is best to use an initial corpus of texts created by human domain experts. After all, domain experts usually have a better idea than software developers of what should be in the generated texts.

It can take considerable effort to build a target text corpus with which both the developer and the users feel comfortable. However, this is time well spent, and a good corpus makes it much easier to develop a good NLG system. We will return to uses of this corpus in subsequent chapters of this book.

Summary:

The month was rather dry with only three days of rain in the middle of the month. The total for the year so far is very depleted again.

Figure 2.3   An example target text in the WEATHERREPORTER domain.

2.4 Evaluating NLG Systems

An important part of building a real-world system is evaluation: determining how well the system meets the goals that it was intended to satisfy. Unfortunately, relatively little is known about the best way to evaluate NLG systems.

The ultimate form of evaluation, of course, is acceptance by the relevant user community. So, for example, in the final analysis FOG will be successful if meteorologists use it to help write weather reports; MODELEXPLAINER will be successful if software developers use it to assist their understanding of software models; and so forth.

From a developer's perspective, however, acceptance by a user community has some problems as an evaluation metric. In particular, it usually takes many years to find out if users accept a program or not; and furthermore, user reactions to a program are heavily influenced by nontechnical factors (some of which are discussed in Section 2.5); these may only partially reflect the underlying strengths or weaknesses of the technology and hence the chance of success in other applications. As a consequence, this metric does not provide much help either in fixing the target application (because of the long time delays) or in creating other applications based on the same technology.

For these reasons, other types of evaluation are frequently used, especially when the goal of the evaluation is to judge the strengths and weaknesses of a class of applications or even NLG as a whole. One such type of evaluation is to look at human users' success or failure in performing a task in the application domain using the NLG system in question. For example, IDAS was evaluated by asking a small group of people to use the system as a knowledge source to be consulted in answering a set of questions about a bicycle. The system's performance was measured by the percentage of questions the subjects answered correctly. A much larger task evaluation is planned for the STOP system. In this evaluation, hundreds of letters produced by STOP will be sent to smokers, and the number of people who actually quit after receiving the letters will be measured; this will be compared to the number from a control group whose members receive a standard (nonpersonalised) smoking-cessation letter.

Task evaluations can be expensive – the cost of evaluating STOP is comparable to the cost of developing the software in the first place. Nonetheless, the cost of evaluation is still usually much cheaper than the cost (in reputation as well as in financial terms) of attempting to deploy a system which does not work as it should. Indeed, users may be reluctant even to consider using a system unless it has passed a task evaluation; doctors will not consider using STOP, for example, unless it is shown to be successful in its evaluation.

Another type of evaluation is based on asking human experts to judge the quality of generated texts under various criteria; in many cases, the experts are also asked to evaluate a set of human-written texts under the same criteria, without knowing which texts are human-written and which are computer-generated. A few of the many possible evaluation criteria that have been considered here are content, organisation, correctness, precision, and textual flow. Both ALETHGEN (Coch, 1996a) and KNIGHT (Lester and Porter, 1997), for example, were evaluated in this way, and in both cases the evaluations showed that the machine-generated texts received worse quality scores than the human-written texts, but the differences were not large, at least under the scoring schemes used in these evaluations.

This type of evaluation is appealing because it is relatively cheap and quick to carry out – at least compared to the other alternatives discussed above – and because it can also provide insights as to the general strengths and weaknesses of NLG technology. Unfortunately, it is not clear how best to perform a quality evaluation or even how meaningful the results are in predicting the success or failure of a particular NLG application. It would be very useful to correlate the results of a quality evaluation with the results of a task or user-acceptance evaluation on the same software; at the time of writing, no such comparisons have been reported in the literature.

All of the above evaluations look at the performance of the NLG system as a whole; in other words, they are BLACK BOX evaluations. It is also possible to evaluate the performance of individual components inside an NLG system; this is called a GLASS BOX evaluation. Yeh and Mellish (1997), for example, evaluated the performance of a referring expression generation algorithm by comparing its decisions about which type of referring expression was appropriate in a given context to the decisions made by human writers who were given the same problem.

In the 1990s, evaluation has become an important issue in a great deal of natural language processing research; to a large extent this has arisen as a result of the interest of funders (such as DARPA in the United States) in seeing measurable results. It is too soon to say how long-lived this phenomenon will be or what impact it will have on work in natural language generation.

2.5   Fielding NLG Systems

It can be surprisingly difficult to deploy or FIELD an innovative piece of software such as an NLG system. By 'fielding' we mean the process of deploying the system in the real world so that users regularly use it to help them accomplish some task. Building a system which works and delivers real benefits to the user is only part of the battle. Sometimes potentially useful software simply sits on a shelf because it does not fit the way an organisation or an individual works, or because the person who stands to benefit from the use of the software is not the person who actually has to use it. In other cases, good software may not be used because it is not well supported by documentation, tutorials, training courses, help lines, and other material and services which help users take best advantage of the software. In still other cases, especially if new technology such as NLG is used, people may be reluctant to use the software because they do not completely trust it.

There is currently no widely-available literature that discusses the particular problems of fielding NLG systems. In this section, we draw on some work that examines the problems of fielding advanced mail-merge systems. These are often targeted at the same general problem areas as NLG systems, and so are likely to suffer from similar problems.

A team at the University of Aberdeen (including many of the people now involved in the STOP project) developed an advanced mail-merge system called GRASSIC, which produced personalised asthma information booklets (Osman et al., 1994). GRASSIC was shown to be effective in clinical trials; indeed, severe asthma patients who received booklets produced by GRASSIC had half the hospitalisation rate of a control group of patients. But despite this demonstrable effectiveness, GRASSIC was never fielded. Instead, the conventional booklets were modified to include a single page which a doctor could manually fill in during a consultation. Among the reasons for preferring this option were the following:

> **Cost.** The process of actually fielding GRASSIC was likely to be considerably more expensive than the development costs of the software itself. The manually-personalised booklets, in contrast, could be put in place very cheaply.
>
> **Acceptance.** The GRASSIC team was concerned that many doctors would not be willing to use the system, partially for the reasons discussed in Section 2.2.3. For example, using GRASSIC required changing the way doctors worked, and it also required doctors to accept responsibility for documents they did not produce. The manually-personalised booklets, in contrast, fitted very well into existing procedures, and the doctors had a sense of ownership of the final results.
>
> **Intolerance of computer-generated mistakes.** Another issue was the fact that, at least in health-related contexts, people are far more intolerant of mistakes made by a computer system than mistakes made by doctors. If a doctor makes a mistake once in a thousand cases, he may be praised for doing an exceptionally good job; if a computer system makes a mistake once in a thousand cases, it may be withdrawn from service.

Of course, many of these problems are NLG-specific instances of more general problems that are faced in fielding any computer system. Whenever possible, requirements analysis should look at fielding issues as well as more straightforward user requirements. As has been widely recognised in many other contexts, it is also important that any attempts to implement new technologies of this kind have a 'champion' within the host organisation.

2.6   Further Reading

A good place to start for those interested in requirements analysis for NLG is the general software engineering literature on requirements analysis techniques. Material can be found in many general software engineering textbooks, such as that of Pressman (1997).

While many papers have been written about specific NLG systems, most of these papers have focused on technical issues, not on what makes a particular application promising, or what benefits using NLG brings. Some exceptions to this rule are by Reiter et al. (1995), who discuss the potential benefits of NLG for producing technical documentation; by Coch (1996a) and Springer, Buta, and Wolf (1991) who discuss the benefits of NLG for producing business letters. Goldberg et al. (1994) and McKeown et al. (1994) briefly discuss the application context and why NLG is needed for, respectively, FOG and PLANDOC, which are both fielded systems.

See Section 7.6 for suggested reading on the integration of text and graphics in information presentation systems. Reiter (1995a) provides a general discussion of when NLG might be preferable to mail-merge or template-based systems, and when it is better not to use NLG. Coch (1996a) gives some experimental results showing that the ALETHGEN natural language generation system produces better results than a mail-merge system, and Goldberg et al. (1994) briefly discuss the maintainability advantages of FOG over template-based weather report generators. Reiter et al. (1995) discuss some of the nonmonetary advantages of NLG over manually created documents.

Surprisingly little has been written about using corpus analysis to analyse the requirements of NLG systems, although some form of corpus analysis does seem to have been used by many NLG researchers and developers. McKeown et al. (1994) discuss, albeit fairly briefly, some of the requirements and corpus analysis techniques used in building PLANDOC. Goldberg et al. (1994) touch on these issues in FOG. Forsythe (1995) and Reiter et al. (1997) discuss some of the problems that result from relying exclusively on corpus analysis and describe some other techniques that can be used for knowledge acquisition and requirements analysis.

Dale and Mellish (1998) discuss evaluation of NLG systems in general terms. The evaluations of IDAS, ALETHGEN, and KNIGHT are discussed in Levine and Mellish (1995), Coch (1996a), and Lester and Porter (1997), respectively. Yeh and Mellish (1997) describe a glass-box evaluation of a referring expression generation algorithm.

A more detailed discussion of the problems in fielding GRASSIC is provided in Reiter and Osman (1997).

3   The Architecture of a Natural Language Generation System

A piece of software as complex as a complete natural language generation system is unlikely to be constructed as a monolithic program. In this chapter, we introduce a particular ARCHITECTURE for NLG systems, by which we mean a specification of how the different types of processing are distributed across a number of component modules. As part of this architectural specification, we discuss how these modules interact with each other and we describe the data structures that are passed between the modules.

3.1   Introduction

Like other complex software systems, NLG systems are generally easier to build and debug if they are decomposed into distinct, well-defined, and easily-integrated modules. This is especially true if the software is being developed by a team rather than by one individual. Modularisation can also make it easier to reuse components amongst different applications and can make it easier to modify an application. Suppose, for example, we adopt a modularisation where one component is responsible for selecting the information content of a text and another is responsible for expressing this content in some natural language. Provided a well-defined interface between these components is specified, different teams or individuals can work on the two components independently. It may be possible to reuse the components (and in particular the second, less application-dependent component) independently of one another. And if there is a subsequent requirement to modify the way in which the information is expressed (perhaps by changing the style of presentation or even the particular natural language that is used), it may then be possible to achieve these changes by modifying only the second component while leaving the first component untouched.

At present there is no agreement in detail among NLG researchers as to what constitutes the most appropriate decomposition of the process of generating natural language from some underlying representation. In this chapter, we present in detail a specific architecture that embodies one particular decomposition of the process into distinct modules and one particular set of representations for the information that is passed between these modules. This architecture is by no means the only possible architecture for NLG systems, but it is similar, at least in general terms, to the architecture of a number of existing NLG systems, and it is broadly compatible with a wide range of work in the field.

Our discussion is primarily oriented towards NLG systems that operate in what we might think of as 'single-interaction' mode, where each invocation of the system produces a single text or document. However, natural language generation capabilities may also be required within a larger dialogue system, where the NLG component is a subsystem responsible for producing output utterances in response to user inputs. By and large, the concepts we introduce are just as applicable in this alternative scenario, and all of the component processes we discuss are also implicated in the context of dialogue; however, for simplicity we will frame discussions in a manner that is more natural for NLG applications of the single-interaction variety.

In Section 3.2, we begin by clarifying what we take to be the inputs and outputs of the natural language generation process as a whole. In Section 3.3, we informally describe the architecture and the kinds of processing that take place within it. In Section 3.4, we then describe the architecture more formally, with particular emphasis on the representations that are used to communicate between the component modules; the details of the component modules themselves are the subject of subsequent chapters in the book. Throughout this discussion, we will usually exemplify the issues that arise by means of the WEATHERREPORTER case study, referring to other systems where appropriate. In Section 3.5, we consider some alternative architectural models that have been discussed in the research literature; and in Section 3.6, we provide pointers to work that discusses further a number of the issues raised in this chapter.

3.2   The Inputs and Outputs of Natural Language Generation

3.2.1   *Language as Goal-Driven Communication*

From a theoretical perspective, the process of language generation is often viewed as goal-driven communication. Under this view, the production of an utterance – whether this be a word, a sentence, or a much longer span of textual material, and whether written and spoken – is seen as being an attempt to satisfy some COMMUNICATIVE GOAL or COMMUNICATIVE INTENTION on the part of the speaker. What counts as a communicative goal or intention is somewhat open to interpretation, but the category of such things is generally viewed as including, variously, the goals of informing the hearer of something, of requesting or persuading the hearer to do something, and of obtaining some item of information from the hearer. In order to satisfy such goals, the speaker (whether human or computer) decides that some COMMUNICATIVE ACT must be performed, so that the hearer may understand the speaker's intention and react or respond appropriately. Note that in many cases goals may be achieved by means other than communicative acts. For example, at a dinner party one of the diners might obtain the salt cellar by asking another diner to pass it to her; alternatively, she might achieve the same result by physically reaching across the table and picking the salt cellar up. It is therefore convenient to think of communicative goals and communicative acts as specific kinds of goals and acts more generally.

The view that language use constitutes a kind of action underlies, in particular, SPEECH ACT THEORY, and some of the philosophical and linguistic work in this area has had a considerable influence on research in natural language processing. However, much of this work focuses on single-sentence utterances and has relatively little to say about the kinds of multisentential texts which NLG systems are typically required to generate. There have been some attempts to analyse larger texts from the perspective of the underlying intentions of the speaker, of which perhaps the most influential in NLG is Rhetorical Structure Theory (RST). Work here is underdeveloped in comparison to speech-act theory, and the discourse-level analogues of sentence-level intentions have been subject to much less rigorous formalisation. Nonetheless, the view of language as goal-driven communication provides a useful starting point for thinking about both human and machine language production of multisentential utterances.

To the extent that machines can be said to have goals or intentions, they clearly do not arise in the same way as they do in people. However, by taking a machine's communicative intention as a given, without considering its genesis, we provide ourselves with a convenient way of reasoning about its required behaviour.

3.2.2   The Inputs to Natural Language Generation

Our discussion so far has been characterised in rather abstract terms. Faced with the task of building a working NLG system, we can ask more concretely: What does the process of natural language generation start from? This is an important question. The relative ease or difficulty of the task of generation depends precisely upon the complexity of processing that is required to go from the input to the desired output.

In general terms, we can characterise the input to a single invocation of an NLG system (whether this is an execution of a single-interaction system, as defined above, or a call to generate an utterance or response in the NLG component of a dialogue system) as a four-tuple $\langle k, c, u, d \rangle$, where k is the KNOWLEDGE SOURCE to be used, c is the COMMUNICATIVE GOAL to be achieved, u is a USER MODEL, and d is a DISCOURSE HISTORY. Each of the elements of this tuple merits further explanation, as follows.

The knowledge source is the information about the domain, typically encoded in one or more databases and knowledge bases, that is available to the NLG system. Both the content and the representation of the knowledge source are highly application-dependent; for example, WEATHERREPORTER's knowledge source is a database of numerical sensor measurements made at meteorological stations, while IDAS (see Section 1.3.3) uses as a knowledge source an AI knowledge base which includes information about purpose and usage as well as more straightforward predications of properties of objects. This wide variation amongst the inputs used in different systems means that it is not possible to provide a general formal characterisation of what a knowledge source looks like, other than to say that it contains an encoding of information. We will consider some examples below.

The communicative goal describes the purpose of the text to be generated. This should be distinguished from what we might term the 'overall purpose' of a given NLG system. So, for example, WEATHERREPORTER's overall purpose is to provide historical information about the weather; but the communicative goal c corresponding to a given execution of the system is that of summarising the data for a specified month, which we might represent as SummariseMonth(m). We will say that a structure like SummariseMonth(m) corresponds to a TYPE of communicative goal, which when provided with a specific value for m corresponds to an INSTANCE of a communicative goal.

The user model is a characterisation of the hearer or intended audience for whom the text is to be generated. In many NLG systems, the user model is not explicitly specified, in which case it is effectively hard wired into the system's behaviour; this is the case in WEATHERREPORTER, for example, where we might loosely characterise the intended audience as something like 'layperson interested in weather conditions'. Where a user model is provided explicitly, its content will once again depend on what is important in the context of the given application. For example, the IDAS system utilises a user model which describes the user's knowledge of domain actions and technical vocabulary, the general type of task the user is performing; and some of the user's linguistic and stylistic preferences (for example, whether contractions such as *it's* are considered acceptable).

The discourse history is a model of what has been said in the text produced so far. This allows the system to keep track of already mentioned entities and properties so that it can make appropriate use of anaphoric resources such as pronouns. In single-interaction systems, the discourse history starts out as an empty data structure and is built up and used during the creation of the text being generated. In dialogue systems, the discourse history is sometimes referred to as a dialogue history; this serves as a repository of information about the previous interactions between the user and the NLG system. In systems such as PEBA (see Section 1.3.5), where users are expected to read a series of related texts, the discourse history has properties of both single-interaction systems and dialogue systems. So, for example, the discourse history can be used to allow a new text to appropriately refer to entities and concepts mentioned in the current or earlier texts or to add discourse markers such as *as previously mentioned* in places where the new text repeats information already presented in an earlier text.

In the case of our WEATHERREPORTER case study, we can provide a characterisation of the inputs required in terms of this four-tuple as follows:

- k is a database of records that encode a number of meteorological data values automatically collected at 15 minute intervals over a period of several years, perhaps preprocessed to produce the daily weather records we saw in Section 2.3.
- c is always an instantiation of a communicative goal of type **Summarise Month**(m), where m is the month to be summarised; we can think of this as a more specific kind of **Describe** or **Inform** goal. A particular choice of m results in the selection of a month's worth of data from k.
- There is no explicit user model, so $u = \phi$; this means that no variations in the texts generated are driven by assumed differences in assumed readership.
- Since this is a simple single-interaction system, the discourse history is empty when the system begins execution, so initially $d = \phi$; it is assumed that each text will be read in isolation.

It would, of course, be possible to build a system which used the same input data but which made use of an explicit user model and a history of previous interactions and could also service a wider range of communicative goals:

- A user model could be used to determine what information is to be emphasised in the summary. For example, a summary for farmers might emphasise precipitation and temperature, whereas a summary for mariners might emphasise wind and sea conditions.
- A history of previous interactions could be used to relate the information in one summary to the information presented in previous summaries. For example, if the user first asks for a summary of the weather in May 1994 and then asks for a summary of the weather in May 1995, the response to the second request could contain explicit comparisons to the weather in May 1994.
- The system could respond to different communicative goals, such as those we might gloss as 'describe the weather over a given week', or 'compare the weather this month with last month'.

Such variations have been implemented in other NLG systems. For example, FOG (see Section 1.3.2) produces different types of weather forecasts for different user communities; PEBA (see Section 1.3.5) relates descriptions of animals to animals previously described for the current user; and IDAS (see Section 1.3.3) is able to generate texts that respond to several types of communicative goals, ranging from simple descriptions to requests for usage instructions.

3.2.3   *The Output of Natural Language Generation*

The output of the generation process is a TEXT. From the user's perspective, a text is something which is read from paper, viewed on-line, or listened to. Most NLG systems, however, do not concern themselves with the details of formatting, on-line display, or speech output. Many research systems simply produce a stream of ASCII text for display in a terminal window. For real applications, this is generally inadequate, and attention has to be paid to the rendering of the text in a more useful form. This is typically done by making use of the capabilities of an external package (such as Microsoft Word, Netscape Navigator, or Lucent TTS) to actually format, display, or speak the document; we will refer to these as DOCUMENT PRESENTATION systems. The job of the NLG system is then to produce appropriate input representations for the document presentation system being used. These representations generally consist of a linear sequence of word tokens and punctuation symbols interspersed with mark-up symbols that are understood by the document presentation system.

The word tokens and punctuation symbols which can appear in a text depend, of course, on the output language. A Spanish document, for example, will use a very different set of word tokens than an English document and will also contain some different punctuation symbols (such as '¿'). Some NLG systems can produce output in multiple languages; for example, FOG produces texts in both French and English. In this book, most of our examples are drawn from systems which generate English texts, but the techniques we describe are transferable to systems which produce texts in other languages.

The mark-up symbols which can appear in a text depend on the mark-up language used by the document presentation system; for example, Microsoft Word uses Rich Text Format (RTF), Netscape Navigator uses Hypertext Markup Language (HTML), and Lucent TTS uses SABLE. The set of mark-up symbols available depends partially on the media in which a text is presented; for example, mark-up languages for producing spoken texts (such as SABLE) generally include annotations that control the speed at which words are spoken, but these annotations are inappropriate in mark-up languages for written texts, such as RTF and HTML. We will discuss media-specific mark-up languages in Chapter 7, along with other issues that arise when a text is 'embodied' in a particular delivery medium.

In addition to media-specific annotations, mark-up languages also often specify information about a document's structure; for instance, how the document as a whole is divided up into sections and how sections are divided up into paragraphs. This is important, because an NLG system should be able to specify not just what words, punctuation symbols, and sentences are in a document but also how these are organised into paragraphs, sections, and other such structures. Furthermore, some of these structures may have extra information associated with them in addition to their constituent sentences; for example, sections may have numbers and titles and may have associated formatting requirements.

The particular structures that can be used in a document depend on the application. For example, WEATHERREPORTER produces documents which contain paragraphs but no other structures above the level of the sentence; MODELEX-PLAINER (see Section 1.3.4) produces documents which contain sections as well as paragraphs; and STOP (see Section 1.3.6) produces documents which contain 'text boxes' that are displayed next to a graphic, as well as sections and paragraphs. The Standard Generalised Markup Language (SGML), which is becoming widely accepted as a mark-up language for documents, provides the DOCUMENT TYPE DEFINITION (DTD) as a means of providing a formal description of the types of structures that can be included in a class of documents.

The length of generated texts again varies in different applications. In some application contexts, a single sentence or a subsentential unit – perhaps even a single word, such as *Yes* or *Okay* – may be appropriate as the output of an NLG system; in other contexts an NLG system may be required to produce a text consisting of several pages. Most of the systems we mention in this book fall between these two extremes, producing texts that are longer than one sentence but which can still fit on one page.

3.3   An Informal Characterisation of the Architecture

There are many decisions that need to be addressed when producing an output text from some specified input data and many ways of organising the required decision-making processes into tasks and modules. In this book, we will assume that the generation process can be usefully decomposed into three component modules, which we will refer to as the document planner, the microplanner, and the surface realiser. This is by no means the only way to build an NLG system, but it is broadly consistent with the structure of many systems described in the literature (see (Reiter, 1994) for discussion). We will further categorise the processing performed by these modules in terms of the tasks of content determination, document structuring, aggregation, lexicalisation, referring expression generation, linguistic realisation, and structure realisation.

In this section, we describe this architecture in informal terms: the aim here is to give the reader an intuitive feel for the types of processing that happen in the different stages of an NLG system. Section 3.4 then provides a more formal characterisation, including a specification of the intermediate data structures passed between the modules.

3.3.1   An Overview of the Architecture

In very general terms, the job of the DOCUMENT PLANNER is to produce a specification of the text's content and structure, using domain and application knowledge about what information is appropriate for the specified communicative goal, user model, and so forth. This also requires using knowledge about how documents are typically structured in the application domain. Many of the techniques used in document planning are similar to those used in the world of expert systems. Correspondingly, one should expect domain experts to be heavily involved in the design and construction of document planning components, just as they are in the design and construction of expert systems.

In some cases it may be appropriate for the document planning component to completely specify the content and structure of a document. However, in many cases it is useful for the document planner to leave open some types of decisions which depend on knowledge about language and effective writing. For example, the kind of knowledge required to determine how best to package information into sentences may be more conveniently specified separately and applied at a later stage. In such cases, it is the job of the MICROPLANNER to fill in these missing details. For example, the document planner may specify that the text should include a statement that March 1995 had below-average temperatures, but it may leave to the microplanner the decision as to whether March 1995 should be referred to as *it*, *the month*, *March*, or *March 1995*. Or the document planner may specify that the text should include the above statement and also a statement that March 1995 had below-average precipitation, but leave to the microplanner the decision as to whether these should be expressed in separate sentences or combined together in a single sentence, such as *the month was cooler and drier than average*.

In some systems, the output of the microplanner may be in the form of an actual text. In many cases, however, it is again useful to separate out some specific knowledge such as that required to produce grammatical structures in the language being generated. The microplanner can then produce an abstract specification of the text's content and structure, leaving to the SURFACE REALISER the job of converting this abstract specification into real text. For example, the microplanner may specify the tense of a sentence by means of an abstract category such as **past, present,** or **future**, and leave to the realiser the choice of appropriate verb inflections and addition of any grammatically required auxiliary words, as in *September has never been colder*; similarly, the microplanner may simply state that a set of sentences should be grouped into a paragraph and may let the realiser convert these specifications into the mark-up symbols required by the target document presentation system.

We can further subdivide the processing carried out by these modules in terms of conceptually distinct tasks that need to be attended to. In any real system, these tasks may not be devolved to separate software components, and in some cases they may be quite interleaved; however, by separating them for the purposes of discussion we can examine more closely what is involved in each case. One way of characterising these tasks is to see some of them as being primarily concerned

Module	Content task	Structure task
Document planning	Content determination	Document structuring
Microplanning	Lexicalisation; Referring expression Generation	Aggregation
Realisation	Linguistic realisation	Structure realisation

Figure 3.1 Modules and tasks.

with content and others as being primarily concerned with structure, as summarised in Figure 3.1.

- CONTENT DETERMINATION is the task of deciding what information should be communicated in the output document. We can think of this as the content aspect of document planning.

- DOCUMENT STRUCTURING is the task of deciding how chunks of content should be grouped in a document and how different chunks should be related in rhetorical terms. We can think of this as the structural aspect of document planning.

- LEXICALISATION constitutes the task of deciding what specific words (or other linguistic resources, such as particular syntactic constructions) should be used to express the content selected by the content determination component. It can be thought of as the content side of microplanning.

- REFERRING EXPRESSION GENERATION is concerned with deciding what expressions should be used to refer to entities. It can be seen as another part of the content aspect of microplanning.

- AGGREGATION is the task of deciding how the structures created by document planning should be mapped onto linguistic structures such as sentences and paragraphs. Aggregation mechanisms may also decide in which order information should be expressed, if this has been left open by the discourse structuring component. We can view this as the structural side of microplanning.

- LINGUISTIC REALISATION is the task of converting abstract representations of sentences into the real text; it corresponds to the content aspect of surface realisation.

- STRUCTURE REALISATION is the task of converting abstract structures such as paragraphs and sections into the mark-up symbols understood by the document presentation component; this corresponds to the structural side of surface realisation.

In the remainder of this section, we provide an intuitive description of each of these tasks. We will motivate the discussion here by examining the issues involved in generating three particular WEATHERREPORTER weather texts, shown in Figures 3.2–3.4.

The month was cooler and drier than average, with the average
number of rain days. The total rain for the year so far is well below
average. There was rain on every day for eight days from the 11th
to the 18th, with mist and fog patches on the 16th and 17th. Rainfall
amounts were mostly small, with light winds.

Figure 3.2   The weather summary for February 1995.

3.3.2   *Content Determination*

CONTENT DETERMINATION is the name we give to the problem of deciding what
information should be communicated in a text. Sometimes the host application will
provide a specification of the information to be communicated, but in many cases
the NLG system itself will be responsible for selecting some appropriate subset of
the available information. McDonald (1999) distinguishes these as PUSH versus
PULL uses of NLG technology.

The choice of what content should be expressed in a text is dependent upon a
variety of factors, including at least the following:

- **Different communicative goals** may require different information to be
  expressed. For example, if the NLG system is capable of both describing
  the weather over some period and also of providing definitions and explanations of meteorological phenomena, then quite different content will
  be required in each case. Less radically different communicative goals
  can still lead to quite different content choices. For example, a summary
  of the weather over the previous 24 hours is likely to contain information
  at a finer granularity than would be included in a summary of the weather
  over the previous month.
- **Content** required may depend on assumed or known characteristics of
  the hearer or reader. For example, someone who is considered a novice
  in the domain of application may require more explanatory information
  than someone who is considered an expert.
- **Constraints** upon the output may play a role in determining the content.
  For example, it may be necessary that the text produced fits within a
  constrained space.

The month was our driest and warmest August in our 24 year
record, and our first rainless month. The 26th was the warmest
August day in our record with 30.1 degrees, and our first hot August day (30). The month forms part of our longest dry spell: 47
days from 18th July to 2nd September. Rainfall so far is the same as
at the end of July but now is very deficient. So far this has been our
third driest year.

Figure 3.3   The weather summary for August 1995.

The month was rather wet and cloudy with low maximums in the day and very mild to warm minimums at night. The rainfall was above average, and several thunderstorms occurred.

Figure 3.4   The weather summary for January 1996.

- **The underlying information source** itself plays a significant role in determining what the content of the text should be. What is worth saying will depend on the nature and content of the information available.

This last point can be demonstrated quite clearly in the WEATHERREPORTER case study. In the texts in Figures 3.2 and 3.4, for example, we see that each summary generally contains a description of the overall temperature and rainfall for the month. However, where the underlying data contains something noteworthy, appropriate additional information is included, as in the description of the spell of rainy days in the text in Figure 3.2 and the observation in the text in Figure 3.3 that the month was the driest and warmest on record.

Ultimately, the questions of what information should be included in a text and the circumstances under which it should be included are very application dependent. Obviously, what is worth reporting in the context of a weather summary is quite unrelated to, for example, that which is noteworthy in the context of generating a letter that encourages the reader to give up smoking. Because of this, it is not possible to specify general rules for content determination, although there are vaguely stated principles that one might use as a guide in building a mechanism to determine appropriate content, such as 'report that which is significant', and 'don't state that which is obvious or easily inferable'.

3.3.3   Document Structuring

DOCUMENT STRUCTURING is concerned with the problem of imposing ordering and structure over the information to be conveyed. A text is not just a randomly-ordered collection of pieces of information. That this is so can easily be demonstrated by trying to read a version of a newspaper story where sentences and paragraphs have been arbitrarily reordered. Readers also have genre-dependent expectations about the structure of texts, and meeting these expectations appropriately can make a text much easier to read. There is, then, usually an underlying structure to the presentation of information in a text. In the simplest possible terms, this is akin to a story having a beginning, a middle, and an end, but most texts have much more discernible structure than this.

The most obvious surface manifestation of structuring is the order of presentation of the information. However, much research into discourse analysis suggests that there is more to this than just a question of sequencing. The underlying structure of a text can often usefully be viewed as being hierarchical in nature, with textual elements such as clauses and sentences being viewed as constituents of larger text fragments, which are in turn elements of other, larger still, fragments. A text can then be analysed in terms of a tree structure, where the relationships between the constituents in the tree may be defined in two ways:

- Information may be grouped for presentation in terms of what the information is about. For example, in the case of our weather summaries, all the information about temperature may be collected into one paragraph and presented before another paragraph which presents all the information about rainfall.

- Information may be presented in ways that indicate the particular DISCOURSE RELATIONS that hold between elements of the text. So, for example, a text might characterise the month's temperature in rather general terms and then go on to elaborate on this general characterisation in some detail, as happens in the text shown in Figure 3.3. We can then think of the second part of the text as being related to the first by means of a discourse relation of **Elaboration**.

Figure 3.5 shows a simple characterisation of the structure of the text in Figure 3.2. Here, as is common in our corpus, the text begins with a general characterisation of the month's weather conditions, compared to the average for the month in question; this is then followed by some information about specific weather events during the month, in this case mostly concerned with rainfall. Here, the description of the rainy spell is elaborated with information about mist and fog and a description of the quantities of rain involved.

The particular roles played by the different elements of a text – for example, whether a particular paragraph or sentence serves to exemplify some point being made – may be explicitly signalled by linguistic or typographic means or left for the reader to infer. Figure 3.6 shows a text generated by PEBA, where a bulleted list is used to make clear that a number of items are being enumerated.

3.3.4   *Lexicalisation*

LEXICALISATION is the problem of choosing the content words – nouns, verbs, adjectives, and adverbs – that are required in order to express the content selected by the content determination system. It is convenient to see this task as also including the choice of other linguistic resources which convey meaning, such as particular syntactic structures. For example, we can express information about ownership either via words as in Example (3.1a) or via the possessive construct as in Example (3.1b):

(3.1)   a. the car owned by Mary
         b. Mary's car

Figure 3.5 The structure of the weather summary in Figure 3.2.

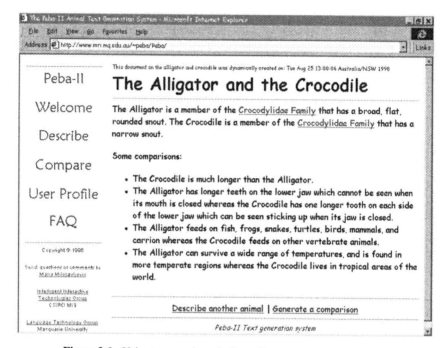

Figure 3.6   Using typography to indicate discourse structure. (Courtesy of Maria Milosavljevic.)

Lexicalisation is an issue because there can be numerous ways in which a piece of information can be expressed; unless the choice is made randomly, we need to provide some mechanism for choosing amongst the alternatives. For example, consider the phrase *There was rain on every day for eight days from the 11th to the 18th* from Figure 3.2. The time period in this phrase can be expressed in many ways, as in the following variations on the original sentence:

(3.2)   a. There was rain on every day for eight days from the 11th to the 18th.
         b. There was rain on every day for eight days from the 11th.
         c. There was rain on every day from the 11th to the 18th.
         d. There was rain on the 11th, 12th, 13th, 14th, 15th, 16th, 17th, and 18th.

Sometimes the choice between possible lexicalisations may be influenced by a contextual model; for example, the repetition in Example (3.2a) (both *for eight days* and *from the 11th to the 18th*) may be useful to some users but annoying to others. Pragmatic factors and communicative goals may also influence the choice process. For example, the explicit day list in Example (3.2d) is clumsy and probably normally should be avoided; however, it may be appropriate if WEATHERREPORTER has the pragmatic goal of emphasising to the reader that there was an unusually long rain spell in this month.

Lexicalisation is hardest in multilingual systems, where the same information must be expressed in different languages. Of course one could simply build completely independent lexicalisation systems for each target language, but this is wasteful; for example, the rule 'avoid long enumerated lists of days unless there are pragmatic reasons to use this construction' probably applies to many other languages in addition to English. Ideally lexicalisation rules should be shared as much as possible across languages, but our understanding of how to do this is still very incomplete.

The exact functionality needed in a lexicalisation process depends, of course, on the application. For example, lexicalisation is fairly simple in WEATHERREPORTER, since it generates text in one language only, with no variations on the basis of user characteristics, pragmatic models, or previous interactions with the system. It is more complex, however, in multilingual systems such as FOG, or systems with rich contextual models such as IDAS.

3.3.5   Referring Expression Generation

Any domain is populated by entities: these are the things that can be talked about, whether concrete or abstract. REFERRING EXPRESSION GENERATION is concerned with how we produce a description of an entity that enables the hearer to identify that entity in a given context. Referring expression generation is an issue for NLG because the same entity may be referred to in many different ways. This is true both when an entity is mentioned for the first time (INITIAL REFERENCE) and when the entity is subsequently referred to after it has been introduced into the discourse (SUBSEQUENT REFERENCE).

In real language use, there are many ways in which we can introduce a given entity into a discourse. An important issue when an entity is referred to for the first time is the choice of what we might think of as 'perspective'. When introducing someone into a conversation, for example, we may be faced with a decision as to whether to introduce her as a computational linguist, a visitor from overseas, or someone interested in Tai-Chi. Which of these or many other possible descriptions are selected will depend on the reason for bringing the person into the conversation and the information we subsequently intend to impart. However, virtually all NLG systems operate only within rather limited contexts, and so the choice of perspective is generally not an issue; the form of initial reference is typically heavily constrained by the domain of application and so can usually be dealt with reasonably straightforwardly.

With subsequent reference, the concern is to distinguish the intended referent from other entities with which it might be confused. Subsequent references are typically abbreviated in some way, and the problem then becomes how to abbreviate a reference without at the same time making it ambiguous.

In many domains there is a choice to be made between the use of a proper name, a definite description, or a pronoun. The form used depends on a variety of factors, but clearly the need to be able to identify the intended referent is a major one. So, for example, WEATHERREPORTER could refer to the specific month March 1995 by means of any of the following expressions depending upon the context of use:

(3.3)   a. March 1995
         b. March
         c. March of the previous year
         d. last month
         e. it

Determining the content of a referring expression generally requires taking account of contextual factors, especially the content of previous communications with the user as maintained in the discourse history. Once we have determined which properties of the entity should be used in a description, we still have to consider how those properties should be realised in the output language; this is the problem of lexicalisation described above.

3.3.6   Aggregation

The output of the document structuring process is usually a tree showing how information is grouped, as in the example shown in Figure 3.5. AGGREGATION is the task of mapping this structure onto linguistic structures and textual elements such as sentences and paragraphs. This might involve, for example, deciding that a single paragraph should be used for the entire structure, and that a single sentence should be used to communicate the **temperature, rainfall,** and **rainydays** information elements, but that the fourth constituent of **general-info,** the **totalrain** element, should be expressed in a separate sentence. We will also take aggregation to include the task of ordering sentences and paragraphs, in cases where this has not been explicitly specified by the document structuring component. An example is deciding that the sentence which communicates the **totalrain** information should follow the sentence which communicates the **temperature, rainfall,** and **rainydays** information.

The best understood type of aggregation is sentence aggregation, which involves the use of linguistic resources to build sentences which communicate several pieces of information at once. In the case of WEATHERREPORTER, for example, suppose we have two pieces of information to be expressed, one which describes the temperature over the month and the other which describes the rainfall over the month. This information might be expressed by means of the following two sentences:

(3.4)   The month was cooler than average.
         The month was drier than average.

This is rather stilted, however. The fluency of the text can be improved by recognising that English allows us to combine these pieces of information linguistically in a variety of ways. Thus, the same content can be expressed by either of the following single sentences:

(3.5)   a. The month was cooler and drier than average.
         b. The month was cooler than average, with less rain than usual.

In each case, we say that sentence aggregation has been performed. Note the interaction with the process of lexicalisation here. The choice of how to describe the information about rainfall has an impact on how this information can be combined with the other information to be expressed. In Example (3.5a) the rainfall is described using an adjectival phrase, whereas in Example (3.5b) it is described using a prepositional phrase. In the former case this means that the content can be more concisely expressed by folding what might have been two adjectival phrases into one.

Natural languages afford many different ways of expressing the same information content; some of these means of expression are more appropriate in some contexts than others. As the preceding examples show, the appropriate use of aggregation can significantly enhance the fluency and readability of a text. The kinds of aggregation we want an NLG system to perform can have a major influence on the kinds of intermediate representations we make use of; we will return to this point in more detail in Chapter 5.

3.3.7   *Linguistic Realisation*

Just as texts are not randomly-ordered sequences of sentences, sentences are not randomly-ordered sequences of words. Each natural language is defined, at least in part, by a set of rules that specify what is a well-formed sentence in that language. These rules of grammar govern both MORPHOLOGY, which determines how words are formed, and SYNTAX, which determines how sentences are formed. LINGUISTIC REALISATION is generally viewed as the problem of applying some characterisation of these rules of grammar to some more abstract representation in order to produce a text which is syntactically and morphologically correct. Just as for NLG as a whole, the complexity of this process once more depends on just how distant from the surface form the abstract representation is.

Some NLG systems, such as PEBA, internally represent sentences by template-like structures; linguistic realisation in such systems is relatively simple. Other systems, such as MODELEXPLAINER, internally represent sentences using abstract syntactic structures. The advantage of doing this is that it allows detailed grammatical knowledge to be encapsulated within the linguistic realiser. For instance, in English the rules for forming negative sentences are not entirely straightforward; in some cases *do* must be added when negating a sentence (as in *I do not like that*), but in other cases this is not necessary (as in *I am not bored*). If an abstract sentence representation is used, then negation can be indicated during content determination, lexicalisation, and so forth simply be setting an appropriate parameter that signals negation within the sentence specification, and the details of how to grammatically implement negation can be left to the linguistic realisation process.

Abstract representations are also useful in multilingual applications. One language may use a syntactic resource to carry information that is indicated by a morphological resource in another language. For example, grammatical function in English is generally indicated by syntactic resources such as word order and the use of prepositions, whereas in German it is indicated by morphological case, realised by means of affixes on the head nouns and morphological properties of their dependents. As a result, if we want to construct a multilingual application, then we may require an input representation at a greater level of abstraction than would be required in a monolingual application.

Even without explicit regard to differences between natural languages, different approaches to linguistic realisation adopt different views as to the most appropriate input to the process. However, most have in common that the input to realisation is a structure that identifies the process to be described in the sentence to be generated and some specification of the participants in that process. The linguistic realiser is left to deal with what are effectively noncontent aspects of the final sentential form. Suppose that earlier stages of generation have determined that we require a sentence that expresses information about a particular rain spell by describing the duration of that spell and its beginning and end; the linguistic realisation process may decide to realise this information via the following sentence.

(3.6)   It rained for eight days from the 11th to the 18th.

Here, the syntactic component of the realiser has decided to add the function words *for*, *from*, and *to* to mark those parts of the sentence which specify the duration, beginning, and end of the spell in question; and the morphological component has produced the past tense form *rained* from the root form *rain*, and the plural nominal form *days* of the root word *day*.

So far we have only mentioned syntactic and morphological aspects of realisation. Less discussed in the literature is the additional requirement that the text produced should be *orthographically* correct. Thus, the first word in a sentence should be appropriately capitalised, and an appropriate sentence terminator should be used. In the example above, the orthographic component has capitalised the first word of the sentence and added a full stop at the end of the sentence. Although this is the most common case, there are other situations – such as capitalisation in section headings, or sentence-final punctuation in the case of exclamations or questions – where an alternative orthography is required.

3.3.8 Structure Realisation

STRUCTURE REALISATION converts abstract specifications of document structures into the annotations required by the document presentation system being used, in an analogous fashion to the way in which linguistic realisation converts abstract specifications of sentences into actual sentences. For example, the input to a structure realisation mechanism might simply state that a group of sentences should be combined into a paragraph; the structure realisation mechanism might then convert this into the appropriate mark-up symbols, such as ⟨P⟩ in HTML (used by Netscape Navigator and other Web browsers), and \par in RTF (used by Microsoft Word).

Some early NLG systems, such as IDAS, included their own document presentation systems; this was generally integrated with the process of structure realisation. However, the now widespread availability and popularity of external document presentation systems removes this requirement. Increasingly, modern NLG systems use these external components; this is the model we will assume in our architecture.

3.4 The Architecture and Its Representations

In this section, we give a more precise definition of our architecture, describing the inputs and outputs of each module. Note that while the architecture we discuss is broadly similar to the architectures of many other complete NLG systems, the details of the representations we use are specific to the particular architecture described here.

3.4.1 Broad Structure and Terminology

As mentioned in Section 3.3, our architecture divides processing into three stages:

- **Document planning.** Determining the content and structure of a document.
- **Microplanning.** Deciding which words, syntactic structures, and so forth will be used to communicate the content and structure chosen by the document planner.
- **Surface realisation.** Mapping the abstract representations used by the microplanner into an actual text.

In our architecture, these modules are connected together into a pipeline. That is, the output of document planning is the input to microplanning, and the output of microplanning is the input to realisation. Furthermore, it is not possible for the microplanner to affect the document planner's behaviour or for the realiser to affect the behaviour of the microplanner or the document planner. Although the pipeline architecture has some limitations, which we will discuss in Section 3.5, it is used in many complete NLG systems, including MODELEXPLAINER, IDAS, STOP, FOG, and PEBA.

An important aspect of any architecture is the definition of the intermediate representations passed between modules. In our architecture, there are two such representations:

- **DOCUMENT PLANS** are the output of the document planner and the input to the microplanner. Document plans consist of a tree whose internal nodes specify structural information (in the sense of Section 3.3), and whose leaf nodes specify content. The leaf nodes of document plans are called MESSAGES.
- **TEXT SPECIFICATIONS** are the output of the microplanner and the input to the realiser. These again are trees, whose internal nodes specify the structure of a text and whose leaf nodes specify the sentences of a text. The leaf nodes of a text specification are called PHRASE SPECIFICATIONS.

The architecture is shown diagrammatically in Figure 3.7. In the rest of this section, we describe these modules and representations in more detail, with a primary focus

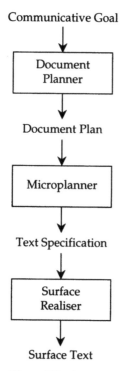

Figure 3.7 An NLG system architecture.

on the representations. Detailed descriptions of the process required to map between these representations are provided in subsequent chapters of this book.

3.4.2 Messages

The notion of a MESSAGE forms a useful abstraction that mediates between the data structures used in the underlying application and the eventual texts to be generated.

The key idea here is that, for any given domain of application, we can define a set of entities, concepts, and relations that provide a conceptual level of representation that characterises the domain in terms that can more easily be mapped into linguistic forms. In some cases, the underlying data elements may already provide such a representation, but in many applications this is not the case. Developing this conceptual representation therefore requires carrying out an exercise in domain modelling, a topic we will discuss further in Section 4.2.

Having established the entities, concepts, and relations we need to make use of, we can then define a set of messages which impose structure over these elements. In the simplest case, a message corresponds to a sentence in the output text. Many natural language generation systems make use of representations that correspond to messages of this kind. However, we can gain more flexibility if we view messages in a more general way as data objects corresponding to the largest distinct linguistic fragments we need in order to generate the variety of the texts we are interested in. Consider again the example text in Figure 3.2. Here, we see that information about the average temperature, rainfall, and number of rainy days is expressed within a single sentence, but in other texts in the corpus, these three pieces of information are distributed across a number of sentences. This argues for having three distinct message types – one that specifies information concerning temperature, one that specifies information concerning rainfall, and one that specifies the number of rainy days. They can then be combined in a variety of ways as specific circumstances demand.

In our architecture, the content of messages is based on the domain modelling process described above. Using this approach, Figure 3.8 shows definitions of WEATHERREPORTER's MonthlyTemperatureMsg and MonthlyRainfallMsg messages, and Figures 3.9 and 3.10 show examples of each of these message types. As in the rest of this section, we will use a object-oriented pseudocode for definitions, and an attribute–value matrix representation for examples.

Both the message-creation process and the form and content of the messages created are highly application dependent, and therefore the specific message representations used in different applications are likely to vary considerably. Section 4.3 looks in detail at how we can determine an appropriate message set for a given domain and application. An important point is that the underlying application's representation of information is likely to be too impoverished to support the distinctions required for generating text, and so typically additional domain knowledge

```
class Message { };

class MonthlyTemperatureMsg extends Message {
    period: Month;
    temperature: Specification;
}
class MonthlyRainfallMsg extends Message {
    period: Month;
    rainfall: Specification;
}

class Specification { };
class RelativeVariation extends Specification{
    magnitude: Measurement;
    direction: one of {+, 0, −};
}

class AbsoluteSpec extends Specification{
    amount: Measurement;
}

class Month {
    month: Integer;
    year: Integer;
}

class Measurement{
    unit: String;
    number: Float;
}
```

Figure 3.8 A definition of some message types in WEATHERREPORTER.

$$
\begin{bmatrix}
\text{type: MonthlyTemperatureMsg} \\
\text{period:} \begin{bmatrix} \text{month: 05} \\ \text{year: 1996} \end{bmatrix} \\
\text{temperature:} \begin{bmatrix} \text{type: RelativeVariation} \\ \text{magnitude:} \begin{bmatrix} \text{unit: degreesCentigrade} \\ \text{number: 2} \end{bmatrix} \\ \text{direction: } − \end{bmatrix}
\end{bmatrix}
$$

Figure 3.9 A MonthlyTemperatureMsg message.

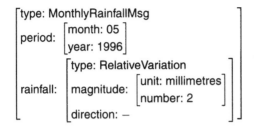

Figure 3.10 A MonthlyRainfallMsg message.

will be brought to bear during the message-construction process. In other words, the construction of messages from the underlying data is usually more than a simple data transformation process.

3.4.3 The Document Planner

The DOCUMENT PLANNER takes as input a four-tuple $\langle k, c, u, d \rangle$, where k is the KNOWLEDGE SOURCE to be used, c is the COMMUNICATIVE GOAL to be achieved, u is a USER MODEL, and d is a DISCOURSE HISTORY. As discussed earlier, in any given application, one or more of these input parameters may be null. The document planner's task is to determine the informational content and the structure of the document that meets the specified communicative goal; this will be output in the form of a document plan, defined in Section 3.4.4.

To construct a document plan, the document planner orchestrates three activities:

- It constructs messages from the underlying source of information.
- It decides which messages need to be communicated in order to satisfy the communicative goal.
- It carries out document structuring to organise the presentation of these messages in such a way that a coherent and fluent text can be generated.

These three component processes can be interleaved within document planning in a variety of ways. In some situations, it makes sense first to construct a set of messages from the input data and then to select messages from this set and organise them into a coherent structure. In other situations, the construction of messages can take place on demand as the plan for the document as a whole is developed. We examine each of these possibilities in Chapter 4.

Document planning is probably the most application-dependent aspect of natural language generation. While microplanning and surface realisation make use of what we can think of as more general linguistic knowledge, document planning is mostly based on application-specific knowledge governing what information is considered to be important, what conventions need to be obeyed in presenting this information, and so forth. These constraints derive both from properties of the application domain and from the specific genre of the texts to be produced.

```
class DocumentPlan {
    children: Constituents;
}

class Constituents { // Constituents of a document plan
}

class NSConstituents extends Constituents{
    // A nucleus and its rhetorical satellites
    nucleus: DocumentPlan or Message;
    satellites: List of SatelliteSpec;
}

class SatelliteSpec {
    // A satellite and its rhetorical relation to the nucleus
    relation: DiscourseRelation;
    satellite: DocumentPlan or Message;
}

class ConstituentSet extends Constituents{
    // A set of constituents, without a nucleus
    relation: DiscourseRelation; // Must be a non-nucleus relation
    constituents: List of DocumentPlan or Message;
}

class DPDocument extends DocumentPlan { // DP for complete document
    title: Message or PhraseSpec;
}

class DPParagraph extends DocumentPlan { // DP for paragraph
    // No extra information needed
}
```

Figure 3.11   A simple document plan representation.

3.4.4   Document Plans

The output of the document planner is a DOCUMENT PLAN. For our architecture, we require a structure that specifies how messages are to be grouped together and related so as to satisfy the initial communicative goal. We represent this in the form of a tree. The terminal nodes of the tree are messages, and the internal nodes of the tree represent groups of related messages. The internal nodes may correspond to structures such as sections and paragraphs. Internal nodes may also specify discourse relations that hold between their daughter constituents.

Figure 3.11 defines a simple set of document plan representations which could be used in WEATHERREPORTER; examples of document plans are shown in Figure 4.3 and Figures 5.2, 5.3, and 5.4. The base class DocumentPlan includes a constituent specification, which can be either of the following:

ConstituentSet. A list of constituents. A discourse relation may be specified that applies to the set as a whole, such as Narrative Sequence.

NSConstituents. A nucleus and a list of satellites; each satellite is linked to the nucleus by a discourse relation. This supports models of discourse relations (such as those proposed in RST; see Section 4.4.1) whose relations generally link a satellite constituent to a nucleus.

DocumentPlan has subclasses for supra-sentential structures found in WEATHER-REPORTER documents:

DPDocument. The complete document; includes a title.
DPParagraph. A paragraph within a document.

This representation can of course be extended in many ways, including to

- Add subclasses for other structures, such as sections and text boxes. Alternatively, we might reduce the number of subclasses if we wish the microplanner to dynamically construct some structures (for example, if we want it to dynamically determine paragraphs).
- Add information to control aggregation and ordering. For instance, we might want to specify a set of constraints which the microplanner must obey when it decides the order in which messages will appear in the generated text.

3.4.5   *Microplanning*

In general, the document plan does not completely specify the final structure and content of the text to be generated; many possible output texts will be compatible with the plan. The purpose of the MICROPLANNER is to refine the document plan so as to produce a more fully-specified text specification. This requires carrying out the following tasks:

- **Lexicalisation.** Choosing which words and syntactic structures should be used to express messages.
- **Aggregation.** Determining how messages should be composed together to produce specifications for sentences or other linguistic units or textual structures.
- **Referring expression generation.** Determining how the entities in the messages should be referred to.

The microplanner also determines those aspects of ordering that were left unspecified in the document plan.

It is possible to construct NLG systems where some or even all of these decisions have already been made during the document planning stage. For example, as was the case in many early NLG systems, messages may correspond directly to propositions that will each be expressed in single sentences, so no aggregation may be required. Our architecture does not rule out these decisions being made during document planning. However, leaving these elements unresolved until this point in the generation of text provides more flexibility in the possible outputs that can be produced.

The interrelationships between the activities carried out by the microplanner are potentially quite complex, and there is no consensus in the NLG community as to how the microplanner should be structured internally. (For more detail on microplanner architecture see Chapter 5.)

The result of the microplanning process is then a text specification containing fully specified phrase specifications; these structures are described in the next two sections.

3.4.6   Text Specifications

A TEXT SPECIFICATION is a data object that provides a complete specification of the document to be generated but does not itself constitute that document. The specification must be mapped into an actual text, that is a sequence of words, punctuation symbols, and mark-up annotations. This is the job of surface realisation; the text specification provides the information required to achieve this goal.

In an analogous manner to document plans, text specifications are usually trees. The leaf nodes of text specifications are phrase specifications; these generally specify individual sentences (see Section 3.4.7). The internal nodes of the text specification specify the structure of the document in terms of paragraphs, sections, boxes, and whatever other structures are used in the target document type.

While the specific structures used in a document are application dependent, most documents have a hierarchical structure; this is why text specifications are usually trees. This book, for example, consists of a number of chapters, each of which is made up of a number of sections; these sections are composed of subsections, and so on down through paragraphs to the individual sentences, which are in turn made up of words. Similarly, a letter typically consists of some header material such as the address of the recipient and the date of writing, and then the body of the letter itself, which begins with some opening salutation, continues with the text of the letter, and ends with a closing salutation; and each of these component parts have lower-level constituents.

This kind of structure is sometimes referred to as the LOGICAL STRUCTURE of the document. This is to be distinguished from the PHYSICAL STRUCTURE of the document, which is concerned with how the material is distributed across pages, columns, and lines. It is the job of the document presentation system (usually an external package such as Microsoft Word or Netscape Navigator) to convert the logical structure specified in the text specification into a physical structure.

Figure 3.12 defines a simple set of text specification representations; examples of text specifications are shown in Figures 5.6 and 6.1. The set of definitions

```
class TextSpec {
    children: List of TextSpec or PhraseSpec;
}

class TSDocument extends TextSpec { // TS for complete document
title: PhraseSpec;
}

class TSParagraph extends TextSpec { // TS for paragraph
    // No extra information needed
}
```

Figure 3.12   A simple text specification representation.

in Figure 3.12 are for the same structures as were supported by the document plan representations shown in Figure 3.11. In comparison to the document plan representations, however, note the following:

- Titles, headers, and leaf children are phrase specifications, not messages. Aggregation may result in several messages in the document plan being replaced by a single phrase specification in the text specification.
- There are no discourse relations. If it is necessary to explicitly communicate a discourse relation, then the microplanner will make appropriate changes at the level of phrase specifications (for example, by inserting a cue phrase such as *However* or *for example*); internal nodes in the text specification do not specify these relations.
- Constituent ordering is fully specified by the order of components in the children list.

3.4.7   *Phrase Specifications*

A PHRASE SPECIFICATION specifies a sentence or some other phrasal unit. Typically a phrase specification which is a leaf node in a text specification will specify a sentence, but a phrase specification which is a title or header may specify a subsentential phrase, such as a noun phrase.

A phrase specification be specified at various levels of abstraction. It may be an orthographic string, a fragment of canned text, or expressed as an abstract syntactic structure or a lexicalised case frame.[1] Mixtures of these representations may also be allowed. Pseudocode definitions of simple versions of these are shown in Figure 3.13. In real applications, the details of abstract syntactic structures and lexicalised case frame representations will depend on the grammatical theory on which the realiser is based (see Chapter 6).

---

[1] All of these notions are discussed in more detail in Section 6.3.

```
class PhraseSpec { };

class PSOrthographicString extends PhraseSpec {
    body: String;
}

class PSCannedText extends PhraseSpec {
    text: String;
}

class PSAbstractSyntax extends PhraseSpec {
    head: Lexeme;
    features: List of FeatureValue;
    subject, object, indirectObject: PhraseSpec;
    modifiers: List of PhraseSpec;
}

class PSLexCaseFrame extends PhraseSpec {
    head: Lexeme;
    features: List of FeatureValue;
    cases: List of CaseFiller;
}

class PSCombination extends PhraseSpec {
    components: List of PhraseSpec;
}

class FeatureValue {
    feature: String;
    value: String;
}

class CaseSpec {
    case: String;
    filler: PhraseSpec;
}
```

Figure 3.13   Some phrase specification representations.

Orthographic Strings

ORTHOGRAPHIC STRINGS specify the phrase as a string, complete with capitals, punctuation symbols, and other orthography. Example 3.7 shows a simple example of an orthographic string

$$(3.7) \quad \begin{bmatrix} \text{type: PSOrthographicString} \\ \text{body: } |\textit{The month had some rainy days.}| \end{bmatrix}$$

Canned Text

CANNED TEXT is the term we use for content specifications where the character sequence to be used has already been determined, although some orthographic processing may still be needed. Example 3.8 shows a simple example of a canned text.

$$(3.8) \quad \begin{bmatrix} \text{type: PSCannedText} \\ \text{text: |the month had some rainy days|} \end{bmatrix}$$

To produce a sentence from this string, it is necessary to capitalise the first word and put a full stop at the end of the sentence, but no syntactic or morphological processing is needed.

Abstract Syntactic Structure

For many applications, a significant part of the value of using NLG techniques comes from the ability to factor out idiosyncrasies of morphology and syntax from the specifications produced by the stages of NLG prior to surface realisation. One representation which supports this is what we will call ABSTRACT SYNTACTIC STRUCTURE.

An abstract syntactic representation describes the linguistic elements to be used in terms of their base LEXEMES (uninflected words) and syntactic constituents, plus a collection of associated features that determine how the required surface forms are to be constructed. A very simple example is shown in Example 3.9:

$$(3.9) \quad \begin{bmatrix} \text{type: PSAbstractSyntax} \\ \text{head: |have|} \\ \text{features: } \begin{bmatrix} \text{tense: past} \end{bmatrix} \end{bmatrix}$$

This specifies that the realiser should produce the past tense version of the verb *have*; that is, the word *had*.

A more complex example of an abstract syntactic structure is shown in Figure 3.14. This again produces the sentence *The month had some rainy days*.

This representation is more complex than canned text or orthographic strings, but it allows the realiser to automatically take care of some of the 'messy details' of grammar. For example, changing the plural feature to singular in the structure whose head is *day* will result in *The month had a rainy day*; in this case not only was *days* changed to *day*, but *some* was also automatically changed to *a*.

Lexicalised Case Frames

A still more abstract representation of phrase specifications is provided by what we will call a LEXICALISED CASE FRAME. These differ from abstract syntactic structures in that phrase constituents are specified by semantic role (for example, possessor) instead of syntactic role (for example, subject). An example of a lexicalised case frame representation for *The month had some rainy days* is shown in Figure 3.15.

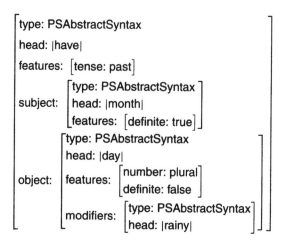

Figure 3.14   An abstract syntactic representation for *The month had some rainy days.*

In this example, the difference between abstract syntactic structures and lexicalised case frames may seem no more than terminological. However, by specifying the content using semantic rather than syntactic categories, the realiser is given more leeway in determining how to realise the given structure. This will be further discussed in Chapter 6.

Combinations

In some applications it makes sense to mix the representations. For example, part of a phrase specification may be represented using canned text, while another part

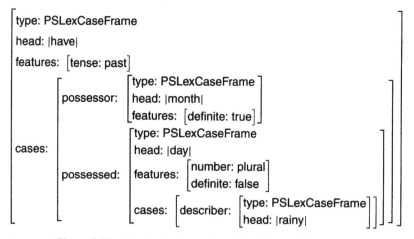

Figure 3.15   A lexicalised case frame for *The month had some rainy days.*

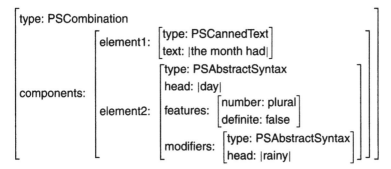

Figure 3.16 Combining canned text and abstract syntactic structures.

may be represented as an abstract syntactic structure. A simple example of this is shown in Figure 3.16. Here we have shown the list of components via pseudofeatures named element1 and element2; element1 is the canned text *the month had*, while element2 is an abstract syntactic representation of the phrase *some rainy days*.

3.4.8   Surface Realisation

The function of the SURFACE REALISATION component is to take the text specification produced by the microplanner and to convert this into text, possibly embedded within some medium. This involves traversing the text specification, typically in a top-down, left-to-right fashion, and producing appropriate output from the nodes encountered during this traversal; the information at the nodes provides a specification of what the realiser needs to do. Since most NLG systems use an external document presentation system, typically the only processing needed for internal nodes (TextSpec and its subclasses) is to generate appropriate mark-up annotations for the presentation system; for example, if Netscape is used as a rendering system, then an HTML ⟨P⟩ mark-up might be produced for a TSParagraph node. This is the process we earlier introduced as structure realisation.

The leaf nodes of a text specification are phrase specifications (PhraseSpec and its subclasses), and these must be mapped into linguistic surface forms; this is the process of linguistic realisation. As noted above, phrase specifications can specify linguistic units at several levels of abstraction. Realisation for orthographic strings is trivial: the result is simply the body of the PSOrthographicString. Realising canned text requires some orthographic processing (in particular, the addition of punctuation and capitalisation) but is still relatively straightforward. Realising abstract syntax or lexicalised case frames is more complex, and generally requires the use of a GRAMMAR, this being a formal description of the syntactic and morphological resources available in the output language.

Linguistic realisation is the most well-established area of NLG. As a result of this, a number of existing systems for carrying out this stage of processing are available in the public domain. For example, the REALPRO system maps abstract syntactic representations to textual forms, while the SURGE and KPML systems can convert lexicalised case frames into text. We will discuss these systems in more detail in Chapter 6.

3.5   Other Architectures

In this chapter, we have described one particular architectural model of the generation process. The decomposition of the process that we have proposed here is roughly compatible with a broad range of research in natural language generation, and, details aside, corresponds to what is probably the most popular architectural model in NLG systems current at the time of writing. However, it is certainly not the only possible architecture for an NLG system. In this section we briefly consider both variations on the architecture presented here and other substantially different architectures.

3.5.1   *Different Representations and Modularisations*

The basic three-stage pipeline model is quite common in NLG systems, but there are many differences in terminology and, more important, in the details of the processing that is performed at each stage and the intermediate representations used. Figure 3.17 shows some of the common alternative terms that can be found in the literature. The correspondences are not exact. For example, in many systems there is a data structure called a text plan that contains elements of both our document plan and our text specification.

Variations in representations and modularisations tend to go together. A significant change in the functionality of a module will almost certainly require a significant change in the input and/or outputs of the module, and vice versa. Below we discuss some of the more common variations of the basic pipeline architecture.

Messages

In our architecture, messages are represented as application-specific data structures, whose structure is determined by domain modelling. Another common form

Our term	Other common terms
document planner	text planner
document plan	text plan
text specification	discourse plan
	text plan
microplanner	sentence planner
phrase specification	sentence plan
linguistic realisation	surface realisation
	realisation

Figure 3.17   Variations in terminology.

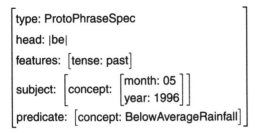

Figure 3.18 A proto-phrase specification representation of the MonthlyRainfallMsg message.

of message representation is to represent messages as what we might call PROTO-PHRASE SPECIFICATIONS. These are structures with the same general representation as phrase specifications but with some details omitted or left underspecified. In our architecture, proto-phrase specifications are used internally inside the microplanner (see Chapter 5); but many systems, including MODELEXPLAINER and FOG, also use proto-phrase specifications to represent messages in document plans.

Figure 3.18 shows an example of how the MonthlyRainfallMsg message from Figure 3.10 might be represented as a proto-phrase specification. The pointers to domain concepts and entities in this structure will be replaced by lexemes and referring expressions (for example, *drier than average* for BelowAverageRainfall, and *the month* for 05-1996) during microplanning, which may also aggregate messages.

From the perspective of modularisation, using proto-phrase specifications to represent messages means that some lexicalisation decisions are made in the document planner, not in the microplanner. For example, the proto-phrase specification shown in Figure 3.18 explicitly states that the message should be expressed with the verb *be*, while the more abstract representation shown in Figure 3.10 does not specify a particular verb. In consequence, the Figure 3.10 representation allows the message to be expressed using other verbs, such as *have* (as in *the month had less rainfall than average*).

The main advantage of proto-phrase specifications as message representations is that they enable the document planner to exert fine control over the precise wording used to express messages. The corresponding disadvantage is that they require the document planner to make decisions about how information is expressed, as well as what information to include in the document. This may make the system harder to maintain and adapt to changing requirements.

If proto-phrase specifications are used to represent messages (and this is a sensible design choice in many applications), it may still be valuable to develop abstract message representations as a paper-and-pencil exercise. This process is discussed further in Chapter 4.

Many mainstream software systems are moving to abstract messagelike representations to specify text (such as prompts and error messages), in order to make it easier to LOCALISE the system to a new human language. The conversion from message to text is usually carried out by means of simple 'fill-in-the-blank' templates, so (using our terminology) microplanning and realisation are quite simple in these systems. However, the part of the system that decides what to say (the document planner, in our terminology) specifies content using structures which are similar in concept (although not necessarily in syntax) to the message representations we use in this book.

Document Plans

In our architecture, document plans are trees whose leaf nodes are messages, and whose internal nodes specify document elements such as paragraphs and sections, and discourse relations between constituent elements. Aspects of the representation of messages were described above; here we turn to the representation of the internal nodes in a document plan.

In many early NLG systems, a text would be represented as a simple list of messages to be expressed. Such an approach is much less popular today, except in systems which generate very short texts. Not only are tree structures a very natural way to specify document elements and their constituency, but they also can provide a convenient way of storing information that the microplanner's aggregation and referring expression generation processes can use.

Many systems do not specify discourse relations between messages; instead, they simply include appropriate cue words (such as *whereas* or *for example*) in messages. This is the case, for example, in IDAS. In principle, the advantages of explicitly specifying discourse relations are as follows. First, the document planner can use these to reason about the text. For example, the document planner might reduce the length of a document by eliminating nodes which are **Elaboration**s of other nodes, if it believes the text is too long. Second, it may be difficult for the microplanner to aggregate messages if they include cue words. This is because many discourse relations are expressed differently depending on whether their participants are aggregated in the same sentence. For instance, a **Contrast** relation may be best expressed as *but* in Example 3.10 when contrasting two phrases in a sentence but best expressed as *However* when contrasting two sentences as in Example 3.11.

(3.10)   I like John, but I dislike Mary.
(3.11)   I like John. However, I dislike Mary.

Perhaps the main disadvantage of using abstract representations of discourse relations is that, given our current understanding of the nature of discourse relations, it can be difficult to specify robust algorithms for mapping them into cue words. In many cases the choice of how to best express a discourse relation depends on subtle pragmatic and semantic factors (see Vander Linden and Martin, 1995; Knott, 1996).

As a result, it may be easier to effectively compile this knowledge into the document planner than to explicitly represent it for the microplanner.

From the perspective of modularisation, if the document planner specifies cue phrases instead of discourse relations, this of course means that the microplanner does not have to lexicalise discourse relations. More subtly, it may also severely restrict the amount of aggregation the microplanner can do (as discussed above), and hence force the document planner itself to make many aggregation decisions.

Phrase Specifications

There are many ways of representing phrase specifications, several of which were discussed in Section 3.4.7. These obviously have an impact on modularisation. For example, using orthographic strings or canned text may require the document planner or microplanner to have a significant amount of knowledge about syntax and morphology. The particular representations we have described are also perhaps best thought of as illustrative points on a spectrum, and certainly there are other plausible representations of phrase specification which fall between the ones we illustrate. For example, the ECRAN system uses a template representation of phrase specifications which includes some structural and syntactic annotations (Geldof and van de Velde, 1997); this lies somewhere between our canned text representation and abstract syntactic structures.

Some realisers can accept what we have called proto-phrase specifications as input; an example of such a system is KPML, which is discussed in Chapter 6. From the perspective of modularisation, this means that the realiser takes over many of the tasks performed by the microplanner. Indeed, if the document planner produces proto-phrase specifications as output and the realiser accepts proto-phrase specifications as input, then there is no need for a microplanner, and the NLG system has two modules instead of three. Such a two-stage architecture was in fact very popular in the 1980s, with the document planner often called the STRATEGIC COMPONENT, and the realiser often called the TACTICAL COMPONENT. It has become less popular in the 1990s but still makes sense for some types of applications, especially systems in which aggregation, lexicalisation, and referring expression generation (the main microplanner tasks) are straightforward. FOG, for example, is a two-stage system of this kind.

Text Specifications

In our architecture, text specifications are trees whose leaf nodes are phrase specifications and whose internal nodes indicate document structure in terms of paragraphs, sections, and other elements relevant to the type of document being produced.

Some NLG systems represent text specifications as a simple list of phrase specifications, perhaps with some annotations such as **Begin-New-Paragraph** included in phrase specifications (or as separate elements in the list). IDAS, for example, used a representation of this kind. Operationally this is not very different from the tree representation presented here, but a tree structure is more in keeping with modern ideas on document structuring and also makes it easier to modify an NLG system when the document structures required change.

3.5.2   *Different Architectures: Integrated Systems*

So far we have discussed variations on the basic three-stage pipeline architecture presented in this chapter. But there also are substantially different architectures which are not simply variations on this basic model. In particular, many researchers have pointed out that pipelines make it difficult for downstream decisions (like realisation) to have an impact on upstream decisions (such as document planning); these researchers argue that systems with richer interactions between modules will produce better output because they do not suffer from this problem.

For a simple example of the interaction problem, suppose an NLG system needs to ensure that its output conforms to a strict size limit; this is the case in STOP, for example, whose output must fit on four A5 pages. The problem is that the main influence on length is the amount of information in the document, which is decided on by the document planner, but the document's length will not actually be known until it has been realised and perhaps even processed by the document presentation system. This means that in a pipeline model the document planner must make decisions about how much information to include without actually knowing whether a document is about to exceed the page limit or not; this is far from ideal.

One solution to this problem is to allow FEEDBACK between the stages. For instance, using the scenario just described, the document planner could create a preliminary version of a document, have it processed by the microplanner and realiser, and then request that the realiser or document presentation system inform it how long the document actually is. If the output document exceeds the length limit, the document planner might then eliminate some information and try again.

A variation of this approach is to have a separate REVISION module which is run after all the other modules have finished. This module examines the generated text for problems (such as a violated size constraint) and signals the appropriate module if a problem is detected; this module is then expected to make appropriate changes to fix the problem.

Although feedback and revision seem like sensible ideas, they have not been widely used in full-blown NLG systems. This is at least in part because revision and feedback can be awkward to implement in practice. For example, in the case of STOP's size limit, it would be reasonably straightforward to inform the document planner via a feedback or revision mechanism if the size constraint was violated. However, it would be more difficult to tell the document planner to what degree each message contributed to a violation (in other words, what the impact would be on document size of removing or replacing specific messages), which is the information that the document planner really needs if it is to modify the document plan so that the resultant document satisfies the size constraint.

A more radical architectural approach is to have no modularisation at all, and instead represent all decision-making processes uniformly as constraint-satisfaction, planning, or theorem-proving tasks. A single reasoning component – a constraint solver, planner, or theorem prover – is then used to find a solution (that is, a text) which simultaneously satisfies all of the constraints. Under this model, a size limit and a content requirement are simply two kinds of constraints, and no assumptions are made about which is processed first (indeed, this may be a meaningless question to ask).

Appelt's KAMP system (Appelt, 1985) is the best example of this kind of architecture to be found in the literature. KAMP uses an AI planner to perform all NLG tasks, and its use of a uniform representation and reasoning mechanism enabled it to generate relatively short texts which satisfied a number of communicative goals. For example, KAMP could generate the sentence *Remove the pump using the wrench in the toolbox* as a means of satisfying the two goals of requesting the user to perform the stated action and informing the user where he will find the necessary tool.

Integrated architectures are theoretically very elegant and in principle should allow NLG systems to generate better texts than pipelined architectures. From a practical perspective, however, they are very expensive to engineer, at least given our current limited understanding of the NLG process.

3.6   Further Reading

Further reading on each of the component problems and generation tasks we have identified in this chapter is provided at the end of the appropriate chapters in the remainder of this book.

The general issue of how best to modularise software systems is discussed in all software engineering textbooks (see, for example, Pressman, 1997).

We have only briefly touched on the extensive literature on communicative acts, intentions, and speech act theory. A good source of further reading on this topic is Cohen, Morgan, and Pollack (1990). Allen and Perrault (1980) discuss how such reasoning can be used to determine helpful responses (in other words, to perform content determination, in our terminology). The most thorough attempt to embody these ideas in a functioning natural language generation system is that of Appelt in his KAMP system (Appelt, 1985). The most widely used model of discourse relations in NLG is rhetorical structure theory. Mann and Thompson (1988) is the central source on RST.

The latest versions of the HTML, RTF, and SABLE mark-up languages can be obtained from the Web. See http://www.w3.org/MarkUp for information about

HTML, and http://www.cstr.ed.ac.uk/projects/sable.html for information about SABLE. As of mid-1998 the most recent specification of RTF was available at http://support.microsoft.com/.

Further information on REALPRO, SURGE, and KPML is given in Chapter 6.

A general description of the three-stage pipeline model, including comparisons to other architectures, is given in Reiter (1994). The two-stage strategy and tactics model (which was very popular in the 1980s) was proposed by Thompson (1977). Numerous papers have argued against pipelines because of interaction problems: see, for example, Appelt (1985) and Danlos and Namer (1988). Rubinoff (1992) and Inui, Tokunaga, and Tanaka (1992) present models of how to implement feedback and revision in an NLG system.

From a psychological perspective, our distinction between document planning and microplanning is in some ways similar to Levelt's (1989) distinction between 'macroplanning' and 'microplanning' in his model of human language production mechanism. We emphasise, however, that our model is not intended to embody any psychological model.

4 Document Planning

In this chapter and the two following, we turn to details of the components that make up the NLG system architecture we introduced in Chapter 3. Our concern in this chapter is with the component we have called the DOCUMENT PLANNER.

The chapter is organised as follows. In Section 4.1, we give an overview of the task of document planning, including the inputs and outputs of this process; this is largely a recap of material introduced in Chapter 3. In Section 4.2, we look at DOMAIN MODELLING and the related task of MESSAGE DEFINITION: Here we are concerned with the process of deciding how domain information should be represented for the purposes of natural language generation. In Sections 4.3 and 4.4, we turn to the two component tasks implicated in our view of document planning, these being CONTENT DETERMINATION and DOCUMENT STRUCTURING. In each case we describe a number of different approaches that can be taken to the tasks. In Section 4.5, we look at how these tasks can be combined architecturally within a document planning module. The chapter ends with some pointers to further reading in Section 4.6.

4.1 Introduction

4.1.1 What Document Planning Is About

In the NLG system architecture we presented in Chapter 3, the document planner is responsible for deciding what information to communicate (this being the task of content determination) and determining how this information should be structured for presentation (this being the task of document structuring). In many applications, the document planner is the most important component of the NLG system. If a generated document presents the necessary information in a reasonably coherent structure, readers may forgive occasional deficiencies in more superficial aspects of the generated texts, such as limited syntactic variety and overly redundant referring expressions. If, conversely, the document does not contain the information the user needs, or the presentation of this information is poorly structured, then it is unlikely to be of much use to human readers no matter how well individual sentences are written.

CONTENT DETERMINATION is the task of deciding what chunks of information, or, as we will term them, MESSAGES, should be included in the generated text. Content determination is a very application-dependent process which may require a considerable amount of general reasoning about the domain and how to best fulfill the system's communicative goal in the current context.

DOCUMENT STRUCTURING is the task of building a structure that contains the messages selected in content determination. This requires grouping the messages to be conveyed. Document structuring may also specify the order that messages appear in; associate groups of messages with suprasentential structures such as paragraphs and sections; and specify DISCOURSE RELATIONS which hold between various messages or groups of messages. Again, the details of this process are very application dependent. Both the domain of application and the genre of the texts to be generated will impose constraints on the kinds of document structures that are appropriate.

There is a growing interest in the research community in applying NLG document planning ideas to the generation of multimodal documents, here meaning documents which contain graphics as well as text, or which are hypertextual in nature. We discuss the generation of multimodal documents in Chapter 7; in this chapter we focus primarily on techniques for generating text alone.

4.1.2   The Inputs and Outputs of Document Planning

The input to the document planner is the same as the input to the NLG system as a whole, since the document planner is the first module in the pipeline. As outlined in Section 3.2, although the precise nature of the input is of course application dependent, we can abstract across differences to characterise the input to the generation process as a four-tuple consisting of the following components:

The knowledge source. This refers to the domain databases and knowledge bases which contain the raw material that will provide the information content for the texts to be generated. WEATHERREPORTER, for example, uses a preexisting meteorological database which records a range of numerical weather measurements over a period of several years, along with other historical data (for an extract from this database, see Figure 1.2). FOG (see Section 1.3.2) and STOP (see Section 1.3.6) also use databases as their main knowledge source. PEBA (see Section 1.3.5) and IDAS (see Section 1.3.3), in contrast, use as their main knowledge source an AI-style knowledge base which encodes the relevant domain information in symbolic terms; an extract from PEBA's knowledge base is shown in Figure 4.1. Other knowledge sources are also possible; MODELEXPLAINER's (see Section 1.3.4) main

```
(ako Echidna Monotreme)
(distinguishing-characteristic Echidna Monotreme
    (body-covering sharp-spines))
(hasprop Echidna (linnaean-classification Family))
(hasprop Echidna (potential-confusor African-Porcupine))
(hasprop Echidna (nose prolonged-slender-snout))
(hasprop Echidna (geography found-Australia))
(hasprop Echidna
    (length (quantity (lower-limit (unit cm) (number 35))
                      (upper-limit (unit cm) (number 60)))))
(hasprop Echidna
    (weight (quantity (lower-limit (unit kg) (number 2))
                      (upper-limit (unit kg) (number 7)))))
(hasprop Echidna (social-living-status lives-by-itself))
(hasprop Echidna (diet eats-ants-termites-earthworms))
(hasprop Echidna (activity-time active-at-dawn-dusk))
(hasprop Echidna
    (colouring browny-black-coat-paler-coloured-spines))
(hasprop Echidna
    (captive-lifespan (quantity (average (unit years)
                                         (number 50)))))
(hasprop Echidna (nails powerful-claws-rapid-digging))
(hasprop Echidna (head small-head))
(hasprop Echidna (teeth no-teeth))
(hasprop Echidna
    (tongue extensible-glutinous-tongue-catching-insects))
```

Figure 4.1 A knowledge base fragment in PEBA. (Courtesy of Maria Milosavljevic.)

knowledge source, for example, is a set of class definitions written in an object-oriented programming language.

The communicative goal. This specifies the purpose for which the text is to be generated; it is often conceived of as a goal which will be satisfied if the text is generated appropriately. For a given invocation of WEATHERREPORTER, for example, this might be the goal SummariseMonth(199505). Goals often consist, as in this example, of goal TYPE (here, SummariseMonth) with one or more parameters (here, 199505). WEATHERREPORTER can cater only for one goal type, but other systems are more flexible; PEBA, for example, can respond to two types of goals, these being Describe(*e*) or Compare(*e*, *f*), where *e* and *f* are particular entities – in the case of PEBA, animals – to be described or compared.

The user model. This model provides information about the user; among other things such a model may give information about the user's task, background, level of expertise, and preferences. WEATHERREPORTER does not make explicit use of a user model; however, this simply means that an implicit notion of the expected audience is hard wired into the operation of the system. IDAS, on the other hand, utilises a user model which records a variety of information; for example, if a user asks IDAS how to perform a task, IDAS's response is influenced by a user model which specifies which tasks the user already knows how to perform.

The discourse history. This gives information about previous interactions between the user and the system. The discourse history is perhaps most important for the task of generating referring expressions (described in Section 5.4), which is part of microplanning; but it can sometimes affect document planning as well. For example, when PEBA describes an animal, it attempts to relate this description to previous descriptions that the user has seen.

The output of the document planner is a document plan. Although the general notion of a document plan as something that dictates text content and structure is quite widespread within the NLG community – sometimes referred to as a discourse plan or a text plan – the specifics of the construct can vary quite significantly from system to system. In our architecture, a document plan is a tree, whose leaf nodes specify messages (content) and whose internal nodes specify structural information such as how messages are grouped, the discourse relations that hold between messages or groups of messages, and suprasentential structures such as paragraphs and sections. A more detailed description of the notion of document plan used in our architecture is provided in Section 3.4.4.

4.1.3   A WeatherReporter Example

For the purposes of producing a summary of the weather over a given month, the information presented in Figure 1.2 is far more detailed than we require. So, rather than work with these source data records directly, WEATHERREPORTER first summarises the data into a collection of DAILY WEATHER RECORDS, an example of which is shown in Figure 4.2. For the remainder of this chapter we will view these daily weather records as the primary knowledge source for WEATHERREPORTER.

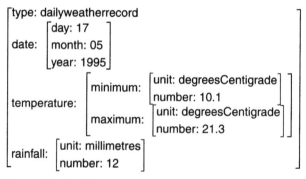

Figure 4.2   A daily weather record.

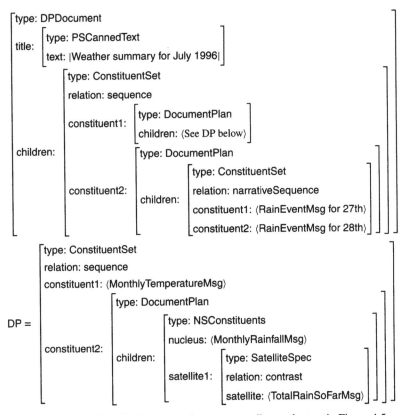

Figure 4.3 The document plan corresponding to the text in Figure 4.5.

An example of a WEATHERREPORTER document plan is shown in Figure 4.3; a schematic version of this is shown in Figure 4.4. This plan relates a set of five messages that have been constructed from the set of daily weather records for a particular month. One text that might be generated from this document plan is shown in Figure 4.5. Figure 4.6 shows two of the constituent messages that make up the plan; the first of these corresponds to the phrase *The month was slightly warmer than average*, and the second to the phrase *Heavy rain fell on the 27th*.

4.2   Representing Information in the Domain

In the context of the kinds of NLG systems we are concerned with here, texts are primarily used to convey information. This information may be expressed in words and sentences, but the words and sentences are not themselves information; the information underlies these linguistic constructs and is carried by them. In this sense, information is the predication of properties to entities or individuals – for example, that a particular month's rainfall was heavy – and the assertion of relationships

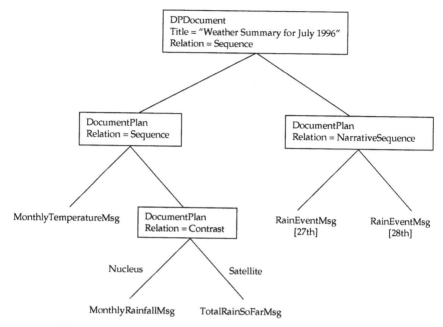

Figure 4.4 A document plan.

between entities – for example, that the echidna's body covering consists of long spines. We are concerned, therefore, with issues of knowledge representation and with the mapping of knowledge structures into semantic representations.

In any given domain, only particular predications or relationships will be of interest. We will conceptualise these significant predications and relationships as MESSAGES, informational elements that are to be considered for inclusion in the generated texts. Other terms sometimes used for these informational elements are FACT or PROPOSITION. We will avoid the second of these because there is a tendency to assume that propositions are expressed via sentences in a one-to-one manner, and, as we will see below, an important characteristic of messages is that they need not correspond to single sentences. By removing the assumption of a one-to-one mapping, we make it possible to contemplate combining messages to make more complex sentences. Messages are the basic elements or packages of information that the NLG system manipulates.

The messages themselves have constituent elements: the entities which are related or of which predications are made, the content of the predications, and the

> The month was slightly warmer than average with almost exactly
> the average rainfall, but rainfall for the year is still very depleted.
> Heavy rain fell on the 27th and 28th.

Figure 4.5 The weather summary for July 1996.

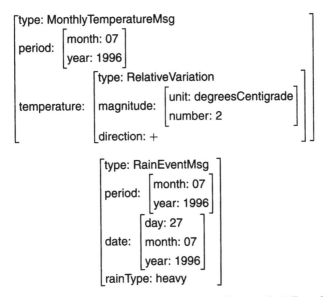

Figure 4.6   Example MonthlyTemperatureMsg and RainEventMsg messages from the document plan shown in Figure 4.3.

particular relationships identified. These are all elements of the DOMAIN. Prior to defining the messages to be used, it therefore makes sense to consider what an appropriate model of the application domain looks like. That is, what kinds of entities are there? what kinds of properties? what kinds of relations? By first developing a clear understanding of the raw material that makes up the domain, we are then in a better position to define the messages that may be derived from the underlying data; the messages are meaningful configurations of these lower-level elements.

Before we look at the process of message definition, we first look in more detail at this process of domain modelling. Both of these tasks are key aspects of the design of a document planner. Domain modelling and message definition are especially important in applications where the input data needs to be summarised or reasoned with before it can be made use of; this is the case in WEATHERREPORTER, for example, where simply reading off the contents of a set of daily weather records would not result in particularly interesting or useful texts. Domain modelling and message specification may appear less critical in systems such as IDAS which just select some information from their domain knowledge base to be communicated in the text. However, in such cases the knowledge base itself is often based on an implicitly-derived domain model. The domain modelling task has already been carried out, and the chunks of information in the knowledge base correspond closely to the packages of information we want to express in the text.

Ultimately, the heart of domain modelling and message definition is the determination of concepts which can be expressed linguistically and are appropriate for expression in the kinds of text to be generated but which can at the same time be derived from the NLG system's input. Thus, the domain model and message definitions form something of a bridge between the representations used in the application's database or knowledge base, which may not be directly expressible in natural language in a way that is useful, and the information communicated in the generated text, which must be based on concepts that can be communicated conveniently in language.

4.2.1   What's in a Domain Model?

When we build a model of a domain, we are in essence asking what there *is* in the domain: What kinds of things are there? This is sometimes described as developing an ONTOLOGY for the domain. Irrespective of the specifics of the domain, there are a number of general categories that recur. As is so often the case, different names may be used for much the same things, although in some cases there are subtle differences of view as to what the most basic distinctions are.

We will identify four principal categories for the elements that make up a domain model:

- ENTITIES (sometimes referred to as INSTANCES). Typically this category includes physical objects, including people and places, and also abstract objects.
- ATTRIBUTES (sometimes referred to as PROPERTIES). This includes physical properties such as colour and size, as well as more abstract attributes such as 'being late' (as might be predicated of a train, for example).
- RELATIONSHIPS. Again, this includes both physical relationships such as something being in a particular location with regard to something else (for example, 'next to') and more abstract relationships such as ownership.
- CLASSES (sometimes referred to as CONCEPTS). It is generally useful to consider classes of which particular entities are instances. Thus, the two authors of this book are entities, and both belong to a number of classes – the class of authors, the class of human beings, and so on.

Classes are generally arranged into a hierarchical taxonomy. Although we have suggested above that only entities belong to classes, in fact we can view attributes and relationships as also belonging to classes. Thus we have the class of colours, of which red and green are instances; and we have the class of locational relationships, which includes being above and being below. Recognising this kind of structure gives us a way of relating the elements of our domain model one to another.

From the point of view of building working NLG systems, we are generally concerned with domain models for specific tasks. A considerable amount of work in knowledge representation and artificial intelligence has tried to identify elements that are useful in many domains. Thus, for example, the CYC project (Lenat,

1995) and the Upper Model underlying the Penman and KPML generation systems (Bateman et al., 1990) attempt to provide what are in effect general-purpose ontologies. In both cases, the idea is that these general-purpose ontologies provide the uppermost levels of a taxonomy of what there is; the elements of any domain can then be subsumed under these categories. This approach has the advantage that information of particular kinds (for example, the fact that the objects related in a locational relationship are physical objects) can be encoded at these higher levels once only and inherited by subordinate concepts.

For many applications, however, the domain model required is sufficiently simple that the incorporation of these more general purpose models may not be warranted. This is a recurrent theme in the construction of working systems: It can be easier to construct a small, tailored resource of some kind than it is to incorporate some preexisting general-purpose resource. One must carefully consider whether the loss of generality is outweighed by the short-term benefits of quicker construction.

In what follows, we will focus on the development of a small, special-purpose domain model for our core case study. In principle, there is no reason why this should not be incorporated within some more general-purpose ontological framework, although if this is ultimately the intention, then a prior examination of how the general-purpose model carves up the world will help avoid unintended incompatibilities.

4.2.2   *Domain Modelling for WeatherReporter*

What do we require, then, in the domain model for WEATHERREPORTER? Since what we need at the end of the day is an inventory of the elements that appear in the texts to be generated, the best place to look for some ideas is the target texts themselves. Analysis of a reasonable sample of these affords the following conceptualisation of the content of these texts:

- Generally the texts are concerned with predicating particular weather characteristics of specific periods of time.
- Some of these periods of time are conventionally defined. Each text is a summary of the weather over a particular month, and specific weather circumstances are ascribed to particular days within that month.
- The texts also often mention specific periods of some number of days in duration.

From this, we can say that our domain model has one principal kind of entity, this being a **time-span**; and that the time spans are of two kinds, which we will refer to as **conventionalised-time-spans** and **ad-hoc-time-spans**. The conventionalised-time-spans are of two types: **months** and **days**. All of these are classes or concepts in the terms introduced earlier; any given day or month is thus an instance of one of these concepts. Any specified time span within a month, often referred to in the texts as *spell*, is an instance of the class ad-hoc-time-span.

Sometimes we compare a property of the current month (for example, its rainfall) to the average of all instances of that month. To cater for this, we will assume that our domain model also has a class generic-month whose instances are january, february, . . . , december; these hold general information about months, such as the average rainfall in this month in past years.

We can also provide some structure over the weather characteristics that populate the domain model. These are predications over time spans, and they are each concerned with some aspect of the weather:

- There is the notion that a month has a total-rainfall, a maximum-temperature and a minimum-temperature.
- generic-months have the attributes average-total-rainfall, average-maximum-temperature and average-minimum-temperature.
- Predicated of each month we also have the number of days on which rain has fallen during that month and the total amount of rain that has fallen from the beginning of the current year to the end of the month being reported. These correspond to the domain model attributes of number-of-rainy-days and total-rain-so-far. Again, corresponding to these we also have average-number-of-rainy-days and average-total-rain-so-far attributes in generic-month.
- Weather characteristics are also predicated of ad-hoc-time-spans; so, a spell may have a rainfall attribute, a wind attribute, or a mist-and-fog attribute.

Each of the attributes identified above has a range of possible values: some of these (such as number-of-rainy-days) are straightforwardly numeric; some are characterised as measurements (here, in millimeters or degrees centigrade, although other measuring schemes are possible in each case); some are best thought of as having symbolic values (so that, for example, the rainfall attribute of a spell could be heavy); and some are binary valued (so that, for example, a spell either does or does not have mist+fog).

4.2.3   *Implementing Domain Models*

For some NLG systems, the process of domain modelling is a paper exercise whose sole function is to clarify the system designer's thinking about the kinds of things that can be communicated in the texts to be generated. Going through this exercise can be very helpful in determining the most useful categories to work with; once these are determined, they can be built into the NLG system code in such a way that they do not figure explicitly in the system's operation.

In other cases, and particularly where the model of the world that underlies the system is more complex, it can be useful to explicitly encode a domain model within the system. This then provides a place where information about entities in the domain can be recorded. Often this is done with an AI knowledge representation language, such as KL-ONE (Brachman and Schmolze, 1985); another approach is to use object-oriented modelling techniques.

Even if a domain model is not explicitly constructed, the exercise of thinking through what the domain consists of puts us in a position where we are more likely to define message types that are not ad hoc in nature. We now turn to this aspect of the problem.

4.2.4 *Defining Messages*

So far we have discussed the kinds of things that populate the domain. When we generate texts about the domain, we express information in the form of particular configurations of these domain elements – for example, we assert that some entity has some property, or that two entities are in some relation. Each such configuration is a MESSAGE. For any given application, we need to construct these messages from the underlying raw data, and so we need to decide what kinds of messages are required.

A key question to be addressed in defining an inventory of message types for a particular application is the decision as to how much information should be communicated in each message. At one extreme, a message could communicate a single atomic fact from the input database or knowledge base; at the other extreme, a single message could contain all the information communicated in a multisentential text.

A pragmatic approach to determining message granularity is to base it on the types of variation expected in the output texts. If a certain set of facts are always described together, then it might make sense to use a single message to communicate them. However, if two facts are sometimes described together but in other cases are described in different parts of the text, then this information will be easier to manipulate if we use separate messages to communicate the two facts.

For example, suppose that WEATHERREPORTER texts always mentioned a month's maximum daytime temperature and total rainfall in the same clause or sentence. In this case, we could use a single message which encoded both the temperature and rainfall information, which we might think of as a **Temperature-AndRainfallMsg**. Because these facts are always expressed together, we do not need to put them into separate messages. If, however, the temperature and rainfall information are sometimes mentioned in different parts of the text, then we need to keep the two items of information in separate messages. This indeed turns out to be the case in WEATHERREPORTER.

From a pragmatic perspective, there is no need for all messages to have the same information granularity. However, aesthetic considerations such as a desire for elegance and consistency may result in the design of a message inventory that is larger than is strictly necessary for the task at hand.

In the case of WEATHERREPORTER, an analysis of the target texts allows us to establish that there are two types of messages we need. First of all, there are the messages that make up what we might think of as the 'standard' reports:

- MonthlyRainfallMsg
- MonthlyTemperatureMsg
- TotalRainSoFarMsg
- MonthlyRainyDaysMsg

These are always constructed for the month to be reported on; we refer to these as the ROUTINE MESSAGES.

The other messages we need are what we refer to as SIGNIFICANT EVENT MESSAGES:

- RainSpellMsg
- TemperatureSpellMsg
- RainEventMsg
- TemperatureEventMsg

We elaborate on an example of each of these message types below; the others in each category are very similar.

MonthlyRainfallMsg

It is on the basis of this message type that we generate clauses like *Rainfall was well above average.* When we talk about a weather parameter like rainfall, there are a number of things we can say about it:

- We can compare it to the average value for this month over the period of record, resulting in descriptions like *well above average, drier than average,* and so on.
- And we can identify it as having a significant value, such as being the rainiest instance of this month on record, the first month of the current year with no rain, or the rainiest month overall.

To cater for these possibilities, the message construction process identifies whether the month is either routine or significant for the meteorological parameter being reported on. What counts as significance depends on the parameter.

We saw a MonthlyRainfallMsg earlier in Figure 3.10. Here, magnitude tells us the variation from the norm, which is determined by comparing the value of this month's rainfall with the recorded average for this month over past years. Notice that magnitude is characterised in purely quantitative terms. It is the role of a later linguistic processing stage to determine how this gets mapped into lexical elements or phrases such as *well above average.*

Temperature	Symbolic Value
Over 40.0	extremelyhot
35.0 to 39.9	veryhot
30.0 to 34.9	hot
25.0 to 29.9	verywarm
20.0 to 24.9	warm
15.0 to 19.9	mild
10.0 to 14.9	cool
05.0 to 09.9	cold
00.0 to 04.9	verycold
Below 00.0	freezing

Figure 4.7   The correspondence of temperature values to categories.

TemperatureSpellMsg

We construct a TemperatureSpellMsg message whenever the daily temperature remains within one band for some sequence of days, where the sequence is longer than the minimum defined spell size. The bands are defined as shown in Figure 4.7. The daily weather records are scanned for spells in any of these predefined ranges, resulting in the construction of a message whenever one is found. The definition of TemperatureSpellMsg is shown in Figure 4.8; an example of such a message is shown in Figure 4.9.

4.2.5   Determining the Degree of Abstraction in Messages

An important question in defining a set of message structures is that of determining how close they should be to the eventual surface forms that will be generated. At

```
class TemperatureSpellMsg extends Message {
        period: Month; //Month was defined in Section 3.4
        spell: Interval;
        temperature: one of {extremelyhot, veryhot, hot, verywarm, warm,
            mild, cool, cold, verycold, freezing};
}

class Interval {
        begin: Date;
        end: Date;
}

class Date {
        day: integer;
        month: integer;
        year: integer;
}
```

Figure 4.8   The definition of TemperatureSpellMsg.

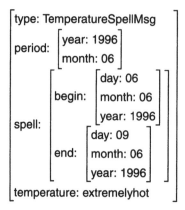

Figure 4.9 A TemperatureSpellMsg message.

one extreme, a message can be nothing more than a specific configuration of data elements in the underlying system's database or knowledge base, perhaps even a complete database record. At the other extreme, a message can be specified as a literal string corresponding to a sentence that may be generated; and there are many points in between. Choosing a point on this spectrum constitutes a decision about the degree of abstraction from the surface. The farther from the surface the abstraction is, the greater the amount of processing that is required to generate texts; and the closer to the surface the abstraction is, the more limited are the possibilities for generating variations in the text.

In the message definitions above, we have chosen a degree of abstraction which is quite close to the underlying data, at least as that data is represented in the daily weather records; the messages are correspondingly quite far from the surface forms of the texts that might be used to realise their content. With the same set of messages, we could have used a much less abstract representation. For example, we could have represented each message with a literal string that expresses its content. An example of such a representation for a monthly rainfall message is shown in Figure 4.10. A text can be produced from this message simply by printing out the **text** attribute; no microplanning or realisation is necessary. On the other hand, if we adopt this approach, there is no scope for variation in the realisation of individual messages, and the enforcement of one message per sentence is likely to result in rather stilted text, even for short texts of two or three sentences in length.

$$
\begin{bmatrix}
\text{type: MonthlyRainfallMsg} \\
\text{text: |The month was drier than average.|}
\end{bmatrix}
$$

Figure 4.10 A message defined as a string.

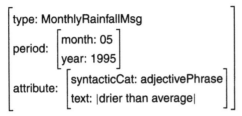

Figure 4.11   A message specified as a month and a textual attribute.

We can overcome this problem to some extent by introducing some internal structure within the message; this corresponds to an increase in abstraction. So, for example, we might instead represent the message under discussion as two components, a month and an attribute. Figure 4.11 shows an example of such a representation, where the month is specified abstractly and the attribute is specified as a text string; the syntactic category of the text string (in this case, adjectivePhrase) is also specified. By representing the message in this fashion rather than as a fully specified sentence, we introduce some scope for the microplanner to optimise the text. For example, the microplanner can decide whether the month should be referred to as *it*, *the month*, or *May*, depending on what was communicated in previous sentences (see Section 5.4). The microplanner may also perform some aggregation (see Section 5.3); for example, if this message is followed by a MonthlyTemperatureMsg message with a similar structure, the microplanner could combine these into a single sentence such as the following:

(4.1)   The month was *cooler than average* and *drier than average*.

This type of aggregation is possible only if the microplanner knows the syntactic categories of the attribute texts; this is one of the reasons for specifying this information as part of the message structure.

The sentence in Example (4.1) is arguably still a little stilted: we might prefer, for example, to generate the following:

(4.2)   The month was *cooler and drier than average*.

In order to be able to do this we need to add yet further abstraction to our message definitions. One possibility is to give more syntactic information about the structure of the attribute texts; here, for example, we would need to separate out the comparative adjective (*cooler*, *drier*) from the phrase that expresses what is being compared to (*than average*). However, analysis of the target texts shows that the same information is sometimes conveyed in quite different ways; so, for example, we may want to be able to generate the following alternative:

(4.3)   The month was cooler than average, with less rain than usual.

It is difficult to realise a message as both *drier than average* and *less rain than usual* if the message is represented as either a text string or a syntactic structure; this level of variation is much easier to support if a more abstract representation is used, such as the one shown in Figure 4.6.

In our architecture, messages are represented at a level of abstraction that supports a broad range of realisation possibilities. The balancing act involved here requires the identification of a level of abstraction that allows the desired variability in output, without adding unnecessary complexity. Of course, the infusion of a little additional generality may help in dealing with unforeseen circumstances. For example, we may discover tomorrow that a further grammatical means of expression is required, and if our representation is insufficiently abstract, we may not be able to cater for this. The addition of apparently unnecessary generality is thus a kind of insurance policy. One has to weigh the alternatives in terms of the real costs and benefits.

The issues here are similar to those that arise in the definition of an interlingua in a machine translation system. An interlingua is in effect a common denominator that allows the content of all the target languages to be represented; similarly, the messages in an NLG system need to be specified in terms that permit the full variety of expressions we want to generate.

4.2.6   *A Methodology for Domain Modelling and Message Definition*

In some cases it is possible to build domain models and define message structures purely on the basis of corpus analysis, but it is usually best to combine corpus analysis with discussions with domain experts. One technique for this is initially to construct models based on corpus analysis and then to ask a domain expert to comment on these models. The models are then revised in light of the expert's comments, and shown again to the expert for further comments; the comment and revision cycle may iterate several times. Figure 4.12 outlines a procedure for this process.

Another approach is to acquire fragments of a domain model directly from the experts or from other sources of domain knowledge such as textbooks. The expert system community has developed many structured KNOWLEDGE ACQUISITION techniques which can help in this regard.

For example, one important modelling issue in the STOP project was the question of how smokers should be classified. Three initial categories (essentially people not intending to quit, people considering quitting, and people who had definitely decided to quit) were obtained from a standard psychological theory of behaviour change, but the STOP team wanted a finer classification than this. So it used SORTING, a knowledge acquisition technique developed by the expert system community. In a typical sorting session, an expert would be given a collection of questionnaires describing individual smokers and asked to sort the collection into two or more groups. The questionnaires all fell into an established category (for

Step 1 Select a small number of texts from the target text corpus; ideally these should be representative of the corpus as a whole.

Step 2 Break each text down into its constituent sentences, and then break each sentence down into a set of phrases which correspond to individual messages. See the discussion in Section 4.2.4 on the question of how much information should be represented in an individual message.

Step 3 Group these messages into classes. There are no hard and fast rules for determining what the best classes are; this is typically based on intuitions that evolve as you become more familiar with the data.

Step 4 Propose a representation for the messages; this should be an abstract representation based on the domain model (see Section 4.2.5).

Step 5 Discuss your analysis with domain experts, and modify it accordingly. If necessary (and it often is necessary), repeat Steps 2–5 until both you and the experts are happy.

Step 6 Repeat Steps 1–5 with a larger selection of texts from the corpus.

> **Figure 4.12** A corpus-based procedure for domain modelling and message definition.

example, all people not intending to quit), so the expert could not simply split the collection based on an already-known category. The experts were then asked what the distinguishing features were of each group, and these features were then used to define additional types of smokers in the domain model. For example, this process suggested that among the people who were not intending to quit, it was useful to distinguish between people who had very few qualms about smoking and those who, although not yet intending to quit, nevertheless were worried by some aspects of smoking.

Of course, the domain modelling and message definition exercises do not have to be based purely on corpus analysis or on knowledge acquisition sessions with domain experts. It often makes sense to use a combination of techniques. The exercise can be a very eclectic one, perhaps starting with models suggested by textbooks or previous research, and then using a combination of corpus analysis, knowledge acquisition sessions, and general brainstorming sessions to revise and improve the models until they seem adequate for the job. And it is by no means uncommon for models to be revised further once prototype versions of the system have been created and evaluated, since this often highlights deficiencies which were not noticed initially.

4.3   Content Determination

Having introduced the kinds of informational elements our document planning component works with – in our terminology, messages – we turn in this section to look at how the document planner can decide which messages should be included in a text.

4.3.1   Aspects of Content Determination

In our terms, content determination is the task of deciding what messages should be included in the generated document. This depends very much on the particular application being developed, its domain, and the genre of texts being generated; this makes it impossible to specify a general algorithm for content determination in any detail. However, content determination usually involves one or more of selecting, summarising, and reasoning with data. Very few NLG systems simply generate messages that communicate all of their input data. Instead, they process this data in some manner, and this processing is the 'value added' of content determination.

Selecting Data

One type of processing performed in content determination is that of *selecting* a subset of the information in the system's domain database or knowledge base for communication to the user. Some examples of selection are described below.

IDAS responds to short questions about an object, represented by queries like WhereIsIt and WhatAreItsParts. Content determination here typically involves the use of a set of rules which identify, in the domain knowledge base, specific attributes of the object in question which need to be communicated in order to respond appropriately to the query. For example, the rule for WhatAreItsParts specifies that IDAS should communicate the value of the object's PartOf attribute in the response.

PEBA generates descriptions or comparisons of animals. For each animal represented in the knowledge base, there is more information available than would typically be included in a generated text. When describing an animal, PEBA sometimes makes use of a CLARIFICATORY COMPARISON (Milosavljevic, 1997), whereby it selects related similarities and differences in order to delimit the information contained in the description. So, for example, if two entities are similar in appearance, then they should be distinguished on the basis of their appearance rather than, say, on the basis of their diet. This is achieved by means of a taxonomisation of the different properties predicated of entities in the domain.

The goal of content selection can be summarised as something like 'provide relevant information'; what counts as relevant depends very much on the context of use.

Summarising Data

Another common type of activity in content determination is that of *summarising* some portion of the system's underlying data or knowledge. This is often necessary if the underlying data is too fine-grained to be reported directly or if some abstraction or generalisation across the data, as opposed to the raw data itself, constitutes the interesting or important information. Some examples of summarisation are described below.

The FOG system generates weather forecasts. From a content determination perspective, the key task here is the choice of a small set of concepts which summarise the most important aspects of the numerical weather data FOG uses as input. For example, an hourly set of wind velocities and directions from 6 A.M. to midnight might be described as *Winds southwest 15 to 20 knots diminishing to light late this evening.* In this example, FOG has summarised a data set of 38 numbers (wind velocity at 6 A.M., wind direction at 6 A.M., wind velocity at 7 A.M., wind direction at 7 A.M., and so on) by stating that initially the wind has direction southwest and speed 15 to 20 knots, and that the speed will change to light in the late evening. Obviously such a summary conveys less information than was present in the original data set; the goal is to summarise the information in a way which does not reduce its utility to the target user community.

The WEATHERREPORTER system also summarises the content of its underlying information source in order to describe interesting patterns in the data. Whereas FOG is concerned with important aspects of predicated weather, WEATHERREPORTER reports on past weather events. As we have seen already, this involves summarising the overall weather for the month and identifying periods of interesting activity. For example, if there are several weeks with no precipitation, this will cause WEATHERREPORTER to include in the text a message about a dry spell.

Summarisation is sometimes guided by a target length for the generated text. For example, human-generated marine forecasts typically convey about 40 items of information (Goldberg et al., 1994); the FOG system therefore uses this measure as a length guideline. This means that minor variations in the weather data may get mentioned on a 'slow' day when there is not much else to report but will not get mentioned on a 'bad weather' day when there are many important messages to communicate.

Reasoning with Data

The processes of selection and summarisation are just special cases of the more general process of reasoning with the underlying data. Many other kinds of reasoning are also possible. For example, if STOP produces a letter for a smoker who has unsuccessfully attempted to quit smoking before, it usually includes in its generated letter a message which attempts to encourage the recipient by pointing out that most people who quit make several unsuccessful attempts first. This reasoning mimics the reasoning performed by experienced health professionals who work with smokers. As such kinds of reasoning become more sophisticated and domain specific, it becomes fruitful to view the development of a content determination process as essentially the development of an expert system.

Tailoring Output for Different Users

Many NLG systems take the user model into account when performing content selection. This can be done either automatically or by giving the user explicit control over the tailoring process.

The EPICURE system (Dale, 1990), for example, automatically tailors cookery recipes using a model of the actions which user is assumed to know how to perform. For example, if an EPICURE user wants to know how to make butter bean soup, EPICURE explains one of the steps in this action as *Prepare the beans* if it believes the user already knows how to prepare beans. However, if the system believes that the user does not know how to prepare beans, then this part of the recipe will be described as something like *Soak, drain, and rinse the beans.*

An alternative approach to user tailoring is to give the user explicit control over the content determination process: instead of the NLG system making possibly incorrect assumptions about the information needed by the user, the user is able to specify directly what content he or she would like to see in the generated text. This approach is taken by MODELEXPLAINER, which allows the user to specify (at a fairly high level) what information will be presented. For example, the user can specify whether she wants detailed information about class attributes to be included in the text and whether the system should include examples of classes.

Some systems support different types of users implicitly by being able to generate different types of output texts, each of which is targeted at a different user community. The FOG system, for example, can produce both general forecasts, which are targeted towards the general public, and marine forecasts, which are targeted towards sailors. Among other differences, the marine forecasts give more detail about wind speed and direction than the general public forecasts, since detailed information about the wind is important to sailors but usually not that important to the general public.

From a more theoretical perspective, many people have argued that content determination systems should be based on a model where the system first attempts to recognise the user's goal and then plans an appropriate response using basic principles about belief and action. The process of identifying the user's goals is usually referred to as PLAN RECOGNITION; because of the substantial amounts of real-world knowledge required to work out what a user really wants, work in this area tends to focus on narrowly specified domains. For example, Allen and Perrault (1980) describe a train inquiry response system where if the user asks, *When does the Glasgow train leave?*, the system will infer that the user has the goal of getting to Glasgow and the plan of achieving this goal via boarding the next train to Glasgow. Having determined this, the system analyses this plan and realises that, in order to satisfy her goal, the user will need a platform number as well as a departure time. The system then generates a response that includes both pieces of information.

4.3.2   *Deriving Content Determination Rules*

As we have now emphasised a number of times, the goal of many NLG systems is to produce documents which are as similar as possible to documents produced by human experts. Since duplicating the performance of human experts in particular domains is one of the goals of expert systems, the domain-dependence of the content determination task encourages us to view this as a specific kind of expert systems task. Irrespective of the kind of technology used to implement an expert system, a key stage in any such development is knowledge acquisition. From the perspective of conventional software engineering, this is part of the problem of requirements analysis.

Just as in other expert system scenarios, the identification of content determination rules is carried out in a context where a domain expert has some knowledge, often implicitly held, which is used in carrying out a specialised task. Almost any knowledge acquisition technique from the expert systems world can be used to acquire content determination rules; see, for example, the techniques described in Scott, Clayton, and Gibson, 1991. In this section, we describe a particular approach which is useful in many situations; for other ideas on knowledge acquisition for content determination, see McKeown et al., 1994; Lester and Porter, 1997; Reiter et al., 1997.

The approach outlined here centres on the idea of analysing texts in the Target Text Corpus, as introduced in Section 2.3, to determine when particular messages are communicated in the text: we use the corpus to construct a set of rules stating which messages should appear in a particular text. Figure 4.13 outlines a procedure that can be used to analyse a set of representative target texts. The rules identified

Step 1 Decompose the text into messages. If necessary, revise the set of message definitions during this process.

Step 2 Relate each message to the source data. Does it directly convey input data, or is some summarisation or processing performed? If summarisation or other processing is performed, try to determine the algorithms used by the human experts. For this exercise, it may be useful to ask experts to 'think aloud' as they create documents.

Step 3 It will often be possible to categorise the texts to be generated into a small number of general types. Try to characterise which classes of messages appear in which types of texts, and try to determine the conditions under which messages appear. The result of this process will be a collection of rules of the form 'a text of type t will contain a message of type m under conditions $c_1, c_2, \ldots c_n$'. As in Step 1, it may be appropriate to revise the set of message definitions, and any taxonomic structure imposed on this set, during this process.

Step 4 Discuss this analysis with domain experts, and modify it accordingly. In most cases, this will require a second pass through Steps 1–4. It may be useful to present the content determination rules to the experts in a semiformal notation which the experts can understand. In some cases, the analysis may suggest modifying the target text corpus, because some texts are either suboptimal or are difficult to generate.

Step 5 When you are satisfied with your analysis, repeat Steps 1–4 with a larger selection of texts from the target text corpus.

Figure 4.13 A corpus-based procedure for identifying content determination rules.

by this procedure then become a specification for a content determination process which indicates what messages should be contained in the text in specified circumstances. This process can be, and often is, integrated with the process of domain modelling and message definition described in Section 4.2, but for expository simplicity we will assume that at least initial versions of the domain model and message definitions are determined before the process of deriving content rules starts.

Regardless of whether the approach outlined here or some other knowledge acquisition technique is used, an essential component of successful knowledge acquisition is becoming familiar with the domain and with the data, which here means the corpus. It takes a considerable amount of time to learn about the domain, to carefully analyse the corpus, and to discuss and verify the observations made with the domain experts. The resource cost of this should not be underestimated; however, there is no easy alternative if the goal is to build a system that delivers appropriate results.

In some cases different domain experts may have substantially different opinions about what should be in the content determination rules. Reiter et al. (1997) suggest that if this happens, it may be useful to describe these differences in terms of parameters and then ask the experts as a group to discuss the best values for these parameters. For instance, in the WEATHERREPORTER domain, if some experts think that a rain spell should be mentioned if it lasts three days and others think that such a period is only worth mentioning if it lasts five days, we could assemble these experts in a room and ask them as a group to discuss what the right value is for the minimal-length-of-rain-spell parameter.

4.3.3   *Implementing Content Determination*

In many cases, the hardest part of building a content determination system is determining what the rules are for determining which messages should be included in a text. Once these rules have been determined, there are a variety of ways in which they can be implemented.

The most straightforward implementation of content determination is simply to write a code which applies the rules to the input data and produces a corresponding set of messages. This can be done either in a conventional programming language or in one of the special languages developed by the AI community to support rule-based programming. This approach was used in MODELEXPLAINER (written in C++, a conventional programming language) and in FOG (written in Prolog, an AI language).

Sometimes it is useful to break down texts into a number of categories and write separate rules for each category, instead of a single set of rules which cover all categories. Rules can of course be shared between multiple categories if necessary, perhaps by using an inheritance mechanism. In this case, it is also necessary to write an additional set of rules that determine which category should be used in which circumstances. This approach was used in IDAS and STOP; IDAS uses an AI classifier in the KL-ONE sense (Brachman and Schmolze, 1985) to select a category, while STOP implements category-selection rules in a conventional programming language (Java).

There are many techniques used for expert system construction which might be adapted to the task of content determination. For example, texts could be generated via case-based reasoning, or sophisticated optimisation and constraint satisfaction algorithms could be used to produce an optimal set of messages given some set of constraints. This is a relatively unexplored research area in NLG.

4.4   Document Structuring

Documents are not just random collections of sentences. They possess coherence and thematic structure, which is to say that the content is expressed in a way that is easy for humans to read and understand. A computer database can accept updates and facts in random order, but a human reader finds information much easier to assimilate if it is presented in a well-structured manner.

For example, many documents have an introduction which gives an overview of the information communicated by the document, and a conclusion which summarises the document's main points. Further, the different parts of the document are often organised by topic, so that related information is presented together. These characteristics can ease a human reader's assimilation of the information presented.

Document structure can be ignored by NLG systems which produce single-sentence outputs; however, most NLG systems need to impart more information than can be realised within a single sentence. This means that we have to consider how a set of messages can be organised or structured to produce a readable and understandable multisentential text. This is the problem of document structuring.

More concretely, in our architecture the task of document structuring is to produce a tree whose leaf nodes are messages and whose internal nodes specify the following information:

- how messages are grouped together thematically;
- the order in which messages (or groups of messages) should appear in the text;
- which groups of messages correspond to document structures such as paragraphs and sections; and
- the discourse relations which hold between messages or groups of messages.

Sometimes the document structuring mechanism may only partially specify some of this information, relying on the microplanner to fill in details. For example, it may specify high-level ordering of message groups but expect the microplanner to order messages within a group; or it may specify higher-level document structures such as sections but expect the microplanner to decide which message groups should be expressed as paragraphs.

4.4.1   Discourse Relations

The notion of a DISCOURSE RELATION – sometimes called a RHETORICAL RELA-TION – is a key concept in any discussion of document structure. Discourse relations specify the relationships that hold between messages or groups of messages. A number of theories of discourse relations have been proposed in the literature; in this book, we will adopt a number of ideas from Rhetorical Structure Theory (RST) (Mann and Thompson, 1988), which has been the most influential such theory in NLG to date.

The basic idea underlying RST is that a text is coherent by virtue of the relationships that hold between the constituent elements of that text. In particular, RST claims that a small number – on the order of twenty-five – of defined rhetorical relations, with names like **Motivation** and **Contrast**, can be used to explain the relationships that hold within an extremely wide range of texts. These relationships hold between TEXT SPANS. For our purposes, we can regard an atomic text span as the text (that is, the actual words) that corresponds to a message. Larger text spans are created by linking together smaller text spans with a rhetorical relation; in the terminology we use here, this corresponds to constructing a group of two or more messages by linking them by means of a discourse relation. Most RST discourse relations are binary, which means that their corresponding message groups will have two components.

For example, consider the following simple text:

(4.4)   a. I like to collect old Fender guitars.
          b. My favourite instrument is a 1951 Stratocaster.

Here, the second sentence is providing an example of the proposition expressed in the first; in RST terms a discourse relation of **Elaboration** or **Exemplification** holds between the two sentences. On the other hand, consider an example like the following:

(4.5)   a. I like to collect old Fender guitars.
          b. However, my favourite instrument is a 1991 Telecaster.

Here, we might say that a discourse relation of **Contrast** or **Exception** holds between the two sentences. Note that particular cue words are often used to signal which discourse relations reside in the text; for example, *however* is commonly used to signal contrast.

relation name:	Elaboration
constraints on N:	none
constraints on S:	none
constraints on the N+ S *combination:*	
	S (the satellite) presents additional detail about the situation or some element of subject matter which is presented in N (the nucleus) or inferentially accessible from N in one or more of the following ways:
	1. N: set; S: member of set
	2. N: abstraction; S: instance
	3. N: whole; S: part
	4. N: process; S: step
	5. N: object; S: attribute of object
	6. N: generalisation; S: specific instance
the effect:	R (the reader) recognises the situation presented in S as providing additional detail for N. R identifies the element of subject matter for which detail is provided.
the locus of the effect:	N and S.

Figure 4.14 The RST definition of Elaboration (adapted from Mann and Thompson, 1987).

More formally, in RST, most rhetorical relations are defined as holding between two portions of a text, called the NUCLEUS and the SATELLITE (N and S). A relation definition has four parts:

- constraints on the nucleus;
- constraints on the satellite;
- constraints on the combination of the nucleus and the satellite; and
- the effect (usually on the reader).

A formal definition of the RST Elaboration relation is shown in Figure 4.14. This attempts to capture something of what is happening in Example 4.4; in this case, the first sentence (*I like to collect old Fender guitars*) is the nucleus, while the second sentence (*My favourite instrument is a 1951 Stratocaster*) is the satellite.

Many NLG systems use the specific set of discourse relations defined in RST as a starting point and modify this set to cater for the idiosyncrasies of a particular domain. The very general descriptions of discourse relations provided by definitions like that given in Figure 4.14 need to be modified and elaborated to be useful in particular domains. For a general discussion of different ways of classifying discourse relations see Maier and Hovy, 1993. Within implemented systems, RST-style rhetorical relations have been 'operationalised' in a number of ways. The orientation of the definitions provided by RST makes them amenable to encoding as AI-style planning operators, with the constraints in the definitions mapping into preconditions on the application of an operator, and the effects mapping into postconditions (see Moore and Paris, 1993, for an exploration of this approach).

RST is not alone in positing the existence of discourse or rhetorical relations. There are different views in the literature as to the size and content of the inventory of discourse relations that can be found in real texts. In implemented systems, designers often choose or create a set that is appropriate for the task at hand. Some common discourse relations which are frequently used are as follows:

- **Elaboration.** One message or group of messages elaborates on the information in another message or group of messages.
- **Exemplification.** One message or group of messages provides an example of the fact stated in another message or group of messages.
- **Contrast.** One message or group of messages provides contrasting information to that provided in another message or group of messages.
- **Narrative Sequence.** A set of messages or groups of messages communicate a time-ordered sequence of events. This is an example of a relation which does not fit the nucleus-satellite model but instead simply applies to a set of constituents.

Rather than relate constituents of a document plan by abstractly-named discourse relations, an alternative approach is to connect the parts by cue phrases directly. This approach is used in STOP, for example, which specifies relations between messages via actual cue phrases such as *however* instead of by abstract discourse relations such as Contrast. With this approach, the microplanner simply inserts the specified cue phrase into the text; it does not need to dynamically choose which cue phrase is the most appropriate expression of the discourse relation in this context. This approach has both advantages and disadvantages. On the one hand, specifying an abstract discourse relation means that the microplanner can vary which cue phrase is used to express this relation according to the context. For example, *however* is a good realisation of Contrast if the two messages are realised in different sentences, but *but* may be more appropriate if the messages are realised in the same sentence. On the other hand, the rules for deciding when particular cue phrases should be used can be quite subtle and are not yet thoroughly understood (see Section 5.2.4); as a result, it may in practice be difficult to write general-purpose microplanner choice rules for discourse relations, and easier to hard code specific cue phrases in the document structuring system.

4.4.2   *Implementation: Schemas*

In many contexts, texts follow fairly regular patterns; acquiring a knowledge of the patterns in any given genre is an important part of the process of learning how to read texts of that type. So, for example, academic articles often begin with an introduction which overviews the subject matter of the article. This is followed by a body of text that provides the main substance of the article and the text generally ends with a section of conclusions where various aspects of the material presented may be drawn together and commented upon. In certain areas of research, the body of the article may often adopt the convention of presenting first an experiment, its results, and then some discussion of those results. Newspaper articles, on the other hand, often follow a pyramid structure, where, beginning with a brief summary of the main points of the story, a number of successively more elaborate iterations through the content are provided.

Predictable structures are also often found at much lower levels in texts. The summaries that make up the WEATHERREPORTER target text corpus, for example, generally first describe the month's overall temperature and rainfall, then go on to compare the month with the same month in previous years, and then describe significant events such as periods of extreme temperature or rainfall, along with any relevant details.

These observations are embodied in the NLG literature in SCHEMA-BASED approaches to document structuring. A schema is a pattern that specifies how a particular document should be constructed from constituent elements, where those constituent elements may be individual messages or, recursively, instantiations of other schemas.

Schemas often include 'optional' elements with associated conditional tests. For example, in WEATHERREPORTER texts, we include significant event messages only if there are significant events which need to be reported. Sometimes a number of patterns are provided for a text, with ACTIVATION CONDITIONS specifying which should be activated in a particular context. For example, if the user asks the WEATHERREPORTER system to describe the weather in a month for which it has no data, this might trigger a special pattern which produces an explanatory message to this effect.

The addition of optional elements and activation conditions gives schemas much of the power of general-purpose programming languages. Many schema systems are in fact implemented as macro or class libraries on top of an underlying programming language.

A set of schemas for a given text type can be viewed as being something like a text grammar, analogous to the grammars used to describe patterns in sentences. Figure 4.15 shows a simple schema as used in PEBA. This defines the structure required for texts which compare two entities, stipulating that any such text first

CompareAndContrast $\longrightarrow$
    DescribeLinnaeanRelationship CompareProperties
CompareProperties $\longrightarrow$
    CompareProperty CompareProperties
CompareProperties $\longrightarrow \phi$

Figure 4.15 PEBA's Compare-And-Contrast schema.

```
Schema DescribeWeather() returns DocumentPlan;
    DocumentPlan DP1 = DescribeMonthOverall();
    DocumentPlan DP2 = DescribeSignificantEvents();
    return newDocumentPlan(DP1, DP2, Sequence);
end Schema;

Schema DescribeMonthOverall() returns DocumentPlan;
    Message M1 = getMessage(MonthlyTemperatureMsg);
    DocumentPlan DP1 = DescribeOverallPrecipitation();
    return newDocumentPlan(M1, DP1, Sequence);
end Schema;

Schema DescribeOverallPrecipitation() returns DocumentPlan;
    Message M1 = getMessage(MonthlyRainfallMsg);
    Message M2 = getMessage(TotalRainSoFarMsg);
    if (M1.rainfall.direction ≠ M2.rainfall.direction)
        then return newDocumentPlan(M1, M2, Contrast);
        else return newDocumentPlan(M1, M2, Elaboration);
end Schema;

Schema DescribeSignificantEvents() returns DocumentPlan;
    List L1 = getAllMessages(RainEventMsg);
    List L2 = getAllMessages(TemperatureEventMsg);
    if (empty(L1) AND empty(L2))
        return null;
    else if (empty(L1))
        return makeSequenceDocPlanFromList(L2);
    else if (empty(L2))
        return makeSequenceDocPlanFromList(L1);
    else begin
        DP1 = makeSequenceDocPlanFromList(L1);
        DP2 = makeSequenceDocPlanFromList(L2);
        return newDocumentPlan(DP1, DP2, Sequence);
        end begin
end Schema;
```

Figure 4.16   A simple set of schemas for WEATHERREPORTER.

defines the two entities in terms of the Linnaean taxonomy, then going on to
compare the properties of these entities. Here, each terminal symbol in the grammar
corresponds to the invocation of a computational procedure that examines the
underlying data source to locate some information that can be included in the text.

Although a representation of this kind can be a very elegant way of captur-
ing structural regularities in texts of a given kind, the computational procedures
underlying the symbols in the grammar can be arbitrarily complex. As an alternative means of representation that foregrounds this aspect of the text structuring
problem, Figure 4.16 shows, in a pseudocode form, the schema elements required
for texts in the WEATHERREPORTER domain. The individual schemas here are as
follows:

DescribeWeather. A simple schema which invokes two subschemas (DescribeMonthOverall and DescribeSignificantEvents), and returns a DocumentPlan which uses a Sequence discourse relation to combine the two DocumentPlans produced by the subschemas.

DescribeMonthOverall. Another simple schema, this one combines a DocumentPlan produced by the DescribeOverallPrecipitation subschema with the MonthlyTemperatureMsg produced by the content determination mechanism for the month in question.

DescribeOverallPrecipitation. This schema combines the Monthly-RainfallMsg and TotalRainSoFarMsg produced by the content determination mechanism. The messages are combined with either an Elaboration or Contrast discourse relation, depending on whether the direction fields of these messages are the same or not. This is a simple example of a conditional test in a schema.

DescribeSignificantEvents. The most complex of the schemas shown, this first retrieves a list of all RainEventMsgs and a list of all TemperatureEventMsgs produced by the content determination mechanism. If there are no significant events, an empty DocumentPlan is returned. If there are just RainEventMsgs or just Temperature-EventMsgs, then a DocumentPlan which links these with event messages with a Sequence relation is returned. If both kinds of event messages exist, then a DocumentPlan is constructed around each set of event messages, and the schema returns a combined document plan which links these two DocumentPlans with a Sequence relation.

As the example illustrates, a schema thus can be considered to be a program which is executed to produce a particular document structure. It can be started after a content determination process has already decided what messages to include in the text. It is also possible, however, for the schema system to request the construction of messages 'on demand' when it finds it needs a particular type of message. These alternatives will be discussed further in Section 4.5.

4.4.3 Implementation: Bottom-up Techniques

Schemas work well when the structure of texts is predictable and can be captured by predetermined patterns. However, they are less well suited to applications where text structures vary a great deal, especially if the variation is difficult to predict in advance. In such cases it may be better to use a 'bottom-up' approach to document structuring. Instead of the top-down expansion of an initial schema like DescribeWeather, these approaches combine messages in a bottom-up fashion until a document plan which includes all the messages produced by the content determination mechanism has been constructed.

Let POOL = *messages produced by content determination mechanism*
while (size(POOL)≥1) **do**
    find all pairs of elements in POOL which
        can be linked by a discourse relation
    assign each such pair a desirability score,
        using a heuristic preference function
    find the pair E_i and E_j with the highest preference score
    combine E_i and E_j into a new DocumentPlan E_k,
        using an appropriate discourse relation;
    remove E_i and E_j from POOL and replace them with E_k;
end while

Figure 4.17   A bottom-up discourse structuring algorithm.

A variety of bottom-up document-structuring approaches have been proposed in the literature. In general, they all assume the following:

- the content determination mechanism has produced a set of messages which are required to be included in the final document plan; and
- the NLG system has a means of determining what discourse relation (if any) can be used to link two particular messages or component document plans.

Given these assumptions a simple version of a bottom-up algorithm is shown in Figure 4.17. A key element of this algorithm is the heuristic scoring function used to decide which elements should be combined at each step when there are several candidate pairs which can be combined. One approach is to base this on the preferences shown by human authors; Marcu (1997) describes how a scoring function based on human authors' preferences can be constructed by statistically analysing a corpus of human-authored texts. Marcu also points out that bottom-up document structuring can be viewed as an optimisation problem, with the goal being to find the document structure which has the highest overall score according to some scoring function. As such, it may make sense to use sophisticated search, optimisation, or constraint satisfaction techniques in this process.

A simple WEATHERREPORTER example is as follows. Suppose that we know that components can be linked with discourse relations under the following circumstances:

- **Elaboration Rule.** A TotalRainfallMsg can be added as an Elaboration to a MonthlyRainfallMsg if both messages have the same value for Direction (the direction of variation).
- **Contrast Rule.** A TotalRainfallMsg can be added as a Contrast to a MonthlyRainfallMsg if the two messages have different Direction values.
- **Sequence Rule.** A MonthlyTemperatureMsg (or a DocumentPlan whose nucleus is a MonthlyTemperatureMsg) and a MonthlyRainfallMsg (or a DocumentPlan whose nucleus is a MonthlyRainfallMsg) can be combined using the Sequence relation.

Step 1 POOL is initialised to contain E_1, E_2 and E_3.

Step 2 Two elements are selected from POOL and combined. There are two possibilities: We could combine E_2 and E_3 under the Sequence Rule, with a score of 1; or we could combine E_2 and E_3 under the Contrast Rule, with a score of 2. Since the latter combination has the higher score, these elements are combined. The result is a new document plan E_4, whose nucleus is E_2, which replaces the constituent elements in the pool.

Step 3 POOL now contains E_1 and E_4. Since E_2 is the nucleus of E_4, these can be combined via the Sequence Rule, producing a new document plan E_5.

Step 4 POOL now contains just one element, E_5, so the document structuring process terminates.

Figure 4.18   Bottom-up construction of a document plan.

Furthermore, assume that the heuristic scoring function assigns a score of 3 if an Elaboration relation is used; 2 if a Contrast relation is used; and 1 if a Sequence relation is used. This means that joining elements via Elaboration is preferred to joining elements using the Contrast relation, which in turn is preferred to joining elements using Sequence. Finally, suppose that the content determination system has produced just three messages: E_1, a MonthlyTemperatureMsg; E_2, a MonthlyRainfallMsg with a Direction of +; and E_3, a TotalRainSoFarMsg, with a Direction of −. Bottom-up document structuring might then operate as shown in Figure 4.18.

4.4.4   A Comparison of Approaches

The idea of bottom-up text structuring is theoretically elegant and very appealing but has some practical disadvantages, at least if the generated texts are greater than a few sentences in length:

- Bottom-up systems can be very slow if they need to perform extensive search or optimisation.
- It can require a considerable amount of effort to create a comprehensive set of rules that specify when a discourse relation can be used to link two elements. This task may become easier in the future if research in the area leads to the development of applicability rules and relation definitions which are easily ported to new domains.
- It can also require a lot of effort to create an appropriate heuristic scoring function; again, this may become easier in the future as our understanding of how such functions vary in different genres and applications grows.
- Many document structuring tasks need to produce document structures such as paragraphs and sections. This is easy to do with schemas but can be more difficult with bottom-up techniques, especially since such document structures often have internal structures of their own (for example, topic sentences in paragraphs, introductory paragraphs in sections).

- In many applications, documents must contain particular elements for bureaucratic, legal, or conventional reasons. For example, STOP starts its letters with a message which thanks recipients for having filled out the smoking questionnaire; this follows the DOMAIN COMMUNICATION KNOWLEDGE (Kittredge, Koreloke, and Rambow, 1991) that letters generated in response to a questionnaire should first thank people for having completed the questionnaire. This type of knowledge is very easy to include in a schema, but it is less clear how to incorporate it in a bottom-up approach based on discourse relations.

For these reasons, schemas are generally the more practical alternative given our current understanding of the nature of discourse structure. Of course, as mentioned above, schemas have disadvantages as well. In particular, they are relatively rigid, and they cannot produce truly novel structures. As NLG spreads to more complex types of applications, the limited flexibility of schemas may become a real bottleneck.

4.4.5   *Knowledge Acquisition*

Given our current patchy understanding of discourse relations and the other theoretical underpinnings of document structuring, it is not possible today to build domain-independent document structuring systems. Instead, NLG system developers must build document structuring systems based on specific domain-dependent schemas, or specific domain-dependent rules which state when a discourse relation can be used to link components in bottom-up document structuring.

The determination of the rules required can be achieved using the same basic methodology as described in Section 4.3.2 but with the focus on determining regular patterns of messages (and hence schemas) or on determining under what circumstances particular discourse relations are used (for bottom-up structuring). It often makes sense to combine this process with the knowledge acquisition process for content determination, so that the rules for selecting messages and the rules for putting messages together into texts are determined simultaneously.

4.5   Document Planner Architecture

How does document structuring interact with content determination? In the literature, there are two clear alternatives:

- Some content determination process first identifies the messages to be expressed in the text, and a document structuring process then combines these messages into a coherent text.
- The document structuring process begins with a notion of what a well-formed text would look like and then requests a content determination process to find or create appropriate messages for insertion into this structure.

	Content determined ...	
	before document structuring (*data-driven*)	during document structuring (*hypothesis-driven*)
Schema-based	TEXT (McKeown, 1985)	MODELEXPLAINER
Relations-based	Hovy's (1988) Text Structurer	PEA (Moore, 1994)

Figure 4.19 Different combinations of document structuring and content determination.

We might think of the first approach as being data driven, and the second as being hypothesis driven. Data driven architectures are pipelined in nature. First the content determination task does its work, and then the document structuring task takes the results and builds a document plan. Hypothesis-driven architectures are more interleaved; such systems switch back and forth between document structuring and content determination.

Figure 4.19 summarises some different combinations that can be found in the literature. Note that while bottom-up document structuring as described in Section 4.4.3 must be data driven, it is possible to build a top-down hypothesis-driven system which is based on models and applicability rules for discourse relations; PEA (Moore, 1994) is probably the best-known example of such a system.

Both data-driven and hypothesis-driven architectures have advantages and disadvantages. In particular, the clean separation between content determination and document structuring in data-driven document planners makes it easier to modify just one of these components. For example, we should (at least in principle) be able to change content determination rules in a data-driven system without having to make any changes to the document structuring rules. In hypothesis-driven systems, in contrast, because content determination and document structuring closely interact, changing one of these components typically requires making changes to the other component as well.

A drawback of data-driven document planners is that the document structuring process may find it is not able to create a coherent text which includes all of the messages produced by the content determination system. For instance, consider again the simple example shown at the end of Section 4.4.3. If the content determination mechanism produces only two messages, these being E_1 (a MonthlyTemperatureMsg) and E_3 (a TotalRainSoFarMsg), then it is impossible, using the rules given in the example, to combine these messages into a single DocumentPlan. The rules allow a TotalRainSoFarMsg to be combined with a MonthlyRainfallMsg, and the resultant structure to be combined with a MonthlyTemperatureMsg; but there is no rule which allows a MonthlyTemperatureMsg to be directly combined with a TotalRainSoFarMsg.

Of course, this problem could be solved by adding additional rules; for example, we could add a rule which allows a MonthlyTemperatureMsg and a TotalRainSoFarMsg to be combined with a Sequence relation and give this rule a low heuristic score so that it will only be used if the system is stuck and can make no other combinations. It should be clear that careful testing is required to ensure that a document structuring rule set is adequate, and that it handles unusual and boundary cases as well as more typical cases.

Another possibility is to combine data-driven and hypothesis-driven techniques. The natural language analysis community has developed algorithms of this sort for parsing syntactic structures, of which the best known is perhaps Earley's chart parsing algorithm (Earley, 1970); a potentially fruitful line of enquiry would be to apply these techniques to the document planning problem.

4.6   Further Reading

Surprisingly little has been written about domain modelling and message definition in NLG. Kukich and her colleagues have probably published the most on this issue: see for example Kukich et al., 1997. Bateman and his colleagues have published a number of papers on the idea of basing NLG domain models around a linguistically-based conceptual hierarchy called the Upper Model (Bateman et al., 1990). The broader AI literature contains a substantial amount of work on domain modelling and related issues; Uschold and Gruniger (1996) provide a useful survey of much of this work. The software engineering literature also contains many techniques that can be applied to the construction of domain models for NLG systems; textbooks on object-oriented modelling (such as Booch, 1994) and entity–relationship modelling (such as Barker, 1990) are good places to look.

There is a larger literature on the problem of content determination. Most of this work describes how content determination is performed in specific systems, including EPICURE (Dale, 1990), IDAS (Reiter et al., 1995), FOG (Goldberg et al., 1994), and PEBA (Milosavljevic and Dale, 1996). The original work on the use of planning and plan-recognition techniques to determine appropriate content is described by Allen and Perraut (1980); Moore (1994) describes more recent and NLG-oriented work in this area. Paris (1988) discusses how content determination should be affected by user models. Reiter et al. (1997) describe some knowledge acquisition techniques that can be used for content determination.

There is a large body of work on what we have called document structuring, often referred to as TEXT PLANNING in the literature. Hovy (1993) provides a general discussion of the use of discourse relations in NLG. Mann and Thompson (1988) describe RST in particular. Schemas were originally proposed by McKeown (1985). Kittredge et al. (1991) argue that document structuring largely depends on domain-specific knowledge. Lester and Porter (1997) describe a specific schema language, EDP, and also discuss the process of developing EDP schemas in a particular domain. The original work on using discourse relations for bottom-up document structuring was by Hovy (1998); our presentation of this approach is partially based on Marcu's work (1997).

One area which has not been much discussed in the research literature is knowledge acquisition for document structuring. Probably the most useful sources here are descriptions of how particular systems were built; see, for example, Goldberg et al. (1994), McKeown et al. (1994), Lester and Porter (1997).

Allen's textbook on natural language understanding (Allen, 1995) is a good starting point for information on parsing algorithms, including Earley's chart parser.

5   Microplanning

In the preceding chapter, we looked at how the document planning component of
an NLG system can produce a document plan that specifies both the content and
overall structure of a document to be generated. The task of the microplanning
component is to take such a document plan and refine it to produce a more detailed
text specification that can be passed to the surface realisation component, which
will produce a corresponding surface text.

The document plan leaves open a number of decisions about the eventual form
of the text in the document to be generated. These finer-grained decisions are made
by the microplanning component. In the NLG system architecture used in this book,
the MICROPLANNER is concerned with

> **LEXICALISATION.** Choosing the particular words, syntactic constructs,
> and mark-up annotations used to communicate the information en-
> coded in the document plan.
>
> **AGGREGATION.** Deciding how much information should be communi-
> cated in each of the document's sentences.
>
> **REFERRING EXPRESSION GENERATION.** Determining what phrases should
> be used to identify particular domain entities to the user.

The result is still not a text. The idiosyncrasies of syntax, morphology, and the target
mark-up language must still be dealt with. However, once the text specification
has been constructed, all substantive decisions have been made. It is the job of the
surface realiser, discussed in Chapter 6, to then construct a document in accordance
with these decisions.

We begin this chapter by presenting our view of the microplanning task in
Section 5.1. We go on to discuss lexicalisation, aggregation, and referring expression generation in Sections 5.2, 5.3, and 5.4, respectively. In Section 5.5, we
review some limitations of the approach to microplanning presented here, and we
describe some alternative approaches. Finally, in Section 5.6, we provide some
pointers to relevant material in the literature.

5.1   Introduction

5.1.1   Why Do We Need Microplanning?

In the 1970s and 1980s, most NLG systems did not contain distinct microplanning components. Echoing Thompson's (1977) distinction between the decisions of 'what to say' and 'how to say it', most complete NLG systems contained some kind of document planner (following Thompson, often referred to as a STRATEGIC COMPONENT), concerned with questions of text content and structure; and some kind of linguistic realiser (often referred to as a TACTICAL COMPONENT), concerned with issues of grammar and morphology. We will refer to this as the TWO-STAGE MODEL of natural language generation. The division of labour embodied in the two-stage model made it possible for researchers to focus their attention on problems or phenomena which properly seemed to belong exclusively in one category or the other.

In the 1990s, however, many groups working on natural language generation have recognised that there are a number of NLG issues which do not seem to be centrally concerned with text content and structure, nor with sentence-level syntax and morphology, but which are nonetheless important in building systems that produce high-quality texts.

Where Does Referring Expression Generation Belong?

As one example, it is not clear in a two-stage model where the task of referring expression generation should fit. There is some sense in which this is a content determination task, since it involves deciding which properties of an entity should be used in describing it. From this perspective, we might choose to see referring expression generation as part of the document planning process. At the same time, however, it seems to be a more fine-grained issue than those normally dealt with at the level of document planning. In many systems the result of the document planning process is a tree where each leaf node is a simple predicate–argument structure; the predicate typically corresponds to a verb, but the arguments are often represented simply as atomic internal symbols that correspond to the in-tended referents. From this perspective, we might choose to view referring ex-pression generation as a process carried out during the surface realisation of these predicate–argument structures. An interesting solution to this problem proposed by Appelt (1985) involved an interleaving of the processes of content determina-tion and surface realisation, so that whenever the surface realiser reached a point in the processing of a predicate–argument structure where a noun phrase referring expression had to be generated, the text planning component would be invoked to determine the content of that referring expression. Once this task was complete, control would revert to the surface realisation component, which would proceed to generate a surface form corresponding to the newly created content specification for the referring expression in question.

Where Does Aggregation Belong?

A second aspect of natural language generation that proved to be difficult to accommodate within the two-stage model was the set of processes that have become known collectively as AGGREGATION, whereby a number of informational elements which could have been expressed by individual sentences are combined grammatically to produce a single, more complex sentence structure. The problem here manifested itself as a result of two developments. First, researchers constructing NLG systems began to attempt the generation of richer, longer, and more fluent texts. Under these circumstances, it soon became apparent that mapping propositions into sentences in a one-by-one fashion led to somewhat stilted and choppy texts. Second, as researchers increasingly relied less and less on handcrafted underlying representations as input, it became apparent that host systems would be unlikely to deliver information for presentation in chunks that would correspond neatly to surface-form sentences. There thus arose a need to provide some mechanism for combining these informational elements to produce more sophisticated grammatical structures. This could be seen as part of the document planning task, and indeed, when present, this is where this kind of work tended to be placed in many systems. At the same time, however, the considerations that are relevant in such a process are strictly more grammatical than the kinds of knowledge more generally used in the document planning stage of natural language generation. On the other hand, placing this processing within the surface realisation component complicates the kinds of decision making that the realiser needs to carry out. Within the field, the realisation process was generally taken to involve the application of a relatively straightforward repository of information about how to map semantic structures into grammatical ones. This typically involves the assumption that the input structures are already packaged into sentence-sized pieces. The incorporation of aggregation into the realisation component then adds a requirement to carry out some preparatory processing to combine the input semantic structures into a form where these realisation mappings can be applied, but this extra processing might then as well be seen as a separate stage in the generation task.

5.1.2   *What's Involved in Microplanning?*

Given considerations like the above, researchers in NLG have increasingly incorporated within their systems a third component that lies between the document planner and the surface realiser. This is often referred to as the SENTENCE PLAN-NER, although we prefer to use the term MICROPLANNER, recognising that some of the issues dealt with – for example, the segmentation of a text into paragraphs – lie beyond sentential level concerns. At the time of writing, there is no strong consensus as to the specific nature of the tasks that should be carried out as part of microplanning. The discussion above suggests that aggregation and referring expression generation might fall into this category. To this we will add the task of lexicalisation, since, as we will argue below, the choice of which words to use to realise concepts has a subsequent impact on the other microplanning tasks. Indeed, it can be argued that these three tasks – lexicalisation, aggregation, and referring expression generation – are not at all independent of one another.

There are no hard and fast rules we can use to determine which tasks belong within microplanning and which more properly belong in the domain of document planning or surface realisation; it is clear that many research groups are still exploring the issues here. For our present purposes, we have adopted the simplifying heuristic that document planning can be viewed as primarily relying on domain knowledge, whereas surface realisation relies primarily on linguistic knowledge; microplanning is then concerned with those tasks that require attention being paid to interactions between domain knowledge and linguistic knowledge. This is a rather vague characterisation, of course. One could argue that all NLG tasks depend to some degree on both domain knowledge and linguistic knowledge. However, it is not uncommon, for example, for systems that generate multilingual output to use the same document planner for all output languages, which suggests that the impact of detailed syntactic knowledge on document planning is limited. Similarly, linguistic realisers are often intended to be used in many domains and applications; this suggests that they are influenced to only a limited extent by domain knowledge, although they are very dependent on detailed linguistic knowledge.

In contrast, the microplanning tasks of lexicalisation, referring expression generation, and aggregation are very dependent on both linguistic knowledge and domain knowledge. Lexicalisation, for example, requires mapping from concepts in the domain to lexical elements that satisfy the required collocational and syntactic constraints and so requires knowledge of both. The generation of referring expressions requires knowledge about which domain entities are salient and what properties they have but also knowledge about the syntactic implications of using specific referential forms such as pronouns and *one*-anaphora. Finally, aggregation requires both linguistic knowledge about how different types of aggregation can be carried out syntactically but also domain knowledge about whether the informational elements in question possess the relevant properties that would licence application of an aggregative operation.

5.1.3   *The Inputs and Outputs of Microplanning*

Given the current level of interest in the area, we can expect significant developments in our understanding and conceptualisation of the task of microplanning over the next few years; but for the moment, the answers to many questions remain unclear. For the purposes of this book, we will adopt some simplifying assumptions

The month was slightly warmer than average, with the average number of rain days. Heavy rain fell on the 27th and 28th.

Figure 5.1   A simple weather summary.

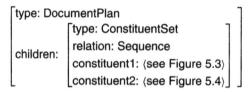

Figure 5.2   The top-level document plan for the text in Figure 5.1.

to enable us to provide a detailed characterisation of the task; we will return to discuss alternative and more complex views in Section 5.5. Before discussing the architecture of the microplanner in Section 5.1.4, however, we first review the inputs and outputs of microplanning.

As described in Chapter 4, the output of the document planning process is a document plan, which places the constituent messages to be expressed within some structure. The microplanner takes this structure as input and provides as output a text specification made up of phrase specifications that can be passed to a surface realisation component. Figures 5.2, 5.3, and 5.4 show a simple document plan which corresponds to the text in Figure 5.1; a schematic version of this

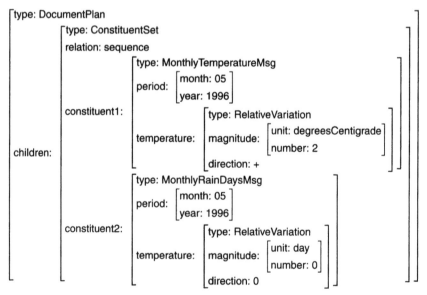

Figure 5.3   The first constituent of the document plan corresponding to the text in Figure 5.1.

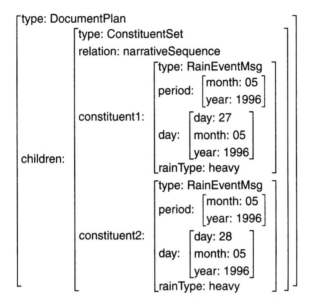

Figure 5.4 The second constituent of the document plan corresponding to the text in Figure 5.1.

document plan is shown in Figure 5.5. The document plan contains four messages: a MonthlyTemperatureMsg, a MonthlyRainDaysMsg, and two RainEventMsgs. The first two messages, which give general information about the month, are grouped together beneath Constituent1 in the top-level document plan. The last two messages, which describe significant events, are beneath Constituent2 in the

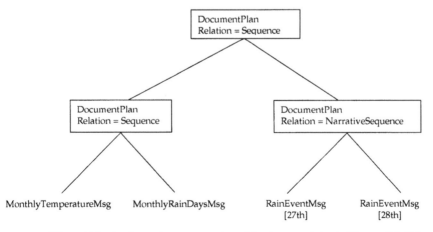

Figure 5.5 A schematic representation of the document plan in Figures 5.2–5.4.

$$
\begin{bmatrix}
\text{type: TextSpecification} \\
\text{Constituent1: } \langle \text{Sentence1} \rangle \\
\text{Constituent1: } \langle \text{Sentence2} \rangle
\end{bmatrix}
$$

Figure 5.6 The top-level text specification corresponding to the text in Figure 5.1.

top-level plan. Note that the messages specify the information to be communicated abstractly. They do not, for example, specify which words should be used to communicate the notion of average temperature, or which words should be used to refer to the fifth month of 1996. The grouping in the document plan reflects general semantic similarity; in this case all general information messages are under top-level Constituent1, while all significant event messages are under top-level Constituent2.

Figures 5.6, 5.7, and 5.8 show the text specification that might be built from this document plan. The top-level text specification (shown in Figure 5.6) is simply

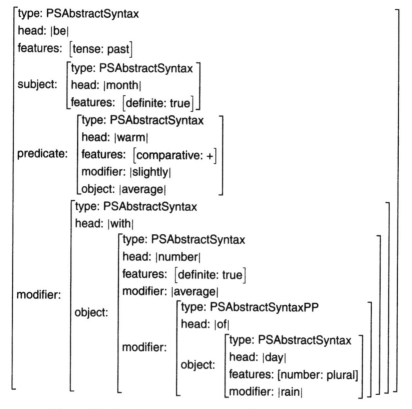

Figure 5.7 The phrase specification for Sentence1 in Figure 5.6 (*The month was slightly warmer than average, with the average number of rain days*).

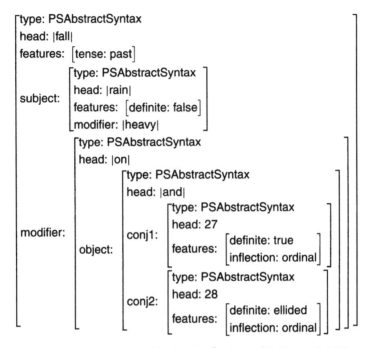

Figure 5.8 The phrase specification for Sentence2 in Figure 5.6 (*Heavy rain fell on the 27th and 28th*).

a list of two phrase specifications, each of which describes a sentence. The first phrase specification (shown in Figure 5.7) specifies the sentence *The month was slightly warmer than average, with the average number of rain days*. It illustrates the various processes which happen in microplanning:

- This sentence communicates two of the messages in the input document plan (the MonthlyTemperatureMsg and the MonthlyRainDaysMsg); combining the messages in this way is an example of aggregation.
- The sentence uses the term *slightly warmer than average* to communicate the fact that the average temperature in the month was two degrees higher than usual (the information in the MonthlyTemperatureMsg); this is an example of lexicalisation.
- The sentence uses the phrase *The month* to refer to May 1996 (the 5th month of 1996); this is an example of referring expression generation. The use of this particular form of reference is only possible if the context makes clear that *the month* refers to May 1996; in the case of WEATHER-REPORTER, this context comes from the title *Weather Summary for May 1996*.

The phrase specifications shown in Figures 5.7 and 5.8 are ABSTRACT SYNTAC-TIC STRUCTURES; see Chapters 3 and 6 for further discussion of this form of representation. The surface realiser converts these phrase specification representations into the final text. For example, it is the job of the realiser to produce the ordinal number *28th* from the conj2 element at the bottom of Figure 5.8.

5.1.4   The Architecture of a Microplanner

As we have already suggested, there are unresolved questions as to how the three processes of lexicalisation, aggregation, and referring expression generation should best be integrated. Wanner and Hovy (1996) suggest using a blackboard architecture which allows very flexible interactions between the processes; a graphical depiction of such an architecture is shown in Figure 5.9. In this architecture, no specific ordering is imposed over the application of the lexicalisation, aggregation, and referring expression generation processes as a whole. Rather, each process opportunistically carries out operations on the data to be expressed, with this data being present on a blackboard that is accessible to all three processes. So, for example, an aggregation operation might be applied to the initial set of data, followed by a lexicalisation operation, followed by some other aggregation operation whose applicability only becomes clear once the preceding lexicalisation operation has been performed.

The working out of such a model is not a trivial matter. Among other things, it is necessary to define a uniform representation which is the input and output of all three processes and which allows decisions of one type to be made without constraining decisions of other types. For example, the result of an aggregation operation should not restrict the applicability of lexicalisation operations unless this really is a necessary consequence of the aggregation operation.

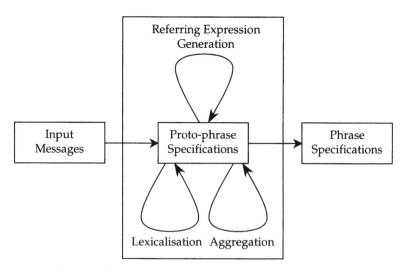

Figure 5.9   A blackboard architecture for a microplanner.

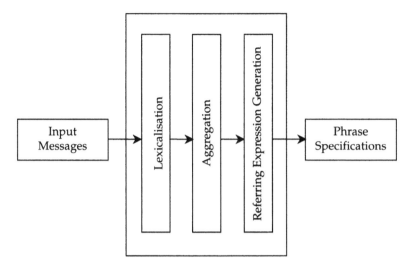

Figure 5.10 A simple microplanner architecture.

Although the architecture shown in Figure 5.9 is theoretically elegant and appealing, in practice it is often easier to build a microplanner as a pipeline, where the different operations happen in a fixed sequence. In this book, we will assume a very simple, pipelined model of the microplanning process which is less flexible, but easier to build (and to explain) than the architecture shown in Figure 5.9. This model is shown in Figure 5.10. The ordering of the microplanning processes can be summarised as follows:

- First, a lexicalisation process chooses the words and syntactic structures that will be used to express each message. We will refer to the result of this process as a PROTO-PHRASE SPECIFICATION. The main difference between this and a real phrase specification is that it may contain references to domain entities; these will be processed by the referring-expression generation process.
- Then, a set of aggregation rules considers the set of proto-phrase specifications that result from lexicalisation, and, where appropriate, combines two or more such specifications into a single proto-phrase specification.
- Finally, a process concerned with the task of referring expression generation takes each proto-phrase specification and replaces references to domain entities with the phrase specification corresponding to a noun phrase that will identify that entity for the reader. The result of this is a full phrase specification, which can then be processed by the surface realiser.

This process is sketched diagrammatically in Figure 5.11. This is clearly a very simple model of microplanning; however, for our present purposes it is sufficient. We will return to consider problems that arise from these simplifications in

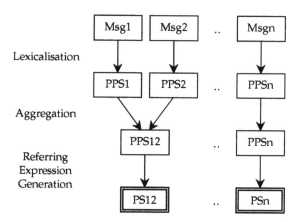

Figure 5.11   Simplified microplanning.

Section 5.5. In the immediately following sections, we look in more detail at the component processes in microplanning as they might be instantiated in this simple architecture.

5.2   Lexicalisation

Lexicalisation is the process of choosing words and syntactic structures to communicate the information in a document plan. This means mapping the messages in the document plan, which are expressed in terms of a domain model, into words and other linguistic resources which make sense to the intended user of the document.

As mentioned above, there is considerable debate in the research community as to whether lexicalisation should be performed in the document planner, microplanner, or surface realiser; or indeed whether different aspects of lexicalisation should be performed in different modules. For simplicity of exposition, we will assume here that all of lexicalisation is performed in the microplanner.

5.2.1   Simple Lexicalisation

The simplest form of lexicalisation is when templates for proto-phrase specifications are associated with each message; lexicalisation then consists of instantiating the template with the particulars of the message to be expressed.

For example, Figure 5.12 shows a simple template which can be used to lexicalise a **RainEventMessage**. In this and other figures in this chapter, the **PPS** prefix in type names indicates that the structure is a proto-phrase specification; so, a structure of type **PSAbstractSyntax** is a phrase specification, while a structure of type **PPSAbstractSyntax** is a proto-phrase specification. Figure 5.14 shows the result of applying this template to the example message shown in Figure 5.13.

$$
\begin{bmatrix}
\text{type: PPSAbstractSyntax} \\
\text{head: |fall|} \\
\text{features: } \begin{bmatrix} \text{tense: past} \end{bmatrix} \\
\text{subject: } \begin{bmatrix}
\text{type: PPSAbstractSyntax} \\
\text{head: |rain|} \\
\text{features: } \begin{bmatrix} \text{definite: false} \end{bmatrix} \\
\text{modifier: lexicalise(rainType)}
\end{bmatrix} \\
\text{modifier: } \begin{bmatrix}
\text{type: PPSABstractSyntax} \\
\text{preposition: |on|} \\
\text{object: } \begin{bmatrix} \text{type: ReferringNP} \\ \text{object: day} \end{bmatrix}
\end{bmatrix}
\end{bmatrix}
$$

Figure 5.12   A simple template for RainEventMsgs.

$$
\begin{bmatrix}
\text{type: RainEventMessage} \\
\text{period: } \begin{bmatrix} \text{month: 05} \\ \text{year: 1996} \end{bmatrix} \\
\text{day: } \begin{bmatrix} \text{day: 27} \\ \text{month: 05} \\ \text{year: 1996} \end{bmatrix} \\
\text{rainType: heavy}
\end{bmatrix}
$$

Figure 5.13   A simple message.

$$
\begin{bmatrix}
\text{type: PPSAbstractSyntax} \\
\text{head: |fall|} \\
\text{features: } \begin{bmatrix} \text{tense: past} \end{bmatrix} \\
\text{subject: } \begin{bmatrix}
\text{type: PPSAbstractSyntax} \\
\text{head: |rain|} \\
\text{features: } \begin{bmatrix} \text{definite: false} \end{bmatrix} \\
\text{modifier: |heavy|}
\end{bmatrix} \\
\text{modifier: } \begin{bmatrix}
\text{type: PPSAbstractSyntax} \\
\text{head: |on|} \\
\text{object: } \begin{bmatrix} \text{type: ReferringNP} \\ \text{object: } \begin{bmatrix} \text{day: 27} \\ \text{month: 05} \\ \text{year: 1996} \end{bmatrix} \end{bmatrix}
\end{bmatrix}
\end{bmatrix}
$$

Figure 5.14   The proto-phrase specification produced by applying the template to a message.

The template includes a recursive invocation of the lexicalisation procedure, lexicalise(rainType); this returns an adjective which expresses the rainType field of the message. In the simplest possible model, the possible values of rainType in the domain model may just be the appropriate adjectives; in this case, lexicalise(rainType) would simply return *heavy*.

The template includes a ReferringNP structure; this will be replaced by a noun phrase which refers to the specified day during the process of referring expression generation (discussed in Section 5.4). If the message occurs in the document plan shown in Figure 5.4, it will be combined with the other RainEventMessage during the aggregation process (discussed in Section 5.3); the final resulting phrase specification is as shown in Figure 5.8.

As we have described it here, simple lexicalisation is in some ways analogous to the techniques used to support localisation of software. For example, the MessageFormat class in Java allows Java programmers to define 'patterns' for expressing a message in different languages; in our terminology, these patterns are basically lexicalisation templates for phrase specifications represented as strings instead of as abstract syntactic structures.

5.2.2   Simple Lexical Choice

In the previous example, there was only one way to lexicalise the message, but in many cases there are several ways of expressing a message or message fragment, and the NLG system must choose which to use. Sometimes this choice can be made straightforwardly, but in other cases it depends on complex contextual and pragmatic factors.

Figure 5.15 shows a lexicalisation template for RainSpellMsgs. This in itself is quite simple, but it contains a recursive call to lexicalise(spell); this is a more complex procedure, for there are many ways of describing contiguous sequences of days. For example, the most appropriate way of describing a spell depends to some extent on the length of that spell. We would not want to generate *from the 10th to the 10th*, for example, since the *from . . . to . . .* construct is not appropriate for a one-day spell. A simple lexical choice algorithm based solely on the length

```
⎡type: PPSAbstractSyntax                              ⎤
⎢head: |fall|                                          ⎥
⎢features: [tense: past]                               ⎥
⎢            ⎡type: PPSAbstractSyntax          ⎤       ⎥
⎢            ⎢head: |rain|                      ⎥       ⎥
⎢subject:    ⎢features: [definite: false]       ⎥       ⎥
⎢            ⎣modifier: lexicalise(rainType)   ⎦       ⎥
⎣modifier: lexicalise(spell)                           ⎦
```

Figure 5.15 A simple template for RainSpellMessages.

if spell.begin = spell.end **then**
    return a proto-phrase specification for *on the ith*
else if spell.begin is the day before spell.end **then**
    return a proto-phrase specification for *on the ith and jth*
else
    return a proto-phrase specification for *from the ith to the jth*

Figure 5.16   An algorithm for lexicalising spells.

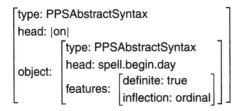

Figure 5.17   A template proto-phrase specification for *on the ith*.

of the spell might use the logic shown in Figure 5.16; this logic can of course be reused for other messages, such as **TemperatureSpellMsg**s, that express spells. Figure 5.17 shows the template proto-phrase specification for expressions of the form *on the ith*, and Figure 5.18 shows the template for expressions of the form *on the ith and jth*.

It may also be appropriate to create different lexicalisation templates for different syntactic categories. For example, suppose we had a **WettestSpellMsg** which stated that a particular spell was the wettest spell of this length seen so far this year, as might be expressed in the following sentence:

(5.1)   The 12th, 13th, and 14th was the wettest three-day period seen so far this year.

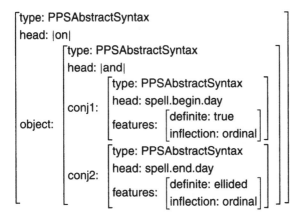

Figure 5.18   A template proto-phrase specification for *on the ith and jth*.

In this context, the spell is being expressed by means of a noun phrase (*the 12th, 13th, and 14th*) rather than by a prepositional phrase (*from the 12th to the 14th*). Clearly, implementing this requires that we create a set of lexicalisation templates which express spell as a noun phrase as well as a set of lexicalisation templates which express spell as a prepositional phrase.

5.2.3   *Contextual and Pragmatic Influences on Lexical Choice*

There are many other influences on lexical choice in addition to syntactic context and the specific parameter values present in a particular message. For instance, the following example shows just a few of the numerous ways of describing a particular RainSpellMsg:

(5.2)   a. It rained for seven days from the 20th to the 26th.
b. It rained for seven days from the 20th.
c. It rained from the 20th to the 26th.
d. It rained on the 20th, 21th, 22th, 23th, 24th, 25th, and 26th.
e. It rained during Thanksgiving week.

The choice between these alternatives is partially determined by the conventions that hold in the genre of the texts to be generated. For example, an analysis of the WeatherReporter corpus shows that spells of this length are usually described using the *from . . . to . . .* construct, as in Example (5.2c). This is therefore the most appropriate default form; however, in certain contexts it may be appropriate to use other forms. Here are some possible considerations:

> **Pragmatic communicative goal.** The explicit list of days in Example (5.2d) may be appropriate if it is important to emphasise to the user that there was an unusual rainy period in this month.
>
> **User knowledge.** Sometimes there are special ways of describing a spell, such as *Thanksgiving week* in Example (5.2e). Such descriptions should be used only if the user will understand and correctly interpret them; for example, Canadians interpret *Thanksgiving week* differently from citizens of the United States, and many British people are not familiar with the term at all.
>
> **Repetition vs. conciseness.** The repetition in Example (5.2a) may be appropriate in order to reduce the possibility of misunderstanding; conversely, the more concise forms in Examples (5.2b) and (5.2c) may be more appropriate where space is limited.
>
> **Consistency with previous text.** If a particular realisation has been used in a previous message for another instance of the concept, it may be best to use the same realisation again, especially if the system wishes to enable the user to compare the two spells. Example (5.3) demonstrates this.

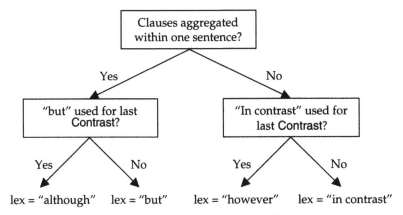

Figure 5.19 A decision tree for realising the Contrast relation.

(5.3)   a. It snowed for five days from the 10th, and it rained from
            the 20th to the 26th.
         b. It snowed for five days from the 10th, and it rained for
            seven days from the 20th.

Consistent realisation may also make it easier to aggregate the content
of phrases: see Section 5.3 in this regard.

The research literature describes many different ways of representing the choice
mechanisms required, including discrimination nets, decision trees, and systemic
networks. An example of a simple decision tree, used here to select an appropriate
cue phrase for a discourse relation, is shown in Figure 5.19.

5.2.4   *Expressing Discourse Relations*

Lexicalisation is often taken to include the task of choosing appropriate cue words
(or other linguistic resources) to express discourse relations such as Contrast
or Elaboration. For example, a contrast relation could variously be realised as
follows:

(5.4)   a. The month was much wetter than average, *but* rainfall for the year is
            still very depleted.
         b. The month was much wetter than average; *however*, rainfall for the
            year is still very depleted.
         c. The month was much wetter than average, *although* rainfall for the
            year is still very depleted.
         d. *Although* the month was much wetter than average, rainfall for the
            year is still very depleted.

Note that different lexical realisations of the contrast relation are appropriate in
different syntactic contexts. Example (5.4d) would not be acceptable with *however*

or *but* as a replacement for *although*. A simple decision tree for choosing an appropriate cue phrase to express Contrast is shown in Figure 5.19. This decision tree is partially based on the rule that cue phrases should be varied; other things being equal, it is best to use a variety of cue phrases instead of reusing the same cue phrase again and again.

One problem with lexicalising discourse relations is that the rules for deciding which cue word to use to express a discourse relation can depend on subtle pragmatic and domain factors (Vander Linden and Martin, 1995; Knott, 1996). For example, the decision tree shown in Figure 5.19 assumes that *but* and *although* can be used interchangeably, but consider the following sentences (from Knott, 1996):

(5.5)   a. She's part time, *but* she does more work than the rest of us put together.
         b. She's part time, *although* she does more work than the rest of us put together.
         c. She does more work than the rest of us put together, *but* she's part time.
         d. She does more work than the rest of us put together, *although* she's part time.

Knott argues that the formulations in Examples (5.5a) and (5.5d) are preferable to those in Examples (5.5b) and (5.5c), which suggests that *but* and *although* are not in fact synonyms.

Unfortunately, the rules for deciding when a particular cue phrase should be used to express a discourse relation are still in general unclear; this makes it difficult to write general-purpose algorithms for choosing cue phrases. On the other hand, it is often less difficult to develop limited algorithms which are targeted towards specific applications.

5.2.5   *Fine-Grained Lexicalisation*

So far we have assumed that the lexicalisation process operates on messages. These are relatively coarse-grained chunks of information with a domain-dependent structure. Another view of lexicalisation is that it operates on fine-grained chunks of information, expressed in terms of what are sometimes considered to be SEMANTIC PRIMITIVES.

For example, instead of operating on a message structure like that shown in Figure 5.13, a lexicalisation process may be required to produce an expression for the following conjunction of predicates:

(5.6)   *precipitationEvent(e)* $\land$ *precipitationSubstance(e, s)* $\land$ *material(s, water)* $\land$ *state(s, liquid)* $\land$ *precipitationIntensity(e, heavy)* $\land$ *eventTime(e, time1)* $\land$ *timeIsDay(time1, 27/5/96)*

If the lexicalisation system individually realised each predicate and then relied on an aggregation mechanism to put the individual predicate realisations together, the result would be something along the lines of the following:

(5.7)   Heavy precipitation of liquid water occurred on the day 27/5/96.

This is not very desirable. But the lexicalisation system can produce a better text if it performs the following operations:

- Look for single words which express multiple predicates. In this example, for instance, the word *rain* can be used to describe a precipitation event whose substance was liquid water (in other words, the first four predicates in the conjunction in Example (5.6)).
- Enforce COLLOCATION constraints and preferences; these are cases when a meaning is expressed with different words depending on the content of other parts of the clause. In this example, for instance, the verb *fell* is more appropriate than the verb *occurred* if the noun is *rain*; if the noun were *fog*, however, it would be more appropriate to use the verb *descended*.
- Omit information which the user can obtain from context. For example, if it is clear from context that the text describes events in the month May 1996, then the date can simply be expressed as *the 27th*; the word *day* can also be omitted if context makes it clear that *the 27th* refers to a day (instead of, say, the 27th applicant for a job).

The result of these operations would then be a proto-phrase specification for the sentence *Heavy rain fell on the 27th*, which is a much better expression of this information.

This type of processing is the subject of a considerable amount of research in the NLG community (Nogier and Zock, 1991; Stede, 1996; Elhadad, McKeown, and Robin, 1997). In very general terms, such systems work by continuously 'rewriting' the input structure, using a dictionary which expresses the meaning of every word in terms of input predicates and also any constraints (such as collocation) on the use of individual words. Sophisticated search techniques can be used to determine the order in which rewriting operations should be performed (see, for example, Elhadad et al., 1997).

Fine-grained lexicalisation seems especially useful in systems which need to encode as much information as possible within a limited number of words, such as is the case in STREAK (Robin and McKeown, 1996). It also seems likely to be useful in multilingual generation, when the same conceptual content must be expressed in different languages. A common problem here, referred to as LEXICAL DIVERGENCE, is the phenomenon whereby different languages offer quite different means of expressing the same content. To repeat an oft-cited example, the English sentence *He swam across the river* can be expressed in French as *Il a travers la rivière à la nage* (literally *He crossed the river by swimming*); these two messages are informationally equivalent, but not word-for-word isomorphic. The two sentences can,

The month was slightly warmer than average. It had almost exactly
the average rainfall. Heavy rain fell on the 27th. Heavy rain fell on
the 27th.

Figure 5.20   The weather summary for July 1996 without aggregation.

at least in principle, be generated from the same input, if fine-grained lexicalisation
techniques are used. Stede (1996) presents an exploration of this problem.

5.3   Aggregation

In the previous section we saw how a lexicalisation process can be used to map input
messages into proto-phrase specifications. These phrase specifications might then
be sent directly to the surface realiser; however, the resulting one-to-one mapping
of messages to sentences can lead to stilted texts. Figure 5.20 shows how the
example text shown in Figure 5.1 might look if we chose to express each message
by means of a separate sentence.

The text shown in Figure 5.20 might be appropriate in some circumstances. For
example, because it uses short sentences, it may be well suited for people with
limited reading ability, such as small children. For most readers, though, the use
of short sentences becomes irritating; the reader's capacity to take on board the
information in larger chunks is not being exercised, and the relatively flat syntactic
structure means that the potential for giving clues as to the relative importance of
different elements of the underlying content is lost. From the perspective of an
NLG system, an important role of microplanning is to take a set of simple phrase
specifications and to combine them in various ways to permit the generation of
more complex sentence structures. This is the process of AGGREGATION, whereby
the microplanner decides how messages are distributed across sentences.

Although the construction of complex sentences is the most widely discussed
aspect of aggregation in the literature, it is not the only one. In particular, if the
document plan does not specify the order in which messages should be expressed,
then the aggregation module should decide this, perhaps on the basis of placing
similar messages together so that they can be combined into one sentence. In some
cases, it may also be possible for the aggregation process to create higher-level
structures such as paragraphs, although our understanding of the considerations
involved in creating such structures is still somewhat limited.

We focus in this section on sentence formation, which is the best understood
aspect of aggregation. We discuss both the linguistic mechanisms which can be
used to combine multiple proto-phrase specifications into one sentence, and the
principles which can be used to decide when proto-phrase specifications should be
aggregated and, if so, which linguistic mechanism should be used. We then briefly
discuss ordering and paragraph formation.

For expository convenience, we will generally talk of the effects of these operations as being fully realised texts, rather than proto-phrase specifications. However,

it should be borne in mind that the microplanner only deals with phrase specifications and proto-phrase specifications; it is the surface realisation process that then renders these phrase specifications as surface text.

5.3.1 Mechanisms for Sentence Formation

From a linguistic perspective, there are a number of mechanisms that can be used to combine multiple proto-phrase specifications in a single sentence; or, more precisely in the terms of the idealised model of microplanning we presented earlier, there are a number of mechanisms by means of which simpler proto-phrase specifications can be combined to make more complex proto-phrase specifications. In the literature, these mechanisms have generally been referred to collectively by the term AGGREGATION, although it is often not clear exactly what kinds of structures these operations are intended to apply to. In our discussion of the various kinds of aggregation operations, we will refer to them as applying to the relatively neutral category of INFORMATIONAL ELEMENTS so as to avoid a commitment to any particular representation.

Descriptions of aggregations often have the flavour of transformations in transformational grammar, and in such cases they appear to apply to what we might think of as deep syntactic structures. In some cases, however, as we will show below, aggregation operations also need to be aware of semantic aspects of the representations they operate upon. In other cases, the effects of possible aggregation operations might be better seen as the results of activities carried out as part of the initial content determination stage of NLG.

We will discuss aggregation operations under the following categories:

- simple conjunction;
- conjunction via shared participants;
- conjunctive via shared structure; and
- syntactic embedding.

Once each of the basic mechanisms has been described, we go on to look at how one might decide when aggregation operations should be performed, and how one might choose *between* these mechanisms.

Simple Conjunction

The simplest form of aggregation is to combine two or more informational elements within a single sentence by using a connective such as *and*. The particular connective that it is most appropriate to use will depend on the discourse relation that holds between the informational elements. For example, if a discourse relation of Contrast holds between two informational elements, then the word *but* might be used to connect them.

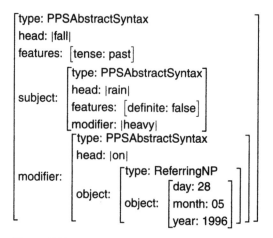

Figure 5.21   A proto-phrase specification for *Heavy rain fell on the 28th.*

So, for example, if we have informational elements that might independently be realised by the clauses in Examples (5.8a) and (5.8b), these can be combined to produce an informational element that could be realised by the sentence in Example (5.9).[1]

(5.8) a. There was a mild spell from the 5th to the 9th.
       b. It was cold at night from the 17th to the 25th.
(5.9) There was a mild spell from the 5th to the 9th, and it was cold at night from the 17th to the 25th.

The implementation of simple conjunction in terms of proto-phrase specifications depends on what representation is used. If an abstract syntactic representation is used, then generally a new proto-phrase specification is created whose top level specifies the conjunct and which includes the original proto-phrase specifications as daughters of the conjunct. Figure 5.22 shows the result of applying simple conjunction to the proto-phrase specifications shown in Figures 5.14 and 5.21 (Figure 5.21 is identical to Figure 5.14, except that it refers to 28th May rather than 27th May). Example (5.10) shows how the proto-phrase specification shown in Figure 5.22 might be realised as a surface form.

(5.10) Heavy rain fell on the 27th and heavy rain fell on the 28th.

---

[1] A sometimes confusing aspect of treatments of aggregation in the literature is that authors easily slip into talking of how some pair of *sentences* can alternatively be expressed as some single sentence. Taken literally, this implies that the aggregative operations are applied to surface strings to produce some new surface string, which is clearly not what is intended. In what follows, we have tried to be as explicit as possible about precisely what it is that aggregative operations apply to; unfortunately, this often results in somewhat long-winded locutions.

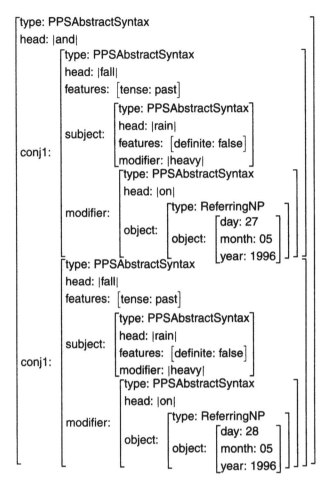

Figure 5.22 The result of a simple conjunction (*Heavy rain fell on the 27th and 28th*).

Simple conjunction makes no changes to the internal syntactic and lexical content of the constituents that are conjoined; precisely because of this, it is a form of aggregation that can be applied to informational elements whose representations are very close to the surface. Even if a system uses canned text (see Section 3.4.7) as representations for phrase specifications, these can still be aggregated with simple conjunction by concatenating the first canned text element, the connective, and then the second canned text element. Because there are orthographic consequences of aggregation (for example, in the aggregated form, the first element will not be terminated by a full stop, and the second element will not begin with an upper case letter), it is less straightforward to use simple conjunction if texts are represented as orthographic strings (see Section 3.4.7). This is one reason for preferring canned text to orthographic string representations for phrase specifications, even if a design decision has been made not to use a grammatical representation such as abstract syntactic structures or lexicalised case frames.

Conjunction via Shared Participants

If two or more informational elements share argument positions with the same content, then it is generally possible to produce a surface form where the shared content is realised only once. The following examples demonstrate this phenomenon, where the first text in each pair shows what would be realised without aggregation and the second text shows the effect of aggregation:

(5.11) a. The month was colder than average. The month was relatively dry.
        b. The month was colder than average and relatively dry.
(5.12) a. January was colder than average. February was colder than average.
        b. January and February were colder than average.
(5.13) a. John gave a book to Mary. John gave a book to Fred.
        b. John gave books to both Mary and Fred.

In Example (5.11), the material which is realised as the subject is shared; in Example (5.12), it is the object that is shared; and Example (5.13) demonstrates that the same behaviour applies to other grammatical roles too.

Within the NLG literature, this form of aggregation has been widely used. For example, in the PLANDOC system (McKeown et al., 1994), we find Example (5.14b) offered as an aggregated alternative to Example (5.14a):

(5.14) a. It requested the placement of a 48-fiber cable from the CO to section 1103. It requested the placement of a 24-fiber cable from section 1201 to section 1301.
        b. It requested the placement of a 48-fiber cable from the CO to section 1103, and the placement of a 24-fibre cable from section 1201 to section 1301.

Note that whether two constituents are considered equivalent for the purposes of aggregation should be judged with regard to their underlying meanings, not with regard to the lexicalisations used to communicate these meanings. This means that the aggregation process needs access to a sufficiently abstract representation of the informational elements; it is not sufficient to know just the lexemes that will be used in the surface realisation. So, for example, the following two utterances do not necessarily mean the same thing:

(5.15) a. John bought a television. Sam bought a television.
        b. John and Sam bought a television.

It would be inappropriate to generate Example (5.15b) in preference to (5.15a), unless Sam and John bought the same television.[2]

The range of constituent structures that can be combined in these ways has been much discussed in the linguistics literature. Quirk (1985) contains a detailed discussion of the phenomenon in terms of a notion of ELISION.

One implementation of this type of conjunction, if proto-phrase specifications are represented as abstract syntactic structures, is to produce the same general type of structure as for simple conjunction, but to mark the repeated elements as elided; the realiser then omits words for these elements when it processes the phrase specification. Figure 5.23 shows the result of applying shared-participant conjunction to the proto-phrase specifications shown in Figures 5.14 and 5.21; Example (5.16) shows how this proto-phrase specification might be realised as a surface form.

(5.16)   Heavy rain fell on the 27th and on the 28th.

In general, conjunction via shared participants is not possible if phrase specifications are represented as canned text (or orthographic strings); some information about syntactic structure is needed. If this type of aggregation is important, a more abstract representation of phrase specifications, such as abstract syntactic structures or lexicalised case frames, is appropriate. Another approach is to use canned text but add structural and syntactic annotations to support aggregation (in this regard, see Geldof and van de Velde, 1997).

Conjunction via Shared Structure

In the examples above, we focussed on cases where the shared elements corresponded to complete top-level grammatical constituents. However, the same conjunctive possibilities are available at all levels of grammatical structure. Consider the following example:

(5.17)   a. January was drier than average. January was colder than average.
          b. January was drier and colder than average.

From the perspective of theoretical linguistics, there is little difference between this form of aggregation and those described in the previous section; however, its implementation can be different. For example, if phrase specifications are represented as abstract syntactic structures, then shared-structure lexicalisation is often implemented by putting an appropriate conjunction inside the proto-phrase specification, instead of at the top level. Figure 5.24 shows the result of applying shared-structure conjunction to the proto-phrase specifications shown in Figures 5.14 and 5.21;

---

[2] If the two sentences are referring to different televisions, then the use of a *one*-anaphoric expression may be appropriate, as in *John bought a television, and Sam bought one too.*

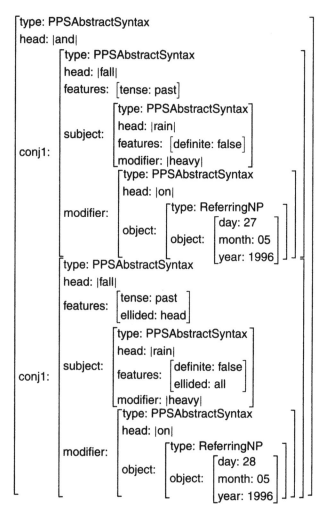

Figure 5.23   The result of a shared-participant conjunction (*Heavy rain fell on the 27th and 28th*).

Example (5.18) shows how this proto-phrase specification might be realised as a surface form.

(5.18)   Heavy rain fell on the 27th and 28th.

One question that arises is whether microplanning is the best way to deal with all apparent cases of aggregation. An alternative to having the microplanner produce the proto-phrase specification shown in Figure 5.24 from the proto-phrase

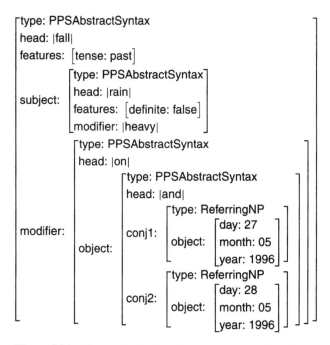

Figure 5.24 The result of a shared-structure conjunction (*Heavy rain fell on the 27th and 28th*).

specifications shown in Figures 5.14 and 5.21 would be to have the content determination process build a single message which specifies that there was heavy rain on both of these days. In other words, the content determination process could build a single **RainSpellMessage** asserting that heavy rain occurred on the 27th and the 28th, instead of two separate **RainEventMessage**s asserting that there were heavy rain events on both the 27th and the 28th. The lexicalisation system could then choose the best expression of this spell, using the techniques described in Section 5.2.

Syntactic Embedding

From a linguistic perspective, the most complex form of aggregation is embedding, whereby an informational element that might have been realised as a separate major clause is instead realised by means of a constituent subordinated to some other realised element. This is sometimes called HYPOTACTIC AGGREGATION.

A common type of hypotactic aggregation is the incorporation of an informational element via a nonrestrictive relative clause, as in the following example:

(5.19) a. September only had 30 mm of rain. It is usually our wettest month.
        b. September, which is usually our wettest month, only had 30 mm of rain.

However, many other grammatical constructions can be used to incorporate information. The following example demonstrates a sophisticated instance of embedding carried out by the MAGIC system (McKeown et al., 1997), where the form in Example (5.20b) is produced as an alternative to the collection of sentences in Example (5.20a):

(5.20)   a. The patient's last name is Jones.
             The patient is female.
             The patient has hypertension.
             The patient has diabetes.
             The patient is 80 years old.
             The patient is undergoing CABG.
             Dr. Smith is the patient's doctor.
         b. Ms. Jones is an 80-year-old, hypertensive, diabetic, female patient of Dr. Smith undergoing CABG.

There are complex and little-understood semantic constraints on embedding. Clearly the predication realised via the embedded structure must be predicated of the same entity as that which is realised as the head of the embedding structure; however, this is only a necessary and not a sufficient condition. For example, an aggregation like that in the following example would be inappropriate:

(5.21)   a. John is lazy.
             John is a pianist.
         b. John is a lazy pianist.

It is difficult to make general statements about how syntactic embedding should be implemented; readers interested in implementing such aggregation are probably best advised to read how it is implemented in specific systems such as MAGIC. Appropriate syntactic embedding seems to require the use of representations that encode relevant semantic as well as syntactic properties; it may therefore be easier if phrase specifications are represented by means of representations which encode some semantic information, such as lexicalised case frames.

5.3.2   *Choosing between Possible Aggregations*

Given all the above aggregation mechanisms, the question arises of how an NLG system can decide which mechanism to use, and indeed if aggregation should be performed at all. In very general terms, two often competing pressures are conciseness and syntactic simplicity.

On the one hand, aggregation is a useful mechanism for making texts shorter, which can be quite important in many applications. For example, MAGIC produces spoken output in a real-time environment; a key requirement is that the texts should be brief, so that they can be spoken quickly (McKeown et al., 1997). Accordingly, MAGIC uses sophisticated aggregation techniques to minimise the size of texts.

On the other hand, aggregation tends to make sentences more syntactically complex, which may not be desirable in some cases. For example, a key design requirement in STOP (see Section 1.3.6) was that its letters be easily readable by a wide variety of recipients, including people with limited education and reading ability. This suggests using short and simple sentences. Accordingly, STOP does not perform any aggregation in the microplanner, although some simple aggregation is carried out in the content determination process.

The types of aggregation which are appropriate can also depend in more subtle ways on the goals of the NLG system. For example, if we look at the ordering issue (discussed in Section 5.3.3), Dixon (1982) suggests that condition–action texts may be more quickly comprehended if the action is specified first, as in *Press the button if the blue light comes on*. However, many technical authors argue that it is best to put the condition first, as in *If the blue light comes on, press the button*, on the grounds that this is less likely to be misinterpreted – if the action is specified first, a reader may execute the action immediately upon reading it, before noticing that there is an attached condition. The best ordering of condition–action texts may thus partially depend upon whether it is more important to minimise reading time or the error rate.

If aggregation is in principle desirable, semantic considerations can play an important role in determining whether particular aggregations can be performed. In particular, aggregation seems to be more acceptable when the messages being aggregated are semantically related. For example, it seems odd to aggregate *I went to the store* and *I play chess* into *I went to the store and play chess*, because these messages are quite distinct in an important respect: The first describes a particular event, whereas the second describes a habitual activity. There is a considerable body of work in linguistics and formal semantics that may be able to provide the relevant semantic distinctions and categorisations required here, but this source of information remains relatively unused in work on aggregation within NLG.

Given all these uncertainties, one approach to determining aggregation choice rules is to use corpus analysis to identify the kinds of aggregations that result in the human-authored texts in the target genre; some of the aggregation rules used in MAGIC, for example, were based on a corpus analysis. However, sometimes the strategies used by human authors may not be optimal. Many of the texts in the MAGIC corpus could have been made shorter and simpler, and Shaw (1998a) suggests this may be because the authors in some cases produced what was easiest for them to write, not what was easiest for other people to read.

Other sources of sentence aggregation strategies are psychological research on reading comprehension and guidelines and style manuals for human readers. The problem with using psychological findings is that it is often difficult to extract detailed rules (as opposed to general observations) from this literature. Scott and de Souza (1990) have hypothesised a number of heuristics, expressed in terms of

When to aggregate. Aggregate messages linked by a rhetorical relation that is expressed by an explicit cue word.

When to aggregate. Do not express more than one rhetorical relation within a single sentence.

How to aggregate. Embedded clauses should only be used for Elaboration relations.

Figure 5.25   Some of Scott and de Souza's heuristics for aggregation.

relations from Rhetorical Structure Theory, which are at least partially motivated by psychological research; some of these are reproduced in Figure 5.25.[3]

Most of the advice given in general style books is, inevitably, vague. However, more specific guidelines for scoping, aggregation, and ordering choices are often given in books aimed at specific genres, as opposed to books concerned with writing in general. A good example of a set of genre-specific writing rules is that provided in the AECMA Simplified English rules for aircraft maintenance manuals (AECMA, 1986); Figure 5.26 presents some extracts from these rules.

5.3.3   Order of Presentation

Many existing natural language generation systems determine the ordering of the constituent elements of the text during the document planning stage. However, sometimes it is best to keep constituency and ordering decisions separate. The rationale for this is that considerations which have an impact on ordering decisions may not be known during the document planning stage, and so a full specification of the ordering of the elements of the text is best left until later in the generation process. The effects of some of the aggregation processes described above are a justification of the appropriateness of this strategy. For example, if an aggregation operation embeds an informational element as a relative clause attached to the subject noun phrase in some other phrase specification, then any previously specified ordering constraint over these two elements would be invalidated.

- Procedural sentences should be 20 words or less.
- Most declarative sentences should be 20 words or less, but one in ten can be up to 25 words long.
- Vary sentence length.
- Paragraphs should not be longer than six sentences. Only one paragraph in ten can consist of a single sentence.
- Two instructions can be aggregated into a single sentence only when they are performed simultaneously.

Figure 5.26   Some example rules from the AECMA Simplified English guide.

---

[3] We have reworded these slightly to be consistent with the terminology used in this book.

The elements in a text specification, however, are fully ordered; and so the microplanner has to add further ordering constraints to those already present. The ordering information present in the developing text specification will be of two kinds. There will be some ordering constraints that were specified during the document planning, and some ordering of elements will follow as a consequence of the aggregation processes described above. However, this may still leave the contents of the document plan largely unordered.

Ordering is also an issue with regard to the structures built by aggregation operations. For example, faced with the following two alternatives, clearly one has to be chosen over the other when realising the information.

(5.22) a. The refinement requested an additional 24-fiber cable in the second quarter of 1994, and an additional multiplexor in the first quarter of 1995.

b. The refinement requested an additional multiplexor in the first quarter of 1995, and an additional 24-fiber cable in the second quarter of 1994.

The first example presents the described actions in temporal order, which is often a sensible thing to do. However, if requesting an additional multiplexor is a more significant act than requesting an additional cable, it may be better to present the more significant act first, as is the case in the second example.

To date, most NLG systems have used one of two approaches to ordering. The first approach, used by MODELEXPLAINER (see Section 1.3.4), has the document planner specify a message order, which the microplanner respects. In effect, this means that ordering is treated as an aspect of document structuring, and is not part of microplanning. The second approach, used by PLANDOC and MAGIC, allows groups of messages within the document plan to be specified as reorderable; the microplanner then reorders these with the goal of maximising sentence aggregation possibilities and hence minimising the total length of the text. Neither of these approaches are very sophisticated; the current research literature offers little in the way of ideas for how this problem is best dealt with.

5.3.4   *Paragraph Formation*

In addition to combining proto-phrase specifications into more complex specifications that will eventually be realised as sentences, the aggregation process may also attempt to distribute the information to be presented across two or more paragraphs. In principle, it could also attempt to create higher-level document structures (such as sections) as well, but we are not aware of any system which does this.

The considerations on which this kind of decision should be based are poorly understood. The most obvious solution is to determine paragraph segmentation on the basis of subject matter and size. A general writing rule is that each paragraph in a text should be about a single topic; in an NLG context this might be translated into a requirement that paragraphs should communicate all messages beneath a particular node in the document plan. Within the framework presented here, size can be determined either in terms of number of messages or number of sentences. However, if size is determined in terms of numbers of constituent sentences, then clearly paragraph determination cannot take place until the sentence formation process has been completed. The ideal size of a paragraph is highly dependent on the genre, although interestingly the number six often seems to recur in this context. For example, on average, human-produced marine weather forecasts mention six events per paragraph (Goldberg et al., 1994), and the AECMA guide (AECMA, 1986) recommends that each paragraph contain no more than six sentences.

5.4   Generating Referring Expressions

5.4.1   *The Nature of the Problem*

Given an input document plan made up of messages to be conveyed, our pipelined microplanner has now lexicalised the messages and aggregated them to produce what is almost the final text specification. There is one more task to be carried out. The symbolic names of knowledge base entities within these messages need to be replaced by the semantic content of noun phrase referring expressions that will be sufficient to identify the intended referents to the hearer.

The process of referring expression generation has to consider questions like the following:

- Can and should a pronoun, such as *he*, *she*, or *it*, be used to refer to an entity?
- Should a proper name, such as *The Caledonian Express* or *Glasgow*, be used?
- Should a full or reduced noun phrase, such as *the Aberdeen train*, *the train on platform 12*, *the express about to depart from platform 12*, or simply *the train*, be used?

In each case, we need to decide upon the appropriate semantic content of the noun phrase used to pick out the intended referent. This means selecting those properties of the entity that will enable the hearer to identify the entity we are talking about.

There are some respects in which referring expression generation is related to lexicalisation. Both are concerned with mapping from abstract elements of an underlying representation language to linguistic material. However, central to our analysis of domain models is a fundamental distinction between concepts, relations, and entities. Lexicalisation is concerned with the linguistic expression of concepts and relations, whereas referring expression generation is concerned

with the identification of entities; the algorithms required are rather different in
nature.

5.4.2   *Forms of Referring Expressions and Their Uses*

Domain entities are, generally, referred to by means of noun phrases. In order to
see what is involved in producing referring expressions, therefore, we must first
briefly survey the world of noun phrases.

Definiteness and Indefiniteness

An important distinction can be drawn between DEFINITE and INDEFINITE noun
phrases. This is a distinction in form, not function; we will return to the functions
of these forms below. Definite noun phrases are prototypically marked by the use
of definite determiners, as in the following examples[4]:

(5.23)   a. *The train* is about to leave.
         b. *This train* will leave before ours.
         c. *That train* will leave before ours.
         d. *These trains* will leave before ours.

However, proper names and pronouns are also important subcategories of definite
noun phrases:

(5.24)   a. *The Caledonian Express* is about to leave for *Glasgow*.
         b. *It* is about to leave.
         c. *They* are about to leave.

Indefinite noun phrases, on the other hand, are signalled by the use of indefinite
determiners:

(5.25)   a. *A train* is about to leave.
         b. *Some trains* will leave before ours.

Generally speaking, indefinite noun phrases are used to introduce into the discourse an entity that has not previously been mentioned – a function we will refer
to as INITIAL REFERENCE – whereas definite noun phrases are used for SUBSEQUENT
REFERENCE, referring to entities that have already been introduced into the discourse. However, there are exceptions to this general rule; in particular, definite
referring expressions can be used for initial reference in a number of circumstances.
For example, definite reference can be used to refer to entities whose existence
can be assumed known or inferable by the hearer, as in the following examples in

---

[4] In each case the noun phrase is in italics, and the determiner is underlined.

contexts where the entities referred to by the italicised noun phrases have not been mentioned in the preceding discourse:

(5.26)   a. Can you tell me where *the railway station* is?
          b. *The station where I boarded this train* was deserted.

It is important to note that not all noun phrases, whether definite or indefinite, are referring expressions in the straightforward sense of picking out some intended referent. However, we will restrict our discussion here to simple initial and subsequent reference to specific entities by means of pronouns, proper names, and full noun phrases, and we will have nothing to say about more complex forms of reference such as nonspecific reference and generic reference (see, for example, Lyons, 1997). We will also leave aside discussion of more complex forms of reference such as deictic terms and the use of *one*-anaphoric expressions.

5.4.3   *Requirements for Referring Expression Generation*

Given a requirement to refer to some entity, the goal is to do this in such a way that the hearer knows what entity is being talked about. Below, we first sketch some relevant background from a computational point of view.

Initial and Subsequent Reference

We have already alluded to the distinction between initial reference and subsequent reference. The function of initial reference is to introduce some entity into the discourse. The generation of referring expressions for initial reference is relatively unexplored in the NLG literature. Generally speaking, entities are introduced into a discourse using properties which are likely to prove useful subsequently in the discourse, effectively setting the stage for what is to follow. However, it seems very likely that the processes involved here are very domain and task dependent, and so from a computational point of view the best strategy is to examine texts in the domain to see what forms of initial reference are generally considered useful. So, for example, in a domain where the entities have proper names, we might choose to always use a full proper name for initial reference, perhaps along with an appositive noun phrase to indicate properties that are deemed relevant in the domain of application:

(5.27)   *Tony Blair, the British Prime Minister,* met ...

Along similar lines, in certain contexts it may be generally appropriate to introduce physical objects by mentioning their location:

(5.28)   You should use *the bicycle in the back of the room.*

Subsequent reference, on the other hand, is generally used to refer to entities which have already been introduced in the discourse. These references are

ANAPHORIC in that their interpretations are dependent upon preceding material in the discourse; for the hearer, interpreting an anaphoric referring expression involves identifying what it refers to, typically by working out what the ANTECEDENT of the anaphor is. The antecedent is some earlier referring expression which CO-REFERS with the anaphoric form.

For an NLG system, there are two issues here. On the one hand, we want to avoid ambiguity, so we must say enough to enable the hearer to distinguish the intended referent from other entities with which it might be confused. If there are two trains about to leave the station and we suggest to hearers that they should aim to board *the train that is about to leave*, this is not very helpful. Of course, on the assumption that every entity is unique by virtue of the complete set of properties that are true of that entity, we could ensure that a description is unambiguous by verbalising every property known to be true of the entity in question. However, this would produce unwieldy descriptions in any context where a realistic amount of information is maintained about any given object. Often, specific items of stored information will be quite irrelevant from the point of view of building a referring expression in a particular context.

This points to the other concern of any process that generates referring expressions. It should avoid redundancy and the inclusion of unnecessary information in descriptions. The minimal descriptive form that most languages offer as a resource for this is the pronoun. Thus we can refer to an entity by means of an expression that provides virtually no content at all, using (in English) the forms *he, she, it*, and so on. However, in many discourse contexts the use of pronouns is ambiguous; consider the following example:

(5.29)   You can take a seat in the first coach or the second coach. It is nonsmoking.

Here, it is unclear which coach is being referred to by means of the pronoun *it* in the second sentence.

So, we need to address two concerns that pull in opposite directions: We want to say as little as possible in order to avoid boring the reader, but we need to say as much as is necessary to enable identification of the intended referent.

The Role of the Discourse Model

If a system is to determine how an entity should be described so that it can be distinguished from other entities with which it might be confused, then the system needs to have some representation of the context. There are two aspects of context that are sources of POTENTIAL DISTRACTORS: the immediate physical context and the preceding discourse.

Most work in NLG has explored the generation of referring expressions with respect to some discourse context rather than with respect to a physical context. There are obvious reasons for this. It is far easier for a computational system to have access to model of the former than of the latter. The relevant aspects of the discourse context are typically maintained in what we call a DISCOURSE MODEL. This stores some representation of the entities that have been mentioned in the discourse so far, perhaps with additional information about when and how they were mentioned. By using this information, the NLG system can determine whether a potential referring expression is likely to be ambiguous.

The simplest possible discourse model is simply a history list of all the entities mentioned in the text so far. Then, for example, if two distinct trains have been mentioned in the preceding discourse, and the system needs to make a subsequent reference to one of them, the discourse model makes clear that the particular train we refer to may need to be distinguished from the other train that has been mentioned.

In effect, the discourse model is an attempt to model the hearer's ATTENTIONAL STATE: a representation of all the entities the hearer is currently attending to, and thus which might be potential distractors for any entity that needs to be identified. A common observation is that the amount of time that has elapsed since an entity was last mentioned makes a difference here. Over time, we forget about things, and other things being equal, entities mentioned more recently are more SALIENT than those mentioned some time ago. More specifically, within the psychological literature, a distinction is often made between SHORT-TERM MEMORY and LONG-TERM MEMORY. It appears to be the case that we are likely to remember the syntactic detail of the immediately preceding utterance, whereas there is a tendency to remember only the content, and not the form of expression, of earlier material in the discourse. An allied observation is that pronouns tend to refer to recently mentioned entities, typically within the current or previous clause.

Discourse models attempt to capture these differences by imposing some structure over the represented information. At the very least, we can draw a distinction between that part of the discourse model that represents the immediately preceding utterance and that which corresponds to the earlier discourse, thus drawing a distinction between two levels of accessibility of previously mentioned discourse entities. Some work goes further than this: Grosz and Sidner (1986) suggest that discourses are hierarchically structured, and that as subdiscourses within this structure are completed, their contents are flushed from the discourse model, or at least made less accessible.[5] This claim is used to support a number of hypotheses about the accessibility of previously mentioned entities within a discourse.

Our document plans and text specifications similarly take the view that discourses have a hierarchical structure; however, the true relationship between this model of discourse structure and that presumed by Grosz and Sidner's model is not clear. In what follows, we will assume a simpler form of discourse model that does not mirror the structure of the discourse being generated; the real impact of

---

[5] The same intuitions are present in the work of a number of authors: see, for example, Fauconnier, 1995; Reichman, 1985; Polanyi, 1988.

discourse structure on discourse models in text generation remains a research issue to be explored.

5.4.4   Generating Pronouns

We turn first, then, to the generation of pronouns. From the point of view of natural language generation, we are concerned with what is sometimes called the PRONOMINALISATION DECISION.

It has been observed that pronouns are generally used to refer to entities which have recently been mentioned in the discourse or are in some other way particularly salient. In English, and in many other languages, pronouns are distinguished by gender (*he* versus *she*), person (*I* versus *you*), and number (*it* versus *they*). Which particular pronoun should be used depends, therefore, on whether the antecedent has the appropriate properties. The syntactic context also has an impact, since pronouns vary according to their grammatical case (*he* versus *him*).

Pronominalisation is also subject to broader syntactic constraints; consider the following examples:

(5.30)   a. The apple had a worm in the apple.
        b. The apple had a worm in it.
        c. It had a worm in the apple.
        d. It had a worm in it.

Examples (5.30b) and (5.30d) are syntactically acceptable, but (5.30a) and (5.30c) are not. Sometimes syntactic constraints can force the use of REFLEXIVE pronouns; for example, we need to say *John saw himself in the mirror*, rather than *John saw him in the mirror*.[6]

This grammatical knowledge is clearly important for a natural language generation system; but the more fundamental question is that of *when* a pronoun can safely be used to refer to an entity without fear of ambiguity in interpretation. We have already noted that pronouns are typically used to refer to entities mentioned in the same sentence or in the immediately preceding sentence. Although instances of LONG-DISTANCE PRONOMINALISATION do occur, it is somewhat unusual, for example, to use a pronoun to refer to an entity last mentioned several sentences ago, even in situations where no other possible antecedents have been mentioned in the interim.

This apparent restriction on the accessibility of previously mentioned entities by means of pronouns has some advantages. It suggests we can develop pronominalisation strategies that do not need to take account of past discourse beyond

---

[6] In a context, of course, where the person John saw was John himself rather than someone else.

that represented in what we might think of as short-term memory. At a first pass, we might then suggest that an appropriate pronominal reference strategy can be captured by the following simple rule:

(5.31)   **if** the intended referent was last mentioned in the previous sentence
          then use a pronoun

Our simple rule above seems to work in a number of cases, such as in the following simple discourse:

(5.32)   a. The train is leaving at 5 P.M.
          b. It arrives in Edinburgh at 7 P.M.

It will also handle some cases where multiple pronouns are involved:

(5.33)   a. John said the train is leaving at 5 P.M.
          b. He thinks it arrives in Edinburgh at 7 P.M.

However, the simple algorithm can very easily generate an inappropriate pronominal reference, as in the example from earlier:

(5.34)   a. You can take a seat in the first coach or the second coach.
          b. It is nonsmoking.

A more cautious algorithm, then, would only use a pronoun if no other entities within the set of potential distractors share the same grammatical properties. However, it turns out that this is, in reality, too restrictive; people additionally use domain and world knowledge when interpreting pronouns, so that instances of pronominalisation which might be thought, on a naïve model, to be ambiguous, are generally not so:[7]

(5.35)   a. Sue$_1$ invited Mary$_2$ over for dinner.
          b. She$_1$ cooked her$_2$ a most amazing meal.
(5.36)   a. The councillors$_1$ refused the women$_2$ a permit because they$_1$ feared revolution.
          b. The councillors$_1$ refused the women$_2$ a permit because they$_2$ advocated revolution.

It is possible, given appropriate contexts, to force alternative interpretations in each case; but there is generally a default interpretation that most readers will agree upon.

The important role of world knowledge in the interpretation of anaphoric references and the difficulties inherent in modelling world knowledge mean that we

---

[7] In each example here we have used subscripts to relate the co-referring noun phrases under the most plausible interpretations of the sentences.

do not currently know how to build an algorithm which produces pronominal references in all and only those cases where pronouns could be used and understood by people. This means that NLG pronominalisation algorithms will make mistakes, which can be characterised as follows:

- **Missed pronouns.** The algorithm decides not to use a pronoun when in fact a pronoun would be perfectly acceptable to the reader.
- **Inappropriate pronouns.** The algorithm decides to use a pronoun inappropriately, in cases where the referent is not clear to the reader.

In many cases there is a trade-off between these two types of mistakes; in other words, we can reduce the number of inappropriate pronouns at the cost of more missed pronouns. This strategy is followed by CONSERVATIVE algorithms which are designed to generate very few inappropriate pronouns at the risk of generating more explicit forms of reference in situations where pronominal reference would be adequate. Conservative algorithms are especially appropriate in many technical and business applications, where the impact of an ambiguous pronoun decision may be large, while the impact of an unnecessarily redundant referring expression may be small (typically, the text will be slightly longer and less fluent than it might have been). A representative conservative algorithm is shown in Figure 5.27. Note that this algorithm, like many conservative algorithms, does not rely on the user using world knowledge to disambiguate pronouns and also uses a very simple model of salience.

A final issue worth mentioning is that it is likely that the sublanguage and genre of the texts to be generated play a role in determining the most appropriate pronominalisation strategies. For example, pronouns seem to be used more often in face-to-face dialogues than in formal technical documentation, where definite noun phrases are preferred; and, as a particular case, cooking recipes often use ZERO ANAPHORA, as in *Bake ϕ for 20 minutes.*

Let:

- C be the set of entities mentioned in the previous utterance;
- r be the internal symbol corresponding to the intended referent; and
- $\langle p_r, g_r, n_r \rangle$ be a triple representing the grammatical properties of person, number, and gender of r.

Then, pronouns can be generated in accordance with the following rule:

- **if** $r \in C \wedge$
  $\neg(\exists x \in C$ such that $x \neq r \wedge \langle p_x, g_x, n_x \rangle = \langle p_r, g_r, n_r \rangle)$
  then use a pronoun
  else use a nonpronominal form of reference

Figure 5.27   A conservative pronoun-generation algorithm.

5.4.5   Generating Subsequent References

Suppose the entity we need to refer to has been mentioned before in the discourse but that our algorithm for pronominalisation has determined that we are unable to use a pronoun to refer to it. Given the simple algorithms we have proposed so far, this is likely to be the case when the intended referent was last mentioned prior to the preceding utterance in the discourse, or if the preceding utterance itself offers potential distractors that make the use of a pronoun an unsafe thing to do.

In either case, we are faced with the question of how the intended referent can be distinguished from all other possible referents. There are three considerations that need to be met:

- The referring expression generated must be ADEQUATE, in that it provides enough information to pick out the intended referent.
- The referring expression must be EFFICIENT, in that it does not provide more information than is necessary in order to identify the intended referent.
- The referring expression should be SENSITIVE to the needs and abilities of the hearer, not making use of properties of the entity that the hearer may not be able to determine.

We begin by characterising the task as being that of constructing a DISTINGUISHING DESCRIPTION of the intended referent. A distinguishing description is one which is an accurate description of the entity being referred to but not of any object in the CONTRAST SET, which is the set of other entities that the hearer is currently assumed to be attending to or which are 'in focus'. The constituency of the contrast set will be determined by discourse model. In the simplest case, it may be every other entity mentioned in the discourse.

Under this model, each property expressed in a referring expression can be regarded as having the function of 'ruling out' members of the contrast set. Suppose a speaker wants to identify a small black dog in a situation where the contrast set consists of a large white dog and a small black cat. She might choose the adjective *black* in order to rule out the white dog and the head noun *dog* in order to rule out the cat. This would result in the generation of the referring expression *the black dog*, which matches the intended referent but no other object in the current context. *The small dog* would also be a successful referring expression in this context. Figure 5.28 presents a more formal characterisation of the requirement to be met by distinguishing descriptions.

There are a variety of algorithms that can be used to identify such collections of properties. Dale (1992a) presents an algorithm whose principal focus is the construction of a minimal distinguishing description (i.e., a description that contains no redundancy). This algorithm begins by examining the set of properties known to be true of the intended referent and determining which of these properties rules out more of the contrast set entities than any other property. This property then

Let r be the intended referent, and C be the contrast set; then, a set L of properties will represent a distinguishing description if the following two conditions hold:

> C1: Every property in L applies to r: that is, every element of L specifies a property that r possesses.
>
> C2: For every member c of C, there is at least one element l of L that does not apply to c: i.e., there is an l in L that specifies a property that c does not possess. l is said to rule out c.

Suppose the task is to create a referring expression for Object1 in a context that also includes Object2 and Object3, where these objects possess the following properties:

- Object1: ⟨type, dog⟩, ⟨size, small⟩, ⟨colour, black⟩
- Object2: ⟨type, dog⟩, ⟨size, large⟩, ⟨colour, white⟩
- Object3: ⟨type, cat⟩, ⟨size, small⟩, ⟨colour, black⟩

In this situation, r = Object1 and C = {Object2, Object3}. The content of one possible distinguishing description is then {⟨type, dog⟩, ⟨colour, black⟩}, which might be realised as *the black dog*. Object1 possesses these properties, but Object2 and Object3 do not.

Figure 5.28   Distinguishing descriptions.

becomes part of the distinguishing description, and the contrast set is reduced by the removal of those entities ruled out. This process repeats with the other properties of the intended referent, until the contrast set is empty and the distinguishing description is complete. By zeroing in on the most distinguishing properties first, the algorithm aims to produce the shortest possible distinguishing description, thus minimising redundancy.

There is a technical problem with the approach just outlined. From a computational perspective, the problem of producing a minimal distinguishing description turns out to be NP-hard (see Reiter, 1990, for discussion). This means that it is of a computational complexity such that we cannot guarantee to find a solution; indeed, the algorithm presented above turns out to produce nonminimal descriptions under certain circumstances. The bottom line is that attempts to produce such minimal descriptions are probably computationally impractical.

From a cognitive perspective, however, it turns out that this may not be an issue. The minimisation of redundancy that the approach above aims to achieve does not, on the available evidence, correspond to the kinds of referring expressions humans construct. Experiments with children have demonstrated that they often construct referring expressions that are not minimal in the sense intended above; instead, they contain informationally redundant elements (see, for example, Sonnenschein, 1985). Intuition and casual introspection suggest that adults also do this, although perhaps to a lesser extent. We might, then, look for an alternative solution to the problem of referring expression generation which is at once both computationally tractable and at the same time more in line with what people appear to do.

We might observe that, in many situations where the intended referent is a visually salient physical object, properties such as colour, size, and location tend to be very useful in identifying entities. In other contexts, for example where the intended referent is not visible or is an abstract object, other properties may conventionally be of use. Generalising a little, we can suggest that, given a domain, we can identify a conventionally useful set of properties to be used in building referring expressions. How such conventions might arise is open to debate, but clearly factors such as likelihood of success on the basis of past usage will play a role. So, for example, perhaps because we have learned through experimentation or some other means, it turns out that using location and colour are often useful ways of identifying physical entities.

On the basis of this observation, we can define an algorithm which simply sequentially iterates through a (task-dependent) list of attributes, adding an attribute to the description being constructed if it rules out any distractors that have not already been ruled out, and terminating when a distinguishing description has been constructed. Figure 5.29 presents such an algorithm; a more sophisticated version of this algorithm that incorporates some reasoning about the hearer's beliefs is presented in Dale and Reiter (1995).

Let L be the set of properties to be realised in our description; let P be an ordered list of task-dependent properties which are generally useful for distinguishing objects, in order of decreasing expected utility; and let C be the set of distractors (the contrast set). The initial conditions are thus as follows:

- $C = \{\langle all\ distractors \rangle\}$;
- $P = \{\langle the\ list\ of\ useful\ properties \rangle\}$;
- $L = \{\}$

In order to describe the intended referent r with respect to the contrast set C, we do the following:

$\boxed{\text{MakeReferringExpression}(r, C, P)}$

$L \leftarrow \{\}$
for each member p_i of list P **do**
   if RulesOut(p_i) $\neq$ nil
   then $L \leftarrow L \cup \{p_i\}$
      $C \leftarrow C - \text{RulesOut}(p_i)$
   endif
   if $C = \{\}$ **then return** L
  endfor
return failure

$\boxed{\text{RulesOut}(p)}$

return $\{x : x \in C \land \neg\text{has-property}(x, p)\}$

Figure 5.29 An algorithm for producing distinguishing descriptions.

1. Initialise L to empty.
2. Initialise C to button2, button3, switch1.
3. Add *button* to L, and remove switch1 from C, since it is not a button.
4. Iterate through the attributes in P:
    (a) We add the modifier ⟨colour, red⟩. This eliminates button3 from C.
    (b) We add the modifier ⟨label, Power⟩. This eliminates button2 from C, which means that C is empty, and we are done.

Figure 5.30   Constructing a referring expression.

This kind of algorithm is used in IDAS (see Section 1.3.3). IDAS generates referring expressions which identify particular switches and buttons on a control panel, using expressions such as *the Reset button*, or *the red switch*. In this case, the context set consists of all buttons, switches, and other elements on the control panel that the user is looking at. Suppose that we need to refer to button1, which is a large red square button with the label 'Power'. Using the algorithm presented above, suppose further that P, the list of preferred attributes to be used for referring to buttons, is the sequence ⟨colour, label, size, shape⟩, and that the context set contains button1, button2 (a small red round button labelled 'Reset'), button3 (a large black square button labelled 'Load'), and switch1 (a large black switch labelled 'Lock'). In this case the algorithm would behave as shown in Figure 5.30; the result of this process is the definite description *the red Power button*.[8] Note that this is not the shortest possible definite referring expression, which would be *the Power button*; however, the inclusion of apparently redundant information may in fact make it easier for the hearer or reader to identify the intended referent.

Beyond Discrimination

So far we have discussed the construction of referring expressions as if the key problem is providing a description that distinguishes the intended referent from other possible referents. There are two points to note here. First, there are often many referring expressions that can perform the required identification task; this leads to the question of how we might choose between such candidates. Second, focussing on the abstract informational aspect of referring expressions is not enough: it is also important that it be easy for the hearer to identify the intended referent. Appelt (1985) gives the illuminating example of a person A asking B on a bus at which stop she should leave the bus in order to reach some specific location. Person B answers as follows:

(5.37)   You should get off at *the stop before mine*.

---

[8] Notice here that, additionally, the head noun *button* is added before the list of properties in P is considered; this reflects the observation that head nouns are generally used in English referring expressions even when other properties used might render the head noun informationally redundant.

Although the referring expression used here by B may indeed be a distinguishing description of the intended referent, it is not a particularly helpful one unless some additional help is provided – by the time B leaves the bus, A will have missed her stop.

The problem here was hinted at in our reference to the need for SENSITIVITY in generating referring expressions. It is not enough that the referring expression generated should in some abstract sense be a distinguishing description; it should also be of a form that is useful to the intended audience.

Where there are multiple possible distinguishing descriptions, this requirement of referring expression generation can be used to choose between otherwise equally appropriate referring expressions. Of course, doing this means that the system needs to have the appropriate user modelling capabilities.

5.5   Limitations and Other Approaches

At the beginning of this chapter, we suggested that the tasks we have placed in the realm of the microplanner – lexicalisation, aggregation, and referring expression generation – may exhibit subtle interdependencies, as a result of which it may not be possible to place a particular ordering over the process as a whole. For example, we have suggested that lexicalisation should happen before aggregation; but the astute reader may have noticed that one box in the example lexicalisation decision tree presented in Figure 5.19 asked whether two messages had been aggregated or not. This question cannot of course be asked if we insist that lexicalisation is done before aggregation.

Strong evidence that there are indeed such interdependencies is harder to obtain than it might at first seem; the above problem, for example, perhaps could be solved by changing representations, or just 'relabelling' the task of choosing cue phrases to be part of aggregation instead of lexicalisation. Nonetheless, there is a great deal of uncertainty over how best to structure the processes involved in microplanning, and it can often seem that microplanning is the 'wastebasket' for unresolved issues in NLG. If we can't easily accommodate some task within a neat model of document planning or surface realisation, then it gets assigned to the no-man's land in the middle, in the same way that tricky aspects of meaning are often assigned to the 'pragmatic wastebasket' when elegant models of semantics seem to have nothing to offer.

In the model we have proposed here, we have side-stepped the issues involved by presenting an architecture where the three processes of lexicalisation, aggregation, and referring expression generation are carried out in the order listed. This ordering seems to us to capture the most obvious interdependencies. Certainly the scope for aggregation is determined on the basis of the identity of referents rather than the surface forms used to refer to them, and in any case it would be pointless to generate a form of reference twice only to collapse it to one occurrence via an aggregation operation. It is also the case that some types of aggregation, such as embedding, may affect which types of referring expressions can be used for a particular component. For example, we cannot attach a relative clause to a pronoun, so if a decision is made to use a pronominal reference before aggregation is considered then that opportunity for aggregation will be lost.

With regard to aggregation and lexicalisation, orderings other than the one we have chosen have been proposed in the literature. In MAGIC and PLANDOC (McKeown, 1994, 1997) for example, aggregation is performed before lexicalisation and referring expression generation. Differences in the representational assumptions made by different systems make it difficult to determine here whether one ordering of the processes is better than any other; there is a significant research task involved in working out the true dependencies between the component processes.

As we noted at the outset, an alternative to using a pipelined architecture is to use a more integrated approach where lexicalisation, aggregation, and referring expression generation take place in an interleaved fashion. Such an approach was used in STREAK (Robin and McKeown, 1996), for example, which integrated lexicalisation and aggregation (referring expression generation was very simple in STREAK's domain). As a result, STREAK could produce highly optimised sentences which made very efficient use of linguistic resources and aggregation possibilities; but on the other hand STREAK could take half an hour of computation time to produce a single sentence (Shaw, 1998a). The pipelined microplanning module in MAGIC, in contrast, does not optimise sentences as highly as STREAK, but it runs in real time.

5.6   Further Reading

In Chapter 3, we pointed out that microplanning has been recognised as a distinct task in NLG only relatively recently; in earlier NLG research, the process of text generation was seen as consisting of only two tasks, roughly corresponding to document planning and linguistic realisation. As we have emphasised in this chapter, microplanning is much less well understood than these other stages of natural language generation.

Historically, one of the first researchers to identify the need for what we now call microplanning was Meteer (1991), who introduced the notion of a 'generation gap' between the stages of document planning and linguistic realisation. Rambow and Korelsky (1992) describe an applied NLG system which includes a 'sentence planning' component; Reiter (1994) summarises approaches to sentence planning in several applied NLG systems.

The notion that one might need to carry out something like aggregation over a set of messages to be conveyed has a long history; the first discussion we are aware of in an NLG context is that of Mann and Moore (1981). However, a long silence on the topic ensued thereafter, with interest being reawakened by the work of Dalianis and Shaw, both of whom have written extensively on this topic (see Dalianis and Hovy, 1996; Shaw, 1998a,b). There is also a considerable amount of work in linguistics that bears on the question of when different types of aggregation can be carried out. Within the NLG literature, an excellent starting point is the work on aggregation choice rules by Scott and de Souza (1990).

Of the topics we have placed within the realm of microplanning, lexicalisation has the longest history. Debates on how to represent word meanings go back at least to Aristotle; Smith and Medin (1981) present a good summary of much of the philosophical and psychological work in this area, although this is now somewhat dated. Cruse (1986) summarises much of the work in the linguistics community on the representation of lexemes. Within NLG, Goldman (1975) was the first to look at lexicalisation issues. Discussions of factors which influence lexical choice can be found in Hovy (1990) and Reiter (1991). Vander Linden and Martin (1995) and Knott (1996) discuss the process of choosing cue phrases to express discourse relations. Elhadad, McKeown, and Robin (1997) is a good recent paper on what we have called fine-grained lexicalisation; Stede (1996) discusses how such lexicalisation can be used in a multilingual NLG system. See http://java.sun.com/docs for information on Java's MessageFormat class and other support for localisation.

Appelt (1985) was amongst the first to seriously explore the generation of referring expressions. Appelt and Kronfeld (1987) discuss how ideas about reference developed in the philosophical literature can be incorporated into a referring expression generator. Several papers on generating referring expressions have been published by the authors of this book, including Dale (1992a) and Dale and Reiter (1995). Horacek has also published a number of papers addressing algorithmic aspects of the generation of referring expressions (see, for example, Horacek, 1997).

Consistent with the lack of consensus in conceptions of microplanning, few papers have described the task as a whole (one exception is Wanner and Hovy, 1996).

6   Surface Realisation

In this chapter we look at the process of mapping an abstract text specification and its constituent phrase specifications into a surface text, made up of words, punctuation symbols, and mark-up annotations. This is known as SURFACE REALISATION. Much of this discussion is centred around three software packages (KPML, SURGE, and REALPRO) which can often be used to carry out part of the mapping process.

6.1   Introduction

In the previous chapter, we saw how a text specification can be constructed from a document plan via the process of microplanning. The text specification provides a complete specification of the document to be generated but does not in itself constitute that document. It is a more abstract representation whose nature is suited to the kinds of manipulation required at earlier stages of the generation process. This representation needs to be mapped into a SURFACE FORM, this being a sequence of words, punctuation symbols, and mark-up annotations which can be delivered to the document presentation system being used.

As described in Section 3.4, a text specification is a tree whose leaf nodes are phrase specifications and whose internal nodes show how phrases are grouped into document structures such as paragraphs and sections; internal nodes may also specify additional information about structures, such as section titles. Phrase specifications describe individual sentences; they may also describe sentence fragments in cases where these fragments are realised as orthographically separate elements (such as section titles or entries in an itemised list). There are many ways of representing phrase specifications; this will be discussed in Section 6.3.

To keep things relatively simple, we will assume that there are two distinct aspects to the processing of text specifications. One is concerned with the mapping of internal text-specification nodes into appropriate annotations for the document presentation system; this is the process of STRUCTURE REALISATION. The other is the process of mapping phrase specifications identical to surface-form sentences

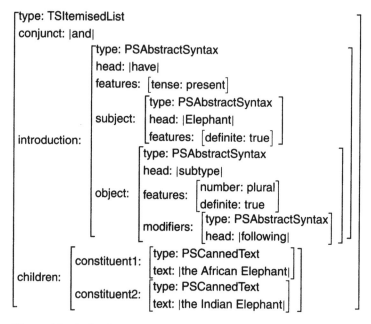

Figure 6.1   A simple PEBA text specification.

or sentence fragments; this is the process of LINGUISTIC REALISATION. Structure realisation is concerned with the process of mapping the internal structure of a text specification into the specific structural resources (such as paragraphs and sections) which the document presentation systems and its mark-up language provides. Linguistic realisation is concerned with the process of mapping a phrase specification into the specific words and syntactic constructs which the target language provides.

To make this discussion more concrete, consider the simple text specification shown in Figure 6.1; this is based on a simplified version of a PEBA text. The surface form corresponding to this text is shown in Figure 6.2; here the annotations are in HTML, which is the mark-up language used by PEBA's document presentation system (a Web browser such as Netscape). Figure 6.3 shows what the user might see after this text is processed by the document presentation system.

The text specification shown in Figure 6.1 contains a single internal node (TSItemisedList) and three leaf phrase specifications, one of which is represented

```
The Elephant has the following subtypes:
<ul>
<li> the African Elephant; and
<li> the Indian Elephant.
</ul>
```

Figure 6.2   A surface form with mark-up annotations for the PEBA text.

The Elephant has the following subtypes:

- the African Elephant; and
- the Indian Elephant.

Figure 6.3 The PEBA text as displayed by the presentation system.

by means of a **PSAbstractSyntax** structure, with the other two being represented by means of **PSCannedText** structures.

Linguistic realisation maps the phrase specifications into words and punctuation symbols. In this case only trivial processing is needed to process the **PSCanned-Text**, and produce the two surface forms *the African Elephant* and *the Indian Elephant*. However, processing the **PSAbstractSyntax** structure in the **introduction** is more complex, and requires the use of a GRAMMAR which tells the realiser that, for example, the **subject** should precede the verb and the **object** should follow the verb, and that the appropriate form of the verb *have* in this context is *has*. The end result of this processing is the surface form *The Elephant has the following subtypes*.

Structure realisation in this example creates a surface form for the **TSItemisedList** node by adding appropriate mark-up annotations and punctuation symbols to the surface forms produced by linguistic realisation from each phrase specification. The result in this case is shown in Figure 6.2. In this case the system has added the HTML mark-up symbols ⟨ul⟩ (start itemised list), ⟨li⟩ (new list element), and ⟨/ul⟩ (end itemised list). It has also inserted a ':' punctuation symbol after the introduction; a ';' punctuation symbol and the conjunct *and* after the first list element; and a '.' punctuation symbol after the second list element.

From a very general perspective, the purpose of realisation is to take care of some of the 'messy details' of ensuring that the output text is correct with regard to both the rules of the target natural language and the rules of the mark-up language. For example, the document planner and microplanner can simply create a **TSItemisedList** structure and rely on the realiser to implement this with appropriate mark-up annotations and punctuation symbols; and the document planner and microplanner can simply specify that the introductory phrase should use the verb *have* and let the realiser choose the appropriate version of this verb (in this case *has*) in this syntactic context.

To date, linguistic realisation has received much more attention in the NLG research literature than structure realisation; indeed, structure realisation is often not considered to be part of the process of natural language generation. We have more to say about the importance of this aspect of the generation task in Chapter 7; in the present chapter, we are concerned mostly with linguistic realisation.

A number of software systems have been built for performing the task of linguistic realisation. These systems vary in terms of both how they represent their inputs (that is, phrase specifications) and how they represent and use grammatical information; these variations are often driven by the particular linguistic theory used for the grammar model. Several of these linguistic realisation systems have been made available to outside users; in many cases no charge is made for research use, although commercial users may be expected to pay a license and support fee.

The existence of these systems means that, at least in principle, NLG system developers and researchers working in other areas of NLG do not need to have a deep understanding of what is involved in linguistic realisation. It is sufficient to know what the various packages do from a functional perspective (including the types of phrase specification representations they expect to see as inputs), and to have an understanding in general terms of how the packages work.

Accordingly, it is not the purpose of this chapter to explain how to build a linguistic realisation component. Rather, we discuss three existing realisation systems:

- KPML, a system based on Systemic Functional Grammar which accepts a number of different types of input, including LEXICALISED CASE FRAMES and also more abstract MEANING SPECIFICATIONS.
- SURGE, a unification-based linguistic realiser which takes Systemic Functional Grammar as its theoretical base and can accept either lexicalised case frames or ABSTRACT SYNTACTIC STRUCTURES as input.
- REALPRO, a linguistic realiser based on Meaning-Text Theory, whose input is in the form of abstract syntactic structures.

In each case we describe the overall functionality of the system, we look at the nature of the inputs required, and we describe how the system works.

6.2   Realising Text Specifications

The idea behind our notion of a text specification is that the document planning and microplanning stages of the language generation process should be concerned with *what* the elements of a text are but not with *how* they will appear on the page. The approach embodies what is sometimes referred to as a distinction between LOGICAL STRUCTURE and PHYSICAL STRUCTURE. In order to realise a text specification, we need, therefore, to map from logical constructs into physical constructs. For example, if a fragment of text has the logical status of being a paragraph, this may be typographically signalled by indenting its first line by half a centimeter; or if a fragment of text has the logical status of being an item within an itemised list, this may be typographically signalled by preceding it with a bullet symbol. Often there are several presentational mechanisms which can be used for a given logical structure, with the choice perhaps being dictated by a governing style or convention. For example, some Web browsers typographically signal a paragraph by preceding it with a blank line, instead of by indenting its first line.

This distinction between logical structure and physical structure is now so well-established in the field of document processing that we do not, as authors, usually need to concern ourselves with low-level formatting issues. The earliest document processing systems removed the need for human authors to be concerned about line-end and page break decisions; within the last twenty years, most document processing systems have moved towards the use of mark-up conventions that further relieve the burden on the author, so that he or she needs simply to indicate, via some special symbols, what the nature of a textual construct is. The document processor then renders this in an appropriate manner on the printed page. So, for example, in LaTeX (Lamport, 1994), we can directly specify structures such as sections and paragraphs, and the formatting system will determine the appropriate typographic properties. The LaTeX construct in Example (6.1), for instance, produced the heading at the beginning of the section you are reading now.

(6.1)   \section{Realising Text Specifications}

The same ideas are now common in word processors through the use of style sheets, although the WYSIWYG nature of most word processors continues to encourage direct manipulation of aspects of physical structure.

Given the availability of document processing systems whose purpose is to provide mappings from logical structures to presentational devices, it is sufficient for NLG systems to know how to map from the logical representations they use to the kinds of mark-up required by these document processing systems as input. In other words, we can use document preparation systems such as LaTeX and Microsoft Word, or Web browsers such as Internet Explorer and Netscape, as postprocessors that will produce the physical documents we need to generate. We will refer to such a system as a DOCUMENT PRESENTATION system.

For example, consider again the text specification shown in Figure 6.1. If the document presentation system is an HTML-based Web browser, the NLG system should convert this into the surface form shown in Figure 6.2. If the document presentation system is LaTeX, then the NLG system should produce the surface form shown in Figure 6.4. And if the document presentation system is Word, then the NLG system should produce the surface form shown in Figure 6.5.[1]

In some situations, it may not be possible to use a document presentation system because the NLG system needs to produce structures which are not supported by any commonly available presentation system. This can in particular happen in systems which mix text and graphics in complex ways, some of which are discussed

---

[1] Note that while LaTeX and HTML are designed to be created and read by humans, Word RTF format is intended to be an interchange format which is created and processed by computers. The meaning of the elements of the RTF version of the surface form are therefore less self-evident to the human reader. Essentially, par means start a new structure, while ls1 means use bullet list format number 1.

```
The Elephant has the following subtypes:
\begin{itemize}
\item the African Elephant; and
\item the Indian Elephant.
\end{itemize}
```

Figure 6.4   The logical structure specification in LaTeX form.

```
{The Elephant has the following subtypes:
\par }\ls1 {the African Elephant; and
\par }\ls1 {the Indian Elephant.
\par }
```

Figure 6.5   The logical structure specification in Word RTF form.

in Chapter 7. In such cases, the NLG system must itself take responsibility for mapping logical specifications into a physical document description language such as PostScript. It is a good idea to encapsulate this processing within the structural realiser or perhaps even within a separate postprocessing system, so that the bulk of the NLG system works with logical structure and is not concerned with the details of physical rendering.

So, we can view the problem of how to realise the logical structure of a text as a (usually reasonably straightforward) process of mapping from constructs in one logical specification language to another. The resulting formatting commands are, however, wrapped around fragments of text to be presented on the page; and these fragments of text are derived on the basis of the phrase specifications that populate the text specification. We turn, next, to the issues to be considered in realising phrase specifications. Within the literature, this is generally viewed as the domain of linguistic realisation.

6.3   Varieties of Phrase Specifications

In the literature, we find a wide range of approaches to characterising the input to linguistic realisation. Sometimes the differences between the representations used in different systems are simply nothing more than notational variations. In other cases, however, the content of the representations vary, signalling deeper differences between the views taken of what is involved in the process of linguistic realisation.

In Chapter 3, we introduced four specific representations for phrase specifications: lexicalised case frames, abstract syntactic structures, canned text, and orthographic strings. In fact these are just a few of the representations which have been discussed in the literature; in particular, much of the research literature has focussed on performing realisation from more abstract structures, such as skeletal propositions and meaning specifications as we will define them below.

Understanding the range of options here adds valuable perspective to the question of what linguistic realisation amounts to.

It is important to realise that there is no one right answer to the question of what the input to linguistic realisation should be. More abstract representations give the document planner and microplanner more flexibility but require more sophisticated realisation systems. Less abstract representations require the document planner and microplanner to do more work, but they also give these systems more control over what the system actually produces. Using more sophisticated representations may also require the developers working on the document planner and microplanner (as well as the realiser) to be familiar with specific linguistic theories; while with less abstract representations it may be sufficient for document planner and microplanner developers simply to have a general understanding of the mechanics of language. We will return to this issue in Section 6.7.

Note also that there is no need for an application to use just one representation; in many cases it makes sense to use a mixture of representations in a phrase specification, as discussed in Chapter 3.

6.3.1 Skeletal Propositions

The most abstract representation we will consider is what we will call a SKELETAL PROPOSITION. This is similar to the representation a logician might use to represent the content of a natural language sentence. As an example, consider the following sentence:

(6.2)   The courier delivered the green bicycle to Mary.

In predicate logic, we might represent this by means of the following proposition:

(6.3) $deliver(c1, p1, m)$

This representation says nothing about the content of the individual noun phrases in the sentence. It abstracts away from detail of this kind, to represent only the essence of the sentence. It indicates that a delivering event took place and identifies the three participants in this event as being entities with the indices $c1$, $p1$, and m, respectively. Note that the symbol *deliver* here is not intended to be a lexical item: the logician would use the same symbol regardless of the source natural language of the sentence that the proposition is intended to represent, and there may well be other lexical items in the same source language that map into this same symbol; again, the representation is intended to abstract away from these differences.

This form of representation is often convenient for logical inference and corresponds to what we might think of as a single fact in the domain. In fact it is close to the notion of a message as discussed in Chapter 3. Using skeletal propositions

$$\begin{bmatrix} \text{predicate: deliver} \\ \text{arguments:} \begin{bmatrix} \text{arg1: c1} \\ \text{arg2: p1} \\ \text{arg3: m} \end{bmatrix} \end{bmatrix}$$

Figure 6.6   A skeletal proposition as an AVM.

to represent phrase specifications thus means that many tasks normally performed by the microplanner, such as lexicalisation and referring-expression generation, are instead performed by the realiser.

To allow easy comparison of the various representations we will consider, we will reexpress the proposition in Example (6.3) using an attribute-value matrix (AVM) which explicitly labels each of the elements, as shown in Figure 6.6.

6.3.2   Meaning Specifications

It is clear that the representation provided in Figure 6.6 does not represent all the information expressed in the sentence in Example (6.2). For example, the representation does not tell us that the object delivered was a package, and it does not tell us that it was green. This, and the other information omitted from the skeletal propositional representation, could be added by conjoining some additional predicates to the representation in Example (6.3), as follows:

(6.4)   *deliver*$(c1, p1, m) \land isa(c1, courier) \land isa(p1, bicycle) \land has\text{-}colour(p1,$
       green$) \land has\text{-}name(m, Mary)$

This additional information might be provided by the document planner or the microplanner as part of the process of generating referring expressions. If it is provided, the realiser can assume that its job is simply to communicate the information in the phrase specification; it does not need to add any further information.

We will refer to this structure as a MEANING SPECIFICATION. Meaning specifications specify all the information that will be communicated in the text. However, they do not specify the actual words or grammatical structures which will be used to communicate this information; for example the realiser is free to express **bicycle** as either *bicycle* or *bike*. Consequently, if phrase specifications are represented as meaning specifications, then it is the realiser, rather than an earlier stage of the generation process, that performs lexicalisation.

We give a concrete example of a meaning specification in Figure 6.7. Note how this has been developed from the previous representation we discussed:

- We have replaced the **predicate** and **arguments** labels in the original structure with the more semantically-loaded terms **process** and

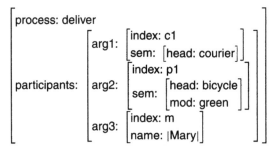

Figure 6.7 A meaning specification.

participants. There is no great significance here, although these alternative labels will be more appropriate later.

- In line with the above, we could also have changed the **arg**n labels to be similar to those used in case grammar, such as **agent**, **patient**, and so on. However, there is considerable variation in the literature with regard to the most appropriate set of case roles to use, and different case roles are appropriate for different verbs; so, for the moment we will retain the rather more neutral labels used here.

The above changes are arguably no more than notational. More significant are our extensions to the representation of the arguments:

- We have elaborated the representation of each argument so that it now specifies both an INDEX and a SEMANTICS. This corresponds to a distinction found in formal logic and the philosophy of language between EXTENSION and INTENSION, or between REFERENCE and SENSE (Frege, 1977; Carnap, 1947). The index is a symbol that uniquely identifies the entity in some real or imagined world; the semantics is a representation of information that can be used to describe that entity. Note that the semantics is not unique to the entity in question. In the case of our example, there may be many other objects in the world that can be referred to as *the green bicycle*. However, there is only one entity labelled $p1$. This name serves as a unique identifier.
- We have imposed some structure over the semantic information, identifying that semantic element that is the HEAD, in contrast to other elements which are viewed as MODIFIERS.
- We have introduced a special element called NAME. Names are somewhat special in this representation: they provide an alternative to semantic expressions as a way of getting to a referent.

Again, this representation is not lexicalised; in principle, each of the semantic elements here could be mapped into different lexical forms, with the possible exception of *Mary*. We can think of this representation as being something like a

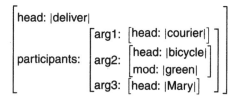

Figure 6.8   A lexicalised case frame.

STRUCTURED LOGICAL FORM, since it indicates how the information is grouped in a way that a simple list of predicates does not.

6.3.3   Lexicalised Case Frames

The structure just presented is still fairly abstract. Many realisers expect the document planner and microplanner to also select the base lexemes to be used in expressing the semantic content, this being the process of lexicalisation we discussed in Section 5.2. Once lexicalisation decisions have been made, the content of the **index** and **sem** features has exhausted its usefulness, and so we will omit them from our representations from here on. Figure 6.8 shows a LEXICALISED CASE FRAME. Note that the base lexemes are not yet words; to achieve this status they need to be subjected to morphological processing, so that, for example, the base lexeme *be* becomes the word *is* in those cases where the syntactic context requires that a third person singular, present tense form is used.

6.3.4   Abstract Syntactic Structures

Representations of the kind just discussed are quite common as inputs to linguistic realisation processes. They are sufficiently abstract that they allow the linguistic realiser to carry out what we might think of as SYNTACTIC INFERENCE. For example, given a structure like that in Figure 6.8 that has been augmented by the addition of some information about which argument of the process is to be placed in focus, the realiser can reason about the syntactic resources that should be used to achieve this effect. If the input structure requires that the second argument be the focus, then the realiser might produce the following sentence:

(6.5)   The green bicycle was delivered to Mary by the courier.

Sometimes, however, it is deemed appropriate for processing carried out prior to the invocation of the linguistic realiser to make such decisions about grammatical structure. In such cases, the role of the realiser is simply to encode knowledge about the grammatical minutiae of the language in question, applying these to an ABSTRACT SYNTACTIC STRUCTURE as input. Figure 6.9 shows an example of such a representation. The realiser converts this into a surface sentence by choosing the

$$
\left[
\begin{array}{l}
\text{head: } |\text{deliver}| \\
\text{subject: } \left[\text{head: } |\text{courier}| \right] \\
\text{object: } \left[
\begin{array}{l}
\text{head: } |\text{bicycle}| \\
\text{modifier: } \left[\text{head: } |\text{green}| \right]
\end{array}
\right] \\
\text{indirectobject: } \left[\text{head: } |\text{Mary}| \right]
\end{array}
\right]
$$

Figure 6.9   An abstract syntactic structure.

correct inflection of the content words, adding appropriate function words, and deciding the order in which the constituent parts of the sentence should appear. A realiser which operates on the basis of inputs like this thus conveniently hides some of the idiosyncrasies of syntax from the rest of the NLG system.

6.3.5   Canned Text

Sometimes the general form of sentences or other constructions in a text is sufficiently invariant that they can be predetermined and stored as text strings. This can be particularly useful for elements of a text for which there is no obvious compositional treatment. So, for example, the closing salutations in a business letter generator – forms like *yours sincerely* and *with best wishes* – might be stored as predetermined text strings for inclusion in the document plan. We will refer to such structures as CANNED TEXT. An example of a canned text representation is shown in Figure 6.10.

As defined here, canned text still needs to be processed orthographically:

- If the phrase in question is a complete sentence, typically the first letter of the sentence will be presented in upper case.
- In certain contexts, if the phrase in question is being used as a title, it may all be upper cased.
- Particular elements of the text may be rendered in bold or italic face to indicate emphasis, or for some other purpose.
- Sentence-final punctuation will depend on whether the sentence is a statement, a question, or an imperative, or whether it serves as the lead-in to an itemised list.

In the case of the canned text shown in Figure 6.10, the result of this processing would be to capitalise the first word of the text and add a period at the end of the sentence.

$$
\left[\text{text: } |\text{the courier delivered the green bicycle to Mary}| \right]
$$

Figure 6.10   A canned text structure.

$$\left[\text{body: } | \textit{The courier delivered the green bicycle to Mary.} | \right]$$

Figure 6.11   An orthographic string structure.

6.3.6   Orthographic Strings

Sometimes it makes sense to specify not just the words in a text but also orthographic information such as capitalisation and sentence-final punctuation. This can be done with an ORTHOGRAPHIC STRING; an example of this is shown in Figure 6.11. Orthographic strings do not need to be processed at all by the linguistic realiser.

6.3.7   Summary

We have surveyed a number of different levels of abstraction at which the inputs to surface realisation can be specified:

- SKELETAL PROPOSITIONS, in which the basic content of a sentence – who did what to whom – is determined, but the specific information required to identify the participants in the represented eventuality is not specified.
- MEANING SPECIFICATIONS, in which the semantic content of the referring expressions to be used in identifying the participants in the eventuality has been decided.
- LEXICALISED CASE FRAMES, in which the semantic content has been mapped into particular base lexemes in the target language.
- ABSTRACT SYNTACTIC STRUCTURES, in which the basic grammatical properties of the sentence to be generated have been specified.
- CANNED TEXT, in which the surface form of the words and phrases to be used has been determined.
- ORTHOGRAPHIC STRINGS, in which the final surface form of the text, including punctuation and capitalisation, is specified.

Given the number of different levels of abstraction we might use to specify the content of a generated text, it is not surprising that different NLG realisation components accept different kinds of input. In the remainder of this chapter, we look at three widely available surface realisation components: KPML, SURGE and REAL-PRO. We begin in Section 6.4 with KPML, since of the three systems this accepts the most abstract representation of phrase specifications as input; the input required by this system is close to what we have called here a MEANING SPECIFICATION. Then, in Section 6.5 we look at SURGE, whose input is close to what we have called here a lexicalised case frame. Finally, we look at REALPRO, whose input corresponds to what we have called here an abstract syntactic structure.

6.4 KPML

6.4.1 An Overview

Komet-Penman Multilingual – the KPML system – is a linguistic realisation component based on the grammatical theory known as Systemic Functional Grammar (Halliday, 1985a). The artifact that is popularly known as KPML in fact contains three elements:

- a computational engine that traverses grammatical resources;
- the collection of grammatical resources that comes with the system; and
- a development environment for writing and debugging new grammars.

We will use the term KPML to refer to all three elements combined.

KPML is a complex and powerful system. Its grammar of English, which is called NIGEL, is probably (as of mid-1998) the largest generation grammar of English ever built; it has been under development since the late 1970s. KPML also includes moderately-sized grammars of German and Dutch; and small illustrative grammars of Spanish, French, and Japanese. Grammars for other languages, including Russian, Czech, and Bulgarian, are under development. One of the long-term goals of the KPML project is to make multilingual generation easy by allowing a single input (in our terms, a phrase specification) to be realised in different languages simply by changing the active grammar being used by the system.

In addition to its grammars, KPML also includes lexicons (for instance, an English lexicon which defines 1,000 common English words), and a sophisticated and powerful development environment for writing and debugging new grammars. This environment includes graphical visualisation tools, static integrity checkers, and testing and verification systems. Again, as of mid-1998, the development environment distributed with KPML is much richer than the development tools distributed with the two other realisers we discuss in this chapter.

6.4.2 The Input to KPML

KPML can accept several types of input. The most common form of input, and the only one we will discuss here, consists of expressions in SPL, the Sentence Planning Language (Kasper, 1989).[2]

The form of SPL expressions is best demonstrated by example. Figure 6.12 shows the SPL required to produce the sentence *March had some rainy days*. Figure 6.13 reexpresses this construct as an explicitly-labelled attribute–value matrix, to make it easier to compare with the various forms of phrase specification we have introduced in this chapter. Figure 6.14 shows an SPL for the more

---

[2] KPML uses the term 'sentence plan' to refer to what we call a phrase specification.

```
(S1 / generalized-possession
  :tense past
  :domain (N1 / time-interval
              :lex march
              :determiner zero)
  :range  (N2 / time-interval
              :number plural
              :lex day
              :determiner some
              :property-ascription
              (A1 / quality :lex rainy)))
```

Figure 6.12   An input to KPML, from which KPML produces *March had some rainy days.*

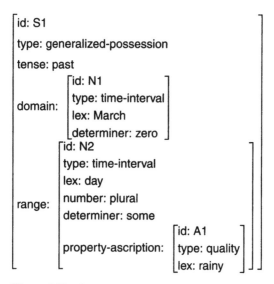

Figure 6.13   An AVM representation of the structure in Figure 6.12.

complex sentence *the month was cool and dry with the average number of rain days.*

Some of the details here warrant some elaboration.

- Every constituent starts off with an id and type. In SPL these are written as a pair of the form id / type, but we have shown them as distinct features in the AVM representation. The id simply associates a name with a constituent; this allows elements of constituents to refer to other constituents where necessary. The type specifies a class in KPML's UPPER MODEL, which we will return to below.
- The type generalised-possession in Figure 6.12 tells KPML that the sentence to be generated asserts that one entity possesses, in some general sense, another entity or set of entities. Note that the verb *have* is not

```
(1 / property-ascription
  :tense past
  :domain (m / one-or-two-d-time
              :lex month :determiner the)
  :range ((c / sense-and-measure-quality :lex cool)
          (d / sense-and-measure-quality :lex dry))
  :inclusive
    (ard / quality
         :lex number
         :determiner the
         :property-ascription
           (av / quality :lex average)
         :part-of (rd / one-or-two-d-time
                      :lex day
                      :number plural
                      :property-ascription
                        (r / quality :lex rain)))))
```

Figure 6.14   A more complex SPL expression (*The month was cool and dry with the average number of rain days*).

explicitly specified in the SPL; its use will be inferred from the presence of the **generalized-possession** type. Similar considerations apply to the type **property-ascription**.

- The attribute–value pair ⟨**tense: past**⟩ indicates that the clause should be in past tense.
- The **domain** attribute describes the entity that is doing the possessing. The type **time-interval** asserts, as might be expected, that this entity is a type of time interval; the attribute–value pair ⟨**lex: March**⟩ tells KPML to use the word *March* in describing this concept, and the attribute–value pair ⟨**determiner: zero**⟩ tells KPML not to insert a determiner before the word *March*.
- The **range** feature describes the entity that is doing the possessing. This is also of type **time-interval**. In a similar fashion to that just described for the **domain** entity, the features specified here tell the system to use the word *day*, to make this plural, and to use the determiner *some*.

KPML can accept both semantic and syntactic information in its input structures. For example, in Figure 6.12, the action that the phrase is describing is specified in abstract semantic terms, as a **generalised-possession**, whereas the determiner *some* in the object noun phrase is specified directly, instead of as a set of semantic features (see below). One of KPML's strengths is its ability to accept a mixture of (using our terminology) meaning specifications, lexicalised case frames, and abstract syntactic structures in its input.

SPL expressions in fact can not literally specify grammatical information. Instead, constructs such as ⟨**determiner: some**⟩ are macros which expand into a set of semantic features which bias the grammar towards selecting a particular grammatical structure. ⟨determiner: some⟩, for example, expands into a set of six semantic features, including ⟨singularity-q: nonsingular⟩ and ⟨amount-attention-q: minimalattention⟩, which strongly bias the grammar towards selecting *some* as a determiner unless this is grammatically impossible.

The semantic types used in KPML are defined in terms of a linguistically-oriented ontology called the UPPER MODEL, represented as an inheritance hierarchy. The ability of subordinate nodes to inherit information from superordinate nodes avoids the need to specify information repeatedly, so that, for example, information about the realisation of temporal concepts like months and days can be specified once only, as properties of the one-or-two-d-time concept.

The Upper Model provides a repository for information about linguistic realisation that can be shared amongst applications. Allowing authors to specify the inputs to realisation in terms of semantic types from this ontology means detailed grammatical specifications can be omitted. For particular applications, further benefit can be achieved by extending the Upper Model by adding a MIDDLE MODEL. This is a set of concepts from the application's domain, subordinated to the elements of the Upper Model in such a way as to allow the appropriate inheritance of information to take place. So, for example, if we augment the Upper Model by adding March as an instance of the concept month, and subordinate the concepts month and day to the Upper Model concept time-interval, then we can generate the sentence *March had some rainy days* using the simplified SPL expression in Figure 6.15. We do not need to explicitly specify time-interval as a type in the SPL expression, since this will be picked up from the augmented Upper Model.

This mechanism is very powerful; however, it comes with a cost. In order to make use of these resources, one needs to have a good understanding of the structure of the Upper Model and the kinds of conceptualisations that underlie KPML's notion of semantic types.

Systemic Functional Grammar

KPML is based on the approach to linguistics known as Systemic Functional Linguistics, and in particular Systemic Functional Grammar (SFG). Systemic Functional Grammar is quite different in orientation to the approaches to linguistic description often adopted in work on natural language analysis (or, more precisely,

```
(S1 / generalized-possession
  :tense past
  :domain (N1 / March)
  :range  (N2 / day
              :number plural
              :determiner some
              :property-ascription
              (A1 / quality :lex rainy)))
```

Figure 6.15   An SPL which exploits a middle model (*March had some rainy days*).

natural language parsing), where researchers have tended to look to the world of generative grammar for ideas and theories about linguistic structure. Chomsky's initial work on transformational grammar began a line of development that was able to provide characterisations of linguistic structure precise enough for embodiment in computational models of parsing. Within this broad area of linguistics, it is now de rigueur for a linguistic theoretician to be concerned about the computational aspects of the grammatical theory he or she is developing. These considerations are at their height in the development of approaches such as Head-driven Phrase Structure Grammar (HPSG), where the formalist's concern with precision means that computational aspects are often developed in lock-step with linguistic descriptions.

That such approaches, with an early emphasis on the autonomy of syntax, should be used in parsing should be of no surprise. These approaches to linguistic description are essentially concerned with cataloguing the surface forms available in the language and with describing these using structures that generalise across instances. Such a view of language is very appropriate when the known is the surface form and the goal is to derive some underlying structure from this surface form.

The task in NLG is different, however; we start with the underlying representation, and our goal is to map this into a surface form. The questions to be dealt with are therefore rather different in nature. Rather than ask, 'What is the structure of this utterance and what is it being used to do?', we ask, 'What resources does the language offer to present the meaning I want to convey?' This leads to a predisposition to categorise the resources of language in terms of their function (more precisely, FUNCTIONAL POTENTIAL) rather than their form. Such a categorisation is precisely what SFG provides.

In Systemic Functional Grammar (as in many aspects of NLG), the central notion is one of choosing from available alternatives. A surface form is viewed as the consequence of selecting a set of abstract functional features from a description of the resources of the language as a whole. In SFG, these resources are represented in the form of a SYSTEMIC NETWORK (in effect, a taxonomy), and linguistic realisation consists of traversing this network. Each divergence in the network represents a choice between minimal grammatical alternatives and results in the addition of small constraints on the final form of the utterance. The information collected as a result of these choices amounts to an interpolation of an intermediate abstract representation. This allows the specification of the text to accumulate gradually, and in principle means that the realisation process does not need to backtrack, since the constraints on the final form of the utterance added at each point are small enough to avoid unwarranted overcommitment.

As just noted, a systemic network is in essence a taxonomy. It categorises the different elements of the language, but it does this in a functionally-motivated way. Technically, a systemic grammar is composed of CHOICE SYSTEMS. Each system is a set of simultaneous alternatives; each alternative is named by a GRAMMATICAL FEATURE and corresponds to a minimal grammatical alternation. Each system has an ENTRY CONDITION; during traversal, this determines which systems may be entered from a given point. From a more declarative point of view, the

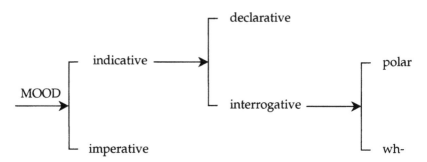

Figure 6.16   The mood system for the English clause.

connectivity of systems expresses the dependencies between linguistic elements. The selection of one alternative determines what further systems may be entered; as we move from left to right in a systemic network, the systems are said to be more DELICATE.

To make all this somewhat more concrete, Figure 6.16 shows a systemic fragment that represents the choices available for mood in the English clause. This indicates that major clauses in English can be indicative or imperative; indicative clauses can be declarative or interrogative; and interrogative clauses can be polar or wh-. Any path through this network thus provides a description of a clause type in English by selecting a feature from each choice system.

Of course, this is only a very small part of a complete grammatical description of the English language. A printed version of the complete NIGEL grammar will easily cover the wall of an average-sized office.

6.4.3   Using Systemic Grammar for Linguistic Realisation

So far we have seen how a particular notation – the systemic network – in conjunction with a terminology that represents a functional view on language can be used to represent the space of meanings that a language makes available. If we are to make use of this to produce surface utterances, we need to add two further elements.

First, we need a mechanism that allows us to traverse the network, guiding decision making at each choice point in the network. Second, each choice should result in some consequences which contribute to the specification of the final surface form.

The general algorithm adopted in KPML for systemic network traversal is quite simple:

- Start with the system of the highest rank appropriate for the semantic input, which is typically the clause (the system network is organised into subnetworks for different grammatical ranks, such as clause and nominal group).

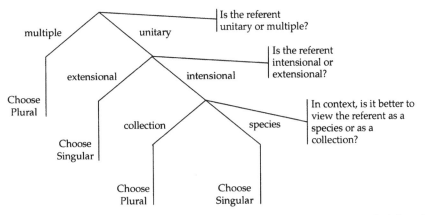

Figure 6.17   A chooser for deciding which determiner should be used. (Adapted from Mann, 1982.)

- Make choices until the maximally delicate distinctions offered have been drawn.

The result of this is a complete description of a linguistic unit at the selected rank. The process then repeats recursively for the elements at the next rank, typically the noun groups that will realise the participants in the sentence.

Whenever we reach a disjunction – a choice point – in the network, a decision must be made. In the KPML framework, this is done using a general approach called INQUIRY SEMANTICS. The bridge between semantics and the choices that affect surface form is provided by specialist pieces of code attached to each choice point that know how to choose between the options available on the basis of various sources of information.

These specialist pieces of code are called CHOOSERS. Each is a small parcel of program code – effectively a decision tree – which, by posing queries of the input SPL expression or of the wider 'environment' in which the system is running, can determine which feature should be chosen. In theory, the answers to these queries could be encoded in the input SPL expression. This is a function of those features whose names end in '-q', such as **command-offer-q**. However, for many queries, it would be unreasonable to expect the constructor of the SPL expression to be able to predict which queries might be relevant. It is generally more convenient for the grammar to determine what information is required at run time, and to obtain this information by posing queries to the environment.[3] Figure 6.17 shows the chooser that decides which form of determiner should be used in referring to a given entity.

---

[3] In fact, the earliest implementation of this model of generation, the PENMAN system, used no explicit input structure at all; traversal of the network was guided completely by an interactive process during which queries were put, one after another, to the user.

Name	Notation/Example	Description
INSERT	+ Subject	Function inserted as constituent of the structure of the unit being specified
ORDER	Subject ∧ Finite	One function ordered to precede another
EXPAND	Mood(Finite)	One function expanded to have another as constituent
CONFLATE	Subject/Agent	One function conflated with another to form the same constituent together
PRESELECT	Subject:singular	A function preselected for a feature; the realisation of the function is constrained to display that feature

Figure 6.18   Some realisation statement operators.

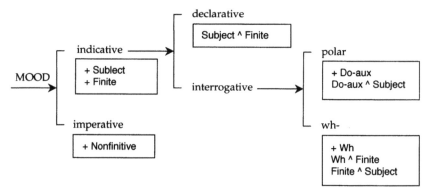

Figure 6.19   Realisation statements in a network. (Courtesy of Elke Teich.)

Choosers, and their underlying inquiry semantics, provide us with a reasoned way of traversing through the systemic network. We still require some means by which the choices made result in the generation of a surface form. In the KPML system, this is achieved by means of REALISATION STATEMENTS. These are low-granularity partial specifications of surface structure attached to the features at each choice point in the grammar; the choice of features during network traversal thus results in the accumulation of a large number of realisation statements each of which adds minimal constraints to the utterance being constructed.

The kinds of operations permitted in realisation statements are shown in Figure 6.18;[4] Figure 6.19 shows the English mood system we saw earlier, but with realisation statements added. The fact that realisation statements allow the determination of surface structure in such small increments means that it is much easier to avoid over-commitment, thus reducing the likelihood that backtracking will be required. Once the entire network has been traversed, the collected realisation statements serve as a set of constraints that determine the surface form of the utterance.

---

[4] This table is derived from Teich (1998).

6.4.4   Summary

We suggested earlier that the function-oriented approach of SFG made it more useful for work in NLG than phrase-structure approaches to linguistic description. We end this section by noting the specific advantages that have been claimed by proponents of SFG.

A significant claim of work in SFG is that it may be more natural and economical to state syntactic regularities in a functional framework. A constituent framework may require additional levels of structure to capture functional similarity. This is perhaps most apparent where cross-language generalisations are desired. These may be better stated in functional terms – by and large, all languages provide ways of doing the same things, but the ways in which these functions are achieved vary. As noted earlier, grammars for languages other than English have been developed for KPML, and some of the current research here explores how portions of the grammatical description can be shared between languages.

One of the characteristic properties of SFG as a linguistic theory is that it attempts to encompass aspects of meaning other than the propositional (or, as it is termed in SFG, the IDEATIONAL). Systemics also considers two other dimensions of meaning: the INTERPERSONAL and the TEXTUAL. Interpersonal meaning is concerned with the relationship between the speaker and his or her audience and the effect this has on the language used; it is this that conditions, for example, the use of honorifics in Japanese, the choice between formal and informal pronouns in French, and in English the firmness with which requests are expressed. Textual meaning is concerned with the way in which information is packaged in a text and how the message conveyed is structured thematically. This aspect of meaning covers, for example, the choice between different syntactic structures which convey the same propositional content.

In SFG, these three aspects of meaning are all represented within one space of grammatical description. This allows an interplay between the dimensions – called in SFG the three METAFUNCTIONS of language – that is not typically addressed by other linguistic theories and, in particular, those that concentrate on the notion of truth conditions as a way of characterising semantics.

6.5   SURGE

6.5.1   An Overview

SURGE – the Systemic Unification Realisation Grammar of English – is a large broad coverage grammar which has been used by a number of research and development groups around the world. It is written in FUF, the Functional Unification Formalism. FUF is in effect a programming language tailored to the needs of grammatical processing and, in particular, to the needs of linguistic realisation in a unification-based framework. It has its origins in Functional Unification

Grammar (Kay, 1979), and uses graph unification to combine an input structure that corresponds to a sentence specification with a grammar of the output natural language, the result being a syntactically-specified structure which is then linearised to produce the required sentence.

Like NIGEL, SURGE embodies a view of language that is based on Systemic Functional Grammar, although the grammar also borrows from HPSG (Pollard and Sag, 1994) and descriptive linguistic works (Quirk, 1985). FUF can be used in conjunction with other grammars, although it is most commonly used with SURGE.

The framework permits phrase specifications to be specified at a variety of levels of abstraction, but most commonly the input expected by SURGE is what we have called a lexicalised case frame – except that a verb is often specified semantically, as a process, instead of directly as a lexeme. This level of representation permits the grammar to make certain decisions about realisation that can be inferred on the basis of the input. An example of this is THEMATISATION. English has several mechanisms which allow the theme or focus of a sentence to be changed, of which perhaps the most common is PASSIVISATION. For example, *John told Mary* and *Mary was told by John* convey the same information, but in the first sentence the focus is on *John*, while in the second it is on *Mary*. SURGE will generate both sentences from what is essentially the same basic input structure, the difference between the two being determined by the value of a focus attribute.

6.5.2   The Input to SURGE

Input to SURGE is in the form of a FUNCTIONAL DESCRIPTION or FD. Formally, this is a collection of attribute–value pairs that together provide a specification of the utterance to be generated. Each such FD must contain a cat feature, which indicates the syntactic category of the form to be produced; the other attributes present depend on the information required by the grammar in order to generate a structure of that category.

Figure 6.20 shows the FD required to produce the sentence *March had some rainy days*; Figure 6.21 reexpresses this FD in a form closer to the AVM notation we introduced earlier. Figure 6.22 shows an FD for the more complex sentence *the month was cool and dry with the average number of rain days*.

```
((cat clause)
 (proc ((type possessive)))
 (tense past)
 (partic ((possessor ((cat proper) (head ((lex "March")))))
          (possessed ((cat common) (head ((lex day)))
                      (describer ((lex rainy)))
                      (selective yes) (number plural)))))))
```

Figure 6.20   An input to SURGE, from which SURGE produces *March had some rainy days*.

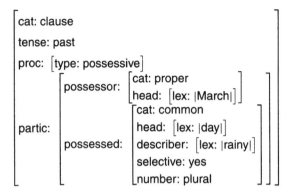

Figure 6.21   An AVM representation of the structure in Figure 6.20.

Just as in the case of SPL, the input specification language used in conjunction with KPML/NIGEL, some of the details here deserve a little elaboration.

- The initial ⟨cat: clause⟩ feature states that this FD should be expressed as a clause (rather than, for example, a noun phrase).
- The ⟨tense: past⟩ feature states that the clause should be in the past tense.[5]
- The proc feature describes the type of PROCESS that the clause describes. In this case, the ⟨type: possessive⟩ feature tells SURGE that the clause is describing a possessive process; this means that the clause will have two participants, a possessor and a possessed, and that in the eventuality to be described by the clause, the possessor participant possesses the possessed participant. Note that the FD does *not* explicitly state that *have* should be used as the verb of the clause; SURGE infers this from the type of process.
- The partic feature describes the PARTICIPANTS in the process, in this case the possessor and the possessed. The possessor is to be realised linguistically by the term *March*, which is a proper noun (indicated by ⟨cat: proper⟩); the possessed is to be realised by the term *day*, which is a common noun (⟨cat: common⟩). The ⟨number: plural⟩ feature tells SURGE to use the plural form, ⟨selective: yes⟩ indicates that determiner *some* should be used, and ⟨describer: rainy⟩ tells SURGE to add *rainy* as an adjective which will modify the head noun *days*.

---

[5] SURGE, like KPML, can also derive tense from temporal information, such as when the event took place, when the sentence is produced, and whether there is a reference time. While both systems allow tense to be specified directly or to be computed, the mechanisms used are different. In KPML ⟨tense: past⟩ is a macro which expands into appropriate semantic features about speech, event, and reference time; while in SURGE specifying ⟨tense: past⟩ 'skips over' the part of the grammar which computes tense from temporal information.

```
((cat clause)
 (tense past)
 (proc ((type ascriptive) (mode attributive)))
 (partic
   ((carrier ((cat common) (lex "month")))
    (attribute
      ((cat ap) (complex conjunction)
       (distinct
          ~(((cat adj) (lex "cool"))
            ((cat adj) (lex "dry")))))))))
 (circum
   ((accompaniment
      ((cat pp)
       (np ((cat common) (head === "number")
            (classifier === "average")
            (qualifier
              ((cat pp) (restrictive yes)
               (np ((cat common) (definite no)
                    (number plural) (head === "day")
                    (classifier === "rain")))))))
       (accomp-polarity +)))))))
```

Figure 6.22   A more complex input to SURGE (*The month was cool and dry with the average number of rain days*).

In contrast to the inputs required by KPML for the same sentences, note that the inputs required by SURGE do not contain explicit references to the semantic entities which take part in the eventualities being described by the sentence. For this reason, we categorise the structures used here as lexicalised case frames.

6.5.3   Functional Unification Grammar

Although the grammatical theory underlying SURGE is, like NIGEL, based on Systemic Functional Grammar, the linguistic resources are represented in a quite different way, in a manner that has its origins in Martin Kay's early work in Functional Unification Grammar (Kay, 1979).

Kay developed the idea of functional unification grammar (FUG) as a means of representing grammatical information that was intended to be neutral between generation and analysis. Although the idea of specifying grammatical knowledge declaratively is now widely accepted, at the time Kay was writing it was still commonplace to embed linguistic knowledge in procedural mechanisms. Functional unification grammar brought together two ideas which are not in fact necessarily related. First, it embodied the idea that grammatical information should include functional aspects: Kay took the view that purely formal descriptions of language were not particularly useful and that primary status should be given to functional aspects of language. This entailed making reference to notions about information structure like 'given', 'new' and 'focus', and concepts such as speech acts that are more traditionally considered part of pragmatics. Second, FUG made use of a notion of UNIFICATION as a process by means of which minimal, conceptually-derived functional descriptions could be fleshed out by merging with the information contained in an appropriately represented grammar. By insisting on a declarative representation of the grammatical knowledge, no specific demands would be imposed on the control structure used for parsing or generation.

Elhadad took these key ideas from Kay, and developed a formalism for expressing linguistic information in a unification-based framework; the result is FUF, which is in effect a programming language that is well-suited to manipulating grammatical information. SURGE is a broad coverage grammar based on systemic ideas, but encoded in a manner appropriate for use by a unification-based process.

6.5.4   Linguistic Realisation via Unification

The view of generation embodied in the SURGE grammar assumes that realisation covers the following tasks:

- the mapping of thematic structure onto syntactic roles;
- the control of syntactic paraphrasing and alternations;
- the provision of defaults for syntactic features;
- the propagation of agreement features;
- the selection of closed class words;
- the imposition of linear precedence constraints; and
- the inflection of open class words.

We noted earlier that the input to SURGE is expressed as a functional description. The grammar itself is also expressed as functional description; realisation is achieved by unifying the functional description that corresponds to the input expression with this second, very large, functional description. The input FD then represents the semantic content of the message to be realised; the grammar FD describes the space of grammatical alternatives and the correspondences of these to semantic elements and contains annotations that provide some control over how the grammar is used. The structure that results from this unification process is then linearised; the output of the realisation process is then a surface sentence expressing the specified meaning according to the grammatical constraints of the language.

In order to give some idea of how this works, we will discuss the process by reference to a much simpler grammar than SURGE itself. Figure 6.24 shows a modified version of one of the example grammars distributed with FUF; we will explore how this grammar is used in conjunction with the simple input FD shown in Figure 6.23, which results in the generation of the sentence *John sells the car*.

The grammar consists of four ALTERNATIONS: one for sentences ($\langle$cat: s$\rangle$), one for noun phrases ($\langle$cat: np$\rangle$), one for verb phrases ($\langle$cat: vp$\rangle$), and one for articles ($\langle$cat: art$\rangle$). When this structure is unified with the input FD, the following happens:

$$
\begin{bmatrix}
\text{cat: s} \\[4pt]
\text{agent:} \begin{bmatrix} \text{head:} \begin{bmatrix} \text{lex: |John|} \end{bmatrix} \\ \text{proper: yes} \end{bmatrix} \\[10pt]
\text{proc:} \begin{bmatrix} \text{head:} \begin{bmatrix} \text{lex: |sell|} \end{bmatrix} \end{bmatrix} \\[10pt]
\text{affected:} \begin{bmatrix} \text{head:} \begin{bmatrix} \text{lex: |car|} \end{bmatrix} \\ \text{proper: no} \end{bmatrix}
\end{bmatrix}
$$

Figure 6.23 An FD for a simple sentence (*John sells the car*).

```
((alt top (

    ;; First branch of the alternative
    ;; Describe the category S.
    ((cat s)
     (agent ((cat np)))
     (affected ((cat np)))
     (proc ((cat vp)
            (number {agent number})))
     (pattern (agent proc affected)))

    ;; Second branch: NP
    ((cat np)
     (head ((cat noun) (number {^ ^ number}))))
     (alt (
       ;; Proper names don't need an article
       ((proper yes)
        (pattern (head)))
       ;; Common names do
       ((proper no)
        (pattern (det head))
        (det ((cat article)
              (lex "the"))))))))

    ;; Third branch: VP
    ((cat vp)
     (pattern (head))
     (head ((cat verb))))

    ;; Fourth branch: ARTICLE
    ;; doesn't do anything
    ((cat article)))))
```

Figure 6.24 A simple FUF grammar. (Courtesy of Michel Elhadad.)

$$
\begin{bmatrix}
\text{cat: s} \\[4pt]
\text{agent:} \begin{bmatrix} \text{head: } [\text{lex: }|\text{John}|] \\ \text{proper: yes} \\ \text{cat: np} \end{bmatrix} \\[12pt]
\text{affected:} \begin{bmatrix} \text{head: } [\text{lex: }|\text{car}|] \\ \text{proper: no} \\ \text{cat: np} \end{bmatrix} \\[12pt]
\text{proc:} \begin{bmatrix} \text{head: } [\text{lex: }|\text{sell}|] \\ \text{cat: vp} \\ \text{number: \{agent number\}} \end{bmatrix} \\[12pt]
\text{pattern: (agent proc affected)}
\end{bmatrix}
$$

Figure 6.25   The result of initial unification of the input FD with the grammar.

- First, the input FD as a whole is compared to the different sections of the grammar. Because the input FD specifies that a sentence is required – this being specified by the ⟨cat: s⟩ feature–value pair in the input FD – the first branch of the grammar is chosen.
- This part of the grammar is unified with the input FD. That is, the features in the input FD are merged with the features in the selected grammar segment, resulting in the combined FD shown in Figure 6.25. The net effect is that the grammar adds some information to the originally input structure. We gain the additional detail that **agent** will be a noun phrase, that the **proc** will be a verb phrase, that the **proc** and the **agent** will have the same grammatical number, and that the **affected** is also to be realised using a noun phrase. The **pattern** feature tells FUF that when this FD is linearised, the **agent** should come first, followed by the **proc**, followed by the **affected**.
- Once the top-level FD has been unified with the grammar, FUF tries to unify all CONSTITUENTS of the FD with the grammar. In simple cases (such as this example), the constituents are all features mentioned in the **pattern** feature: here, **agent**, **proc**, and **affected**. The result of this unification is the FD shown in Figure 6.26. Note that the section of the grammar that deals with noun phrases has two alternations. The first of these (for noun phrases which have the feature ⟨**proper: yes**⟩) is used for the agent *John*, and the second of these (for noun phrases with the feature ⟨**proper: no**⟩) is used for the affected *the car*.
- After all unifications have been completed and the final FD is produced, FUF linearises this FD. This is done by recursively expanding the **pattern** feature until FDs are reached which do not contain a **pattern**. At this point, the particular word to be used is inserted into the output sentence by retrieving the **lex** feature and morphologically inflecting it according to

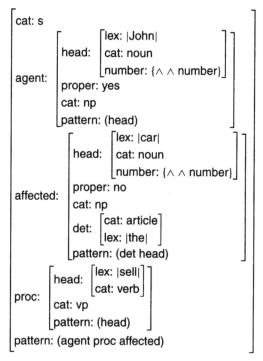

Figure 6.26 The FD in Figure 6.23 after unification with the grammar in Figure 6.24.

features such as number and person. In our simple example this results in the sentence *John sells the car.*

The processing carried out by FUF is generally more complex than this simple example suggests; the reader is encouraged to explore the examples discussed in the FUF system documentation. As with KPML, anyone who expects to use SURGE in an NLG system will have to spend a nontrivial amount of time learning how to use the system.

6.6   RealPro

6.6.1   An Overview

Of the three systems we discuss in this chapter, REALPRO is functionally the simplest. REALPRO looks to Mel'čuk's Meaning-Text Theory (MTT) (Mel'čuk, 1988) for its theoretical linguistic base. The system takes as input a DEEP SYNTACTIC STRUCTURE, termed a DSYNTS in MTT. Oversimplifying to some degree, a DSyntS

help
   (I John [class:proper-noun]
   II Mary [class:proper-noun])

Figure 6.27 The DSyntS for *John helps Mary.*

can be thought of as a parse tree which does not specify function words or word
ordering but does specify content words, syntactic roles (for example, the subjects
and objects of verbs), and syntactic features (for example, tense). REALPRO's task
is to produce a surface sentence from such a structure by adding appropriate function words, deciding on the appropriate inflections to use for content words, and
specifying the order in which the content and function words should appear in the
output sentence.

6.6.2   The Input to RealPro

As just noted, the input to REALPRO is an expression called a DSyntS. Figure 6.27
shows the DSyntS that corresponds to the simple sentence *John helps Mary*, in a
context where the word *help* has been appropriately defined in REALPRO's lexicon.

    This structure states that the head verb of the sentence to be generated is *help*,
that the subject of the verb is *John* (which is a proper noun, that is a name), and
the object is *Mary* (which is also a proper noun).

    So far this is not particularly interesting. The example we have just seen assumes
a number of default values for features that affect the output; by making these
features explicit and giving them values other than the defaults, we can begin to
see the power that comes even from this simple abstraction away from the surface
level of the sentence. Figure 6.28 shows a number of variations on the basic form
used above. In the first example, we add the feature–value pair ⟨**aspect: cont**⟩ to

1 help [aspect:cont]   *John is helping Mary*
     (I John [class:proper-noun]
     II Mary [class:proper-noun])

2 help [polarity:neg]   *John doesn't help Mary*
     (I John [class:proper-noun]
     II Mary [class:proper-noun])

3 help [aspect:cont, polarity:neg]   *John is not helping Mary*
     (I John [class:proper-noun]
     II Mary [class:proper-noun])

Figure 6.28 Variations of the DSyntS in Figure 6.27.

```
HAVE1 [tense:past]
    (I March [class:proper-noun]
    II day [class:common-noun number:pl]
        (ATTR rainy [class:adjective]))
```

Figure 6.29   A DSyntS for *March had some rain days.*

$$
\begin{bmatrix}
\text{head: have} \\
\text{tense: past} \\
\text{I:} \begin{bmatrix} \text{head: |March|} \\ \text{class: proper-noun} \end{bmatrix} \\
\text{II:} \begin{bmatrix} \text{head: |day|} \\ \text{class: common-noun} \\ \text{number: pl} \\ \text{attr:} \begin{bmatrix} \text{head: |rainy|} \\ \text{class: adjective} \end{bmatrix} \end{bmatrix}
\end{bmatrix}
$$

Figure 6.30   An AVM representation of the structure in Figure 6.29.

the verb in order to generate the progressive form of the original sentence. The second and third examples show our first two sentences can be negated simply by adding the feature ⟨polarity: neg⟩. The different syntactic consequences of negation – in the case of the nonprogressive form, the *do* auxiliary verb needs to be added – are handled transparently by the realiser, so that the earlier stages of the generation process do not need to be concerned with these idiosyncrasies.

Figure 6.29 shows the DSyntS corresponding to the sentence *March had some rainy days*; Figure 6.30 reexpresses this in our by now familiar AVM notation. Figure 6.31 shows a DSyntS for the sentence *The month was cool and dry with the average number of rain days.*

```
BE1 [tense:past]
    (I month [class:common-noun article:def]
    II cool [ class:adjective]
        (COORD AND2 [ ]
            (II dry [class:adjective]))
    ATTR WITH1
        (II number [class:common-noun article:def]
            (ATTR average [class:adjective]
            ATTR OF1
                (II day [class:common-noun number:pl article:no-art]
                    (ATTR rain [class:common-noun]))))))
```

Figure 6.31   A more complex DSyntS input to REALPRO (*The month was cool and dry with the average number of rain days*).

6.6.3   Meaning-Text Theory

Meaning-Text Theory is a form of DEPENDENCY GRAMMAR: the analyses the theory provides of sentences do not consist of phrase structure constituency descriptions but instead identify heads and modifiers that are dependent on those heads. Modifiers themselves may have dependent elements, so that quite complex dependency structures can be constructed. These are represented as trees where the nodes are words and the arcs connecting words are the labelled dependencies.

MTT views the generation of language as being a process of mapping iteratively through seven levels of representation. By taking DSyntS structures as input, REALPRO effectively assumes that prior stages in the NLG process have already performed some of these mappings.

A DSyntS is essentially a tree whose nodes represent content words and whose arcs represent the deep-syntactic relations that hold between content words. In a DSyntS for a sentence, typically the verb will be the root of the tree, with its arguments being its daughters, connected by arcs labelled with the grammatical roles of those daughters. Features can be added to nodes to indicate that a particular word should be put into the plural form, put in past tense, and so on. The arcs between words are drawn from a finite set defined in the theory; the most common of these are shown in Figure 6.32.

In the light of this background, we can now further elaborate on some of the elements in the DSyntS for the sentence *March had some rainy days*, as shown in Figure 6.29:

HAVE1. This is the sentence verb *have*, and the root node of the DSyntS. The feature ⟨tense: past⟩ tells REALPRO to put the sentence in past tense; the realiser knows that *have* is an irregular verb and uses the irregular form *had*. Because *have* is a common auxiliary verb in English, it is included in REALPRO's built-in lexicon, under the identifier HAVE1.

March. This is the subject of the sentence, as indicated by the I relation from the verb HAVE1 to this node. The feature ⟨class: proper-noun⟩ tells REALPRO that March is a name; the realiser therefore knows that a determiner is not required.

I	the subject of a clause
II	the object of a clause, or of any other type of phrase which requires an object, such as a prepositional phrase
III	the indirect object of a clause
ATTR	a phrase modifier – an adjective, adverb, prepositional phrase or relative clause
COORD	a conjunction

Figure 6.32   Common relations in MTT's DSyntS.

day. This is the object of the sentence, as indicated by the II relation from
the verb HAVE1 to this node. The feature ⟨class: common-noun⟩
tells REALPRO that day is a common noun. The feature number:pl indicates that the plural form *days* should be used; this information is also
used when selecting the determiner *some*. Note that *some* is not represented explicitly in the DSyntS; because it is a function word rather
than a content word, it is the realiser's job to include it automatically.

rainy. This modifies day, as indicated by the ATTR link from day to this
node. The ⟨class: adjective⟩ feature indicates that this is an adjective;
this causes the realiser to place the modifier before the noun. Other
types of modifiers, such as prepositional phrases, would be placed
after the noun.

The class features in this DSyntS could be omitted if the words in question –
March, day, and rainy – were present in REALPRO's lexicon.

6.6.4   How RealPro Works

As noted earlier, from the perspective of NLG, MTT divides the generation process
into seven steps. Some of these steps are not relevant for systems which generate
written English (as opposed to, say, spoken Japanese), and in fact REALPRO only
implements the following stages:

Deep syntactic component converts the DSyntS into a SURFACE SYN-
TACTIC STRUCTURE or SSyntS. An SSyntS includes function words
(such as *some*), and also uses more specialised arc labels.

Surface syntactic component LINEARISES an SSyntS, that is, it decides
in which order words should appear. Its output is a DEEP MORPHOLOG-
ICAL STRUCTURE or DMorphS.

Deep morphological component applies morphological processing
to produce appropriately inflected words from the contents of the
DMorphS. Its output is a SURFACE MORPHOLOGICAL STRUCTURE or
SMorphS.

Graphical component carries out orthographic processing on the
SMorphS. Its output is a DEEP GRAPHICAL STRUCTURE or DGraphS,
which is a complete representation of the sentence.

There is also an initial preprocessing stage which adds default features (for example, if no number is specified for a noun, it is assumed to have number:sg); and
a final postprocessing stage which converts the DGraphS into a standard mark-up
language such as HTML.

REALPRO's grammar is the set of rules which convert DSyntSs to SSyntSs,
SSyntSs to DMorphs, and so on. These are essentially pattern-matching rules which
in many ways are similar to the production rules used in many expert systems. Two

```
DSYNT-RULE:

    [(X I Y)]                |    [(X [class:verb])]
        <-->
    [(X predicative Y)]

SSYNT-RULE:

    [(X predicative Y)]  |    [(Y [number:?n person:?p])
                                 (X [class:verb])]
        <-->
    [(Y < X)]            |    [(X [number:?n person:?p])]
```

Figure 6.33   Some simple REALPRO grammar rules. (Courtesy of Co Gen Tex, Inc.)

examples of REALPRO rules are shown in Figure 6.33. The first rule is a DSyntS-to-SSyntS rule which replaces the DSyntS I relation with an SSyntS predicative (that is, subject) relation if the source (governor) of the relation is a verb. The second rule is an SSyntS-to-DMorphS rule which states that if a predicative relation occurs between a verb x and some other constituent y, then y should precede x in the sentence, and furthermore that x should have the same person and number features as y. These constraints are reminiscent of the realisation statements found in the NIGEL grammar discussed in Section 6.4.

In Figure 6.34, we show how these rules are used to realise a simple DSyntS which corresponds to the sentence *Sam sleeps*. This example is oversimplified, and we have not, in particular, shown the other rules that would be needed to process this DSyntS, such as the rules which select the correct inflection of the verb.

6.6.5   Summary

Of the systems we have surveyed, REALPRO is the simplest. It takes as input what we earlier termed an abstract syntactic structure, and applies rules of grammar and morphology to this to produce an output sentence. Of the three systems, it correspondingly requires the microplanner to do the most work in constructing input specifications.

REALPRO is also different from KPML and SURGE in that it is based on MTT instead of SFG. Advocates of MTT from a natural language processing perspective (for example, Goldberg et al., 1994) claim that it is well suited to NLG realisation because it modularises the realisation process into well-defined substages. Although REALPRO's input is an abstract syntactic structure, this is not required by MTT; indeed MTT includes a semantic representation level which has been used by other MTT-based realisers, such as ALETHGEN/GL (Coch, 1996b).

It is difficult to compare the pros and cons of SFG and MTT, not least because SFG and MTT advocates mostly compare their theories to the phrase-structure linguistic

System input (DSyntS)

sleep [class:verb]
(I Sam [class:proper-noun])

With defaults added (DSyntS)

sleep [class:verb]
(I Sam [class:proper-noun person:3rd number:sg])

After DSYNT-RULEs applied (SSyntS)

sleep [class:verb]
(predicative Sam [class:proper-noun person:3rd number:sg])

After SSYNT-RULEs applied (DMorphS)

[(Sam [person:3rd number:sg])
 (sleep [person:3rd number:sg])]

Final output

Sam sleeps.

Figure 6.34   Stages of realisation in REALPRO.

models which dominate natural language understanding research. In practice, engineering issues such as speed, reliability, documentation quality, and cost may be more important in choosing a realiser for an NLG system than the grammatical theory on which it is based.

As with the other systems we have described, making use of REALPRO requires a significant investment of time spent learning about both MTT in general as well as the realisation engine itself. Once more, it is important to emphasise that all of these systems require the user to undertake specific theoretical commitments in order to use the machinery in a consistent fashion.

6.7   Choosing a Realiser

We have taken the view in this chapter that it makes sense to use an existing realiser, rather than build one from scratch. How do you decide which realiser to use? Of course, the answer to this question depends on the particular application you are developing.

As we have demonstrated, the three systems we have described differ on two basic dimensions:

- the level of abstraction at which the input structures to the realiser are specified; and
- the particular grammatical theory embodied in the realiser.

There is a third dimension which we have only alluded to in passing: differences in grammatical coverage. The particular coverage offered by any system depends historically on its developmental path. It is a reality of using packages like these that, inevitably, one finds that there are gaps in the systems' grammatical coverage: There will always be grammatical structures that one wishes to build that are not catered for by the existing grammars. This is, of course, no different to the situation that occurs with the use of existing grammars for parsing: No matter how broad coverage such a resource is, one always finds there are structures that it does not cater for. From this point of view, it is best to take the view that the systems described here are still under development. We have found the developers of these systems extremely helpful in assistance with the making of grammatical extensions, but clearly this kind of support is not sustainable on a wider basis unless resources are specifically allocated to the task.

Of course, as time goes on and the development of these systems continues, the effect of this difference will be reduced. The first two differences we identified remain. Unless one has a specific preexisting theoretical commitment that causes one to choose one system rather than the others, the most important issue to consider is thus the level of abstraction of the input specifications the realisers expect. In some systems, phrase specifications are produced from scratch in the microplanner by doing deep reasoning on the information that needs to be communicated and the linguistic resources available to communicate this information. In such systems, it may be best to use a realiser whose input is expressed in fairly abstract terms, such as KPML or SURGE, since these will minimise the amount of work required by the microplanner. In other systems, in contrast, phrase specifications may originally be written in skeleton form by human developers, and then instantiated or otherwise modified by the document planner and microplanner. In such systems it is important that skeleton phrase specifications be easy for human authors to write. This may suggest using a phrase specification representation that is expressed in terms closer to the lay-linguistic terminology one might expect users of the system to be familiar with, and in such cases a realiser like REALPRO which deals in terms of abstract syntactic structures may be most appropriate.

Of course, another possibility is to use a simple phrase specification representation such as canned text or orthographic strings, and hence to have a very simple 'linguistic realiser' which has knowledge of orthography (for processing canned text) but nothing else. In this case there is no need to use a complex realisation package such as KPML, SURGE, or REALPRO.

In summary, to repeat our position at the outset of this chapter: Given the availability of these components, each of which comes with a reasonably broad-coverage grammatical resource, it is not clear that there is much to be gained from building one's own realisation component. The development effort required to build grammars with the coverage of the systems described here should not be underestimated. At the same time, the effort required to come to terms with any of these systems is not insignificant. It should also be realised that these tools are very powerful – perhaps more powerful than many applications require. Indeed, for many NLG scenarios, a simple canned-text realisation component may be sufficient, where the only grammatical processing required is orthographic processing to ensure correct punctuation and capitalisation.

6.8   Bidirectional Grammars

In each of the systems we have described so far, a distinction can be drawn between, on the one hand, the grammatical and lexical resources used to characterise information about language, and on the other, the engine that makes use of those resources. This raises the question of whether the grammar or lexicon in each case is necessarily something that can only be used for generation, or whether it can be viewed as a rather more declarative description that could in principle be used for either natural language generation or natural language analysis.

In the systems we have surveyed, the grammatical resources are not specified in a manner that makes them neutral with respect to their direction of use; in each case there are assumptions made with regard to the processing of the representations that effectively makes them all generation-oriented grammars. However, the idea that one might specify a grammatical resource as something that is independent of this aspect of its use is not new; indeed, as we saw in Section 6.5.3, this very possibility was one of the motivating factors in Kay's original development of Functional Unification Grammar, the progenitor to Elhadad's FUF. The idea has also received attention within work on Machine Translation, where there is a desire to economise on the construction of grammatical resources by allowing a grammatical description of a language to be used both for the analysis of the source language and for the generation of the target language.

In more recent years, the idea of a bidirectional grammar has surfaced in the context of discussion of algorithms for head-driven generation (Shieber, 1988; Shieber et al., 1990). The basic idea here is that a grammar provides a declarative specification of the relationships that hold between meaning and surface form. Some processing engine – a surface realiser or a parser – can then take an expression that is an instance of one of the relata and, given the grammar, produce an instance of the other relatum.

The simplest variants of this idea can easily be explored using Definite Clause Grammars (Pereira and Warren, 1980) in Prolog, where Prolog's top-down backtracking processing regime can be used to perform a mapping from an appropriately expressed surface form to a representation of semantic content or vice versa. More sophisticated work in the area is concerned with issues of the control of search which arise as soon as grammatical descriptions of any complexity are considered.

The ideas here are clearly appealing. It seems redundant to specify grammatical information once for generation and then again for analysis. However, bidirectional systems have not been widespread in the larger context of the kinds of NLG systems we describe in this book.

It is instructive to consider why this is the case. If we look at current experiments in the use of bidirectional grammars, it is immediately apparent that the kinds of representations used as input to realisers based on bidirectional grammars are not the same as the representations (such as SPL or DSyntS expressions) that are generally provided by microplanning components. The mappings encoded in these bidirectional grammars tend to focus on correspondences between logical forms and surface strings, where those logical forms express the propositional content of the corresponding sentences. This is generally deemed appropriate as far as natural language parsing is concerned. However, in NLG systems, there is generally a concern with kinds of information that can be ignored from the point of view of the parsing process. A parser might produce the same logical form for the following three sentences:

(6.6)   a. Mary gave John a ball.
       b. Mary gave a ball to John.
       c. John was given a ball by Mary.

The input to a realiser, however, should explicitly provide a means of choosing among these forms; the alternative is to choose at random.

This point relates to our discussion in Section 6.4.4 of aspects of meaning other than the propositional. Viewed simply from the point of view of propositional content, there are many ways of saying the same thing. Winograd (1983), for example, lists all the following as providing valid descriptions of the same state of affairs in the world:

(6.7)   a. Jon bought a painting for Vina.
       b. Jon bought Vina a painting.
       c. Vina was bought a painting by Jon.
       d. What Jon bought Vina was a painting.
       e. What Vina was bought by Jon was a painting.
       f. It was a painting that Jon bought for Vina.
       g. It was Jon that bought Vina a painting.
       h. It was Vina that Jon bought a painting for.

Although these may all be equivalent in propositional meaning, the sentences are not mutually interchangeable. For example, Example (6.7h) is appropriate as a response to *Who did Jon buy a painting for*, but not as a response to *What did Jon buy for Vina*.

How then do we characterise the differences between these sentences? Generally this is viewed in terms of notions like FOCUS, GIVEN versus NEW INFORMATION, and so on – just those phenomena we earlier referred to as making up textual meaning. This is not to say that there are no random selections to be made between different ways of saying things; however, there is the perception among

NLG researchers that most choices are motivated in some way. The input specification should therefore include whatever information is required in order to generate these different outputs; in a true bidirectional resource, these elements would also be part of the output of analysis.

In practice, this is not the case. There are two related reasons for this. First, much of the work in the area of bidirectional grammars has its origins in the parsing world, bringing with it a focus on concerns like the control of search strategies. Second, the linguistic models adopted in these approaches tend not to highlight these nonpropositional aspects of meaning.

This is not a necessary property of attempts to build bidirectional grammatical resources. Provided we could characterise the correspondences between surface forms and a richer notion of 'meaning' appropriately, we could conceivably have analysis systems which would use such a resource to produce these richer outputs, and at the same time the current source of indeterminacy that arises when these resources are used for generation would be removed. At the current time, however, we do not have appropriate characterisations of the relationships between meaning and surface form.

There is also a less theoretically motivated and more pragmatic reason for the lack of use of bidirectional grammars. For generation we only want to construct grammatical utterances; in real-world natural language analysis systems, however, we need to be able to cope with any sentence which a human user might produce. Grammars for use in parsers therefore often are annotated with information intended to help resolve ambiguities or robustly handle small grammatical mistakes in human-entered text. This kind of information is not required for linguistic realisation in NLG systems.

6.9   Further Reading

The literature on surface realisation is considerable. Just as a significant amount of work in natural language understanding has focussed on syntactic analysis and parsing, it is possible that more has been written on linguistic realisation than any other aspect of NLG. Many grammatical formalisms and theories that have been developed to describe natural languages have been used in the construction of realisation components. Although we have focussed here on the use of Systemic Functional Grammar and Meaning-Text Theory in linguistic realisation, other linguistic formalisms which have been used in parsing frameworks have also been used in realisation: for example, Tree Adjoining Grammars, Categorial Unification Grammar, Lexical Functional Grammar, Government and Binding Theory, and Head-driven Phrase Structure Grammar.

One aspect of surface realisation that has not been explored very much in the literature is structure realisation. Nunberg (1990) provides some interesting discussion on the difference between what he calls LINGUISTIC GRAMMAR and TEXT

GRAMMAR, but the most appropriate characterisation of the relationship between these levels of representation remains to be worked out.

Mellish (1991) provides a good theoretical overview of different approaches to realising phrase specifications; and Reiter (1995a) discusses at a very high level the pros and cons of strings as compared to more abstracted grammatical representations.

Numerous papers have been published on KPML, on its predecessor system PENMAN, and on the NIGEL grammar of English. Matthiessen and Bateman (1991) is the most comprehensive description of these systems in a single volume; Bateman (1997) is a more recent paper which focuses on the KPML development environment. Bateman et al. (1990) describe the Upper Model, while some of the issues in developing multilingual grammars are discussed by Bateman et al. (1991). Additional information about KPML can be downloaded from http://www.darmstadt.gmd.de/publish/komet/kpml.html. Halliday (1985a) is the standard introduction to systemic functional linguistics.

The best introduction to SURGE is Elhadad and Robin (1997); more detailed information about both FUF and SURGE can be downloaded from http://www.cs.bgu.ac.il/surge. Elhadad, McKeown, and Robin (1997) describe a very sophisticated use of SURGE, which illustrates the power of the system.

A general introduction to REALPRO is provided in (Lavoie and Rambow, 1997); more details are available in the system documentation, available from http://www.cogentex.com/systems/realpro. Mel'čuk (1988) describes Meaning-Text Theory, the linguistic theory underlying REALPRO.

The most well-known algorithm for realisation in a bidirectional grammar framework is called SEMANTIC-HEAD-DRIVEN GENERATION; see Shieber et al. (1990) and van Noord (1990) for an introduction to these ideas. Busemann (1996) discusses some of the problems with using realisers based on bidirectional grammars.

Those people who wish to build their own linguistic realisers (a course of action we recommend only if it is not possible to use an existing system) may wish to look at Quirk (1985) for a general description of English syntax. If only morphological and orthographic processing is needed, valuable sources are Ritchie et al. (1992) for morphology, and Nunberg (1990) for punctuation and orthographic processing. White (1995) discusses some of the complexities in implementing Nunberg's ideas in an NLG system.

Relatively little has been written discussing under what circumstances particular approaches to realisation should be preferred, but see Reiter (1995a) and Reiter and Mellish (1993) for some comments on this.

7   Beyond Text Generation

So far in this book we have considered the generation of natural language as if it were concerned with the production of text abstracted away from embodiment in any particular medium. This does not reflect reality, of course: When we are confronted with language, it is always embodied, whether in a speech stream, on a computer screen, on the page of a book, or on the back of a breakfast cereal packet. In this final chapter, we look beyond text generation and examine some of the issues that arise when we consider the generation of text contained within some medium.

7.1   Introduction

Linguistic content can be delivered to a reader or hearer in many ways. Consider, for example, a few of the ways in which a weather report might be presented to an audience:

- **Email.** When delivered as the body of a simple text-only email message, it might consist of nothing more than a sequence of words and punctuation symbols, with blank lines or indentations to indicate some of the structure in the text.
- **Newspaper article.** In this case it could include typographic elements, such as the use of bold and italic typefaces, and accompanying graphics, such as a weather map.
- **Web page.** As well as making use of typographic devices and graphical elements, in this case it could also include hypertext links to related information, such as the weather in neighbouring cities.
- **Radio broadcast.** Prosodic elements such as pauses and pitch changes might be used to communicate emphasis and structure.
- **Television broadcast.** Here, the presenter's speech might be accompanied by (possibly animated) graphics, and the delivery might be supported by means of gestures made by the presenter.

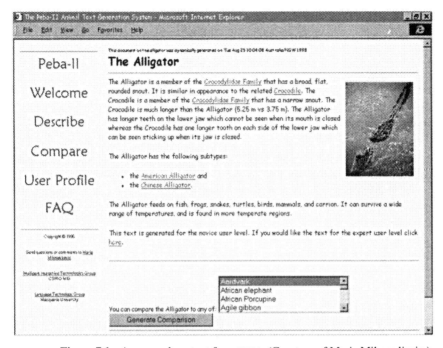

Figure 7.1 An example output from PEBA. (Courtesy of Maria Milosavljevic.)

This is list is by no means complete and, indeed, is growing as technological advances create new presentation media. For our purposes, the most important point is that all of these presentation media except the first include more than just words; and appropriate use of PRESENTATION-SPECIFIC MECHANISMS such as typography, layout, graphics, prosody, gestures, and hypertext links can lead to much more effective documents.[1] Furthermore, document users in the late 1990s usually expect documents to use such devices and may be reluctant to read or listen to a 'document' which consists solely of words.

To give a concrete example, consider Figure 7.1, which is a Web page produced by PEBA (see Section 1.3.5) that describes alligators. This demonstrates several of the mechanisms we have just alluded to:

Typography. The text lists the different kinds of alligator that are present in the system's knowledge base; these are presented typographically by means of a

---

[1] The English language does not offer an appropriate term which conveniently covers instances of output in a wide variety of presentation media. In this book we will refer to the output of systems that attend to the concerns under discussion here as a document, regardless of whether it is an email message, paper document, Web page, radio broadcast, TV broadcast, or some other presentation medium.

bulleted list. This information could have been presented without such a typographic device, using a sentence like the following in the running text:

(7.1)   The Alligator has two subtypes: the American Alligator and the Chinese Alligator.

However, as the number of items to be listed increases, expressing the information in this way becomes unwieldy.

Graphics. A picture of an alligator is included in the document: an image like this often conveys much information that would be difficult or impossible to convey in words. In the general case, knowing what information is conveyed by a graphical element can impact on the system's decisions about what information should be communicated via text.

Hypertext. All underlined words and phrases in the document are hypertext links that correspond to new communicative goals that the user can provide to the system. If the user clicks, for example, on American Alligator, this is considered by PEBA as a request to generate a description of that entity.

Historically much NLG research has ignored presentation media and concentrated on the production of text in the classic linguistic sense: a sequence of words and punctuation symbols. However, real-world applied NLG systems must consider the use of typography, graphics, hypertext, and the other mechanisms mentioned above, unless they are working in a presentation medium (such as simple email) where documents really do consist of just sequences of words and punctuation symbols. They also must consider any constraints imposed by the presentation media; for example, STOP's output must fit on four A5 pages, which limits the amount of information the system can communicate.

This raises several important issues. First, when should typography, hypertext, and so forth be used? For example, it is valuable to use typeface changes to emphasise key phrases, provided this is done in moderation; too much text in bold or italic face may confuse and irritate the reader and actually reduce a document's effectiveness. Second, what constraints do presentation media impose on the content and structure of documents? As mentioned above, written documents may be constrained in size terms. Other examples of such constraints are that it may be best to avoid complex syntactic structures in spoken texts (McKeown et al., 1997) and that on-line documents may be required to include certain information (such as safety warnings) at their beginning, so that this information is visible when the document is first opened.

Last but certainly not least, how should all this be implemented in an NLG system? From a mechanical perspective, presentation-specific mechanisms are usually specified by mark-up annotations. For example, \bf is a LaTeX annotation which specifies boldface; <A HREF> is an HTML annotation which specifies a hypertext link; and <PITCH> is a SABLE annotation which specifies properties of the pitch at which words are spoken. But what changes need to be made to the document planner, microplanner, and realiser to enable the system to decide when to use one of these annotations; and what changes should be made to the content and structure of a document because of presentation media constraints?

It is not possible to discuss here all possible presentation media and their associated mechanisms and constraints. Instead, we examine a few media and mechanisms which have been relatively prominent in the research community: typography (discussed in Section 7.2), graphics (discussed in Section 7.3), hypertext (discussed in Section 7.4), and speech output (discussed in Section 7.5).

7.2   Typography

7.2.1   The Uses of Typography

As a discipline, typography is concerned with the appearance and effectiveness of written documents. This concern covers a wide variety of phenomena at different levels, including the shapes and sizes of individual letterforms; the spaces between letters, words and lines; the lengths of lines and sizes of margins; and the spatial configuration of larger elements of text. Poor typographic choices, or a neglect of the typographic properties of a document, can have a serious impact on the effectiveness of that document.

Typographic choices are motivated by a variety of considerations:

Typographic Conventions. Sometimes typographic properties are dictated by conventions that apply to the kind of text under consideration. In the publishing world, conventions such as these are often collected together and referred to as a HOUSE STYLE, this being a catalogue of rules for the particular ways in which typographic variations should be used. For example, a common house style rule is that references to literary works should be in italic face, as in *Gone with the Wind*. It is important to note that these prescriptions are only conventions, and so there is no one right way of doing things; a different house style, for example, might require that the titles of literary works be presented wrapped in quotes, as in 'Gone with the Wind'. What matters is consistency within a document or collection of documents; this makes it easier for the reader to develop expectations as to what particular typographic variations signify.

Indicating Emphasis. Typography can be used to mark a particular piece of text as being especially important. Figure 7.2 shows a fragment from a conference announcement, where boldface has been used to draw the reader's attention to important dates associated with the conference. Of course, this use of boldface

Important Dates

Paper and electronic submissions must be received by **Friday, November 29, 1996**. Notification of receipt will be mailed to the first author (or designated author) soon after receipt. Authors will be notified of acceptance by **Monday, December 16, 1996**. Camera-ready copies of final eight-page papers must be received by **Monday, January 27, 1997**.

Figure 7.2   Using typeface variation for emphasis.

is itself something of a convention, but the visual salience of this device makes it distinct from many other conventions adopted in written documents, where the function of the convention is primarily to mark distinctions by indicating logical difference via typography. Other typographic devices can be used to draw the reader's attention; for example, text can be underlined, different colours can be used, boxes can be drawn around important elements, and so on.[2]

Indicating Structure. A key use of typography, especially in technical domains but also more generally, is to indicate the logical structure of a document. Headings provide visual cues to the intended segmentation of the textual material, and different sizes or styles in headings are often used to provide an indication of the hierarchical relationships in the document. Typographic devices, such as itemised or enumerated lists, can also be used to indicate the structure of information. For example, it is not uncommon for a sequence of instructions to be presented in list form, so that the scope of each distinct step is made clear visually; various levels of indentation can also be used to indicate the hierarchical relationships between elements of the list.

Enabling Information Access. Just as typographic devices can be used to indicate that which is important, a related use is to help users quickly identify specific pieces of information. For example, presenting information in any regularised form such as a table makes it easier for the reader to access specific elements without having to read the whole text. Figure 7.3 shows the information in our conference announcement expressed in a different way. Here, the significant events that make up the conference reviewing process are used as labels, and the particular spatial configuration used makes it easy for the reader to jump straight to the relevant information. Back-of-the-book indexes are another example of the same device. As the degree of regularity in the information to be presented increases, it becomes more appropriate to provide this information in an explicit table with labelled rows and columns.

---

[2] It is interesting to note that the notion of underlining as emphasis has achieved the status of a metaphor, as in *Let me just underline what I'm saying here.*

Important Dates

Deadline for receipt of paper and electronic submissions. All submissions
must be received by Friday, November 29, 1996. Notification of receipt will
be mailed to the first author (or designated author) soon after receipt.
Notification of reviewing results. Notifications of acceptance or rejection will
be provided to authors by Monday, December 16, 1996.
Camera-ready due date. Camera-ready copies of final eight-page papers must
be received by us by Monday, January 27, 1997.

Figure 7.3   Using a labelled list structure to aid information access.

As a larger example of how typography can be used to achieve different effects,
consider the following text that might be produced by a travel advice organisation:[3]

(7.2)   When time is limited, travel by limousine, unless cost is also limited,
in which case go by train. When only cost is limited a bicycle should be
used for journeys of less than 10 kilometers, and a bus for longer journeys.
Taxis are recommended when there are no constraints on time or cost,
unless the distance to be travelled exceeds 10 kilometers. For journeys
longer than 10 kilometers, when time and cost are not important, journeys
should be made by hire car.

The information expressed in this text can be presented typographically in various
ways, as demonstrated in Figures 7.4–7.6. Each presentation is appropriate in
different circumstances. So, for example, the logical tree structure in Figure 7.4
might be helpful on a reader's first exposure to the information, since it makes
it easy to distinguish those factors the reader considers important. The form in
Figure 7.5 is perhaps better suited to experienced users; and the form in Figure 7.6
offers the most compact solution. Note that in each case, the appropriate use
of typography has resulted in a presentation of the information that is easier to
navigate than the purely textual version shown above.

7.2.2   Typography in NLG Systems

For an NLG system to make use of typographic resources, it must in some sense be
TYPOGRAPHICALLY-AWARE: It must be able to indicate typographic distinctions in
its output, typically by including annotations which are understood by the document presentation system. Figure 7.7 shows some of the annotations used in LaTeX
and HTML to indicate structure. Note that these indicate logical types (as discussed
in Section 6.2); in each case they tell the document presentation system to indicate

---

[3] This example is based on one provided by Crystal (1987).

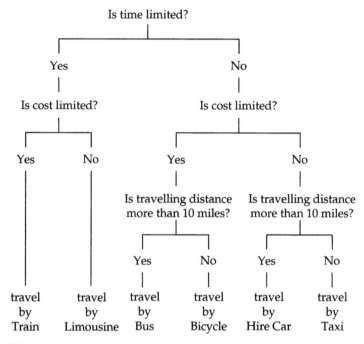

Figure 7.4   Information expressed typographically as a decision tree.

a particular structure, but they do not specify which typographic mechanism should be used to achieve this goal. This information is specified in a STYLE FILE or STYLE SHEET used by the document presentation system; the style file or style sheet is typically prepared by a design specialist, based on the house style of the publishing organisation. LaTeX and HTML can also specify typographic effects directly; some examples are shown in Figure 7.8.

As mentioned above, some uses of typography are determined by convention, whereas others may be the result of conscious decisions made during the

	If journey less than 10 km	If journey more than 10 km
When only time is limited	travel by Limousine	travel by Limousine
When only cost is limited	travel by Bicycle	travel by Bus
When time and cost are not limited	travel by Taxi	travel by Hire Car
When both time and cost are limited	travel by Train	travel by Train

Figure 7.5   Information expressed typographically via a table.

When only time is limited
    travel by Limousine
When only cost is limited
    travel by Bus if journey more than 10 kilometers
    travel by Bicycle if journey less than 10 kilometers
When both time and cost are limited
    travel by Train
When time and cost are not limited
    travel by Hire Car if journey more than 10 kilometers
    travel by Taxi if journey less than 10 kilometers

Figure 7.6   Information expressed compactly.

Element	LaTeX	HTML
Major heading	\section{...}	<h1>...</h1>
Minor heading	\subsection{...}	<h2>...</h2>
Itemised list	\begin{itemize}\item ...	<ul><li>...
Numbered list	\begin{enumerate}\item ...	<ol><li>...

Figure 7.7   Declarative mark-up annotations.

design of a document in order to achieve particular effects. For those aspects of typography based on conventions, the issues that arise when building a natural language generation system are quite simple, provided of course that the system is typographically-aware. If the system is capable of indicating typographic variation in its output, then all that is required is that the appropriate conventions be hard-wired into the system's behaviour. So, for example, whenever the NLG system refers to a literary work or uses a technical term for the first time, it is relatively straightforward for these to be rendered using the predetermined typographic cues.

Typographic issues are more complicated where the meaning-to-form mapping is one to many – that is, when there are different typographical devices available for expressing a given meaning, and the system must somehow choose between these at run time. One such case would be the choice between a long and complex sentence and a more typographically structured presentation of the same information, as we have seen in a number of the examples above. Formulation of the reasoning required in order to make such choices is a relatively unexplored area of NLG research. The appropriate choice of typographic devices from the wide range available is clearly a knowledge-rich decision process, and there are as yet no systems which attempt to

Element	LaTeX	HTML
Emboldening	{\bf ...}	...
Italicisation	{\it ...}	<i>...</i>
Teletype font	{\tt ...}	<tt>...</tt>

Figure 7.8   Physical mark-up annotations.

emulate the complex reasoning processes pursued by a typographer or information design specialist.

7.2.3   Implementing Typographic Awareness

Making an NLG system typographically aware has implications for all parts of an NLG system; we review some of what is involved below.

Document Planning

As discussed in Chapter 4, the document planner is responsible for deciding what information content should be communicated in a text; it also is responsible for imposing some structure over the selected messages. The document planner usually does not explicitly make typographic decisions, but it does make many decisions which have a typographic impact. For example, the document planner may specify that certain groups of messages should be associated with logical document structures such as sections; these structures are usually marked in the final document with typographic means, such as boldface headings for sections. The document planner may also specify that certain messages are especially important; this may result in the texts corresponding to these messages being typographically emphasised, perhaps by putting them in italic face or underlining them.

The document planner must also in some cases be aware of typographic constraints. For example, if the genre of the text to be generated requires that certain kinds of information be presented in tabular form, this may provide a constraint on the content elements that can be selected for expression. Similarly, if there is a size limitation on the text to be generated, this imposes a constraint on the content selection task in terms of the quantity of material it chooses for expression.

Microplanning

The microplanner decides which specific linguistic and structural resources should be used to communicate the abstract content and structure specified by the document planner. Since typography can be regarded as another type of resource which can be used to communicate content and structure, many kinds of typographic decisions fit very naturally into the microplanning process. For example, the microplanner may decide what typographic mechanism (if any) should be used to communicate the fact that a particular message is important; and the microplanner may decide what paragraph structure should be used in the document, based on the message groupings produced by the document planner.

The microplanner may also decide to use typographic mechanisms in the aggregation process. Our discussion of aggregation in Section 5.3 was based on the use of purely linguistic mechanisms such as conjunctions and embedded clauses. In many cases, though, it makes sense to use typographic mechanisms in aggregations, as well as (or even instead of) linguistic mechanisms. Consider the following

The meeting was attended by the following:

Company	Representatives
IBM	Tom Jones
Digital	Cecile Smith, Nancy Robinson
Microsoft	Mike Williams
Sun	Richard Adams, Joe Blackford, Sally Su

Figure 7.9   A tabular presentation of aggregated information.

two examples:

(7.3)   The meeting was attended by Tom Jones from IBM; Cecile Smith and Nancy Robinson from Digital; Mike Williams from Microsoft; and Richard Adams, Joe Blackford, and Sally Su from Sun.

(7.4)   The meeting was attended by:
- Tom Jones from IBM;
- Cecile Smith and Nancy Robinson from Digital;
- Mike Williams from Microsoft; and
- Richard Adams, Joe Blackford, and Sally Su from Sun.

The first of these examples is based on purely linguistic aggregation as discussed in Section 5.3. The second example contains the same words as the first, but a typographic mechanism (an itemised list) is used to show the groupings of the people mentioned. In many situations, the second example may be clearer and easier to understand than the first. The microplanner can also choose to use a purely typographic mechanism, such as a table, to communicate an aggregation; an example of this is shown in Figure 7.9.

Hovy and Arens (1991) have noted that typographic resources can be used instead of, or as a supplement to, cue words when expressing some discourse relations. For example, a Sequence might be expressed by including the sequence elements in a numbered list, instead of (or in addition to) inserting cue words such as *first*, *then*, and *finally*. Thus, where a lexicalisation process might have chosen from amongst different cue words that realise some relation, we now have to countenance the possibility that a nonlexical realisation might be appropriate. Again, this kind of decision is best placed within the microplanner.

Surface Realisation

The realiser must convert the typographic decisions made by the document planner and microplanner into the typographic mark-up annotations which are understood by the document presentation system. Usually this is a straightforward process, although in some cases it is complicated by the need to conform to conventions. For example, aircraft maintenance documents written according to the AECMA Simplified English standard (AECMA, 1986) should use a dash instead of a bullet to mark items in an itemised list, as in the following example:

(7.5)   The meeting was attended by:
  – Tom Jones from IBM;
  – Cecile Smith and Nancy Robinson from Digital;
  – Mike Williams from Microsoft; and
  – Richard Adams, Joe Blackford, and Sally Su from Sun.

Ideally this kind of rule should be specified in a style sheet or style file accessed by the document presentation system, so that these fine details are invisible to the NLG system. In practice, however, it may sometimes be necessary for the realiser to enforce such rules.

7.3   Integrating Text and Graphics

In the previous section we saw how typographic resources can be utilised in an NLG system. Incorporating the use of typography represents a first step towards the generation of documents rather than texts; with this hurdle overcome, a whole new range of possibilities arise for NLG systems. In this section, we build on the preceding material to consider what is involved in having a system generate documents that include graphical elements – diagrams, figures, pictures, and so forth – as well as words.

An example of a MULTIMODAL document generated by the WIP system (Wahlster et al., 1993) is shown in Figure 7.10. This is part of a sequence of instructions for using a modem; the example shown instructs the user to set a particular switch on the modem. In this example, WIP has used graphics to indicate the location of the switch, but it has used text to indicate the action that should be performed on the switch. WIP is also able to describe this instruction purely graphically, as in Figure 7.11, and purely textually, as in Figure 7.12.

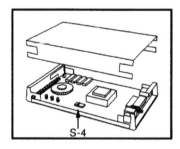

Push the code switch S-4 to
the right.

Figure 7.10   Multimodal output from the WIP system. (Courtesy of Elizabeth André.)

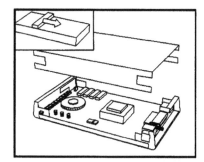

Figure 7.11 Graphics-only output from the WIP system. (Courtesy of Elizabeth André.)

At the time of writing, the automatic generation of multimodal documents constitutes one of the most exciting areas of research in NLG. Research focuses on issues such as the following:

- Which types of information are best communicated textually, and which are best communicated graphically?
- What are the underlying similarities and differences between text and graphics as communication media?
- How can we combine the two in a way which produces truly integrated documents?

7.3.1 The Automatic Generation of Graphical Objects

Considerable research has been carried out in computer graphics to develop systems which automatically create information-conveying graphics. Given a chunk of information that needs to be communicated to the user, or a communicative goal that needs to be satisfied, such systems automatically create appropriate pictures, diagrams, maps, and so on to convey this information. Some results are as follows:

Data Graphics. One of the most common uses of graphics is to display a set of data values. Commonly used techniques for doing this include X–Y plots, bar charts, and scatter plots. Designing an appropriate graphic – i.e., choosing the general type

> Push the code switch S-4 to the right. The code switch is located in front of the transformer.

Figure 7.12 Text-only output from the WIP system. (Courtesy of Elizabeth André.)

of graphic, then determining the most appropriate scale, assignment of axes, and so on – for a particular data set can be a difficult task. Ultimately the choices should be driven by a knowledge of the characteristics of the human visual system, since at the end of the day this is what will determine what works best. In the interim, a substitute in those areas where there is a lack of strong psychological findings are design guidelines proposed by human experts, such as Tufte (1983, 1990) and Bertin (1983); this approach was used, for example, in APT (Mackinlay, 1986).

Node-Link Diagrams. Another common type of graphic is a series of shapes (most often boxes or circles) connected by arrows; examples include entity-relationship diagrams and PERT charts. Creating a good node-link diagram can again be a difficult task, and the research community does not yet have a thorough understanding of what makes such diagrams effective and useful. The best studied aspect of this task is ensuring that diagrams satisfy general aesthetic criteria, such as having as few edge crossings as possible; a popular algorithm based on such criteria is described by Sugiyama, Tagawa, and Toda (1981). However, it is also important to ensure that diagrams conform to the conventions of the target genre (Petre, 1995; Reiter, 1995b).

Pictures and Illustrations. Producing an image of what an object looks like from a digitally-represented model of the object is a well-studied problem, which is discussed in most graphics textbooks. Some research systems – for example, IBIS (Seligmann and Feiner, 1991) – have investigated ways of automatically enhancing images with arrows, highlighting, cut-out views, and all the other techniques that human graphics designers routinely use.

There is, then, a body of work which can help us automatically create a graphical object to express a given set of data. Within the context of natural language generation, the main issues are how we choose between graphical and linguistic representations of information, and how the two forms can best be integrated.

7.3.2   Choosing a Medium

A Chinese proverb says that one picture is worth more than ten thousand words. This is often true; in other cases, however, words can communicate information more effectively than graphics. We do not know all the answers as to when graphics are better than words or vice versa, but it is clear that the following questions are important in determining which form of presentation is most appropriate:

- What kind of information is being communicated?
- How much expertise does the user have?
- Does the delivery medium or user population impose any constraints?

The process of making the required choices here is known in the literature as the MEDIA ALLOCATION problem.

Information Type

Graphics is a very powerful way of communicating some types of information. For instance, in many cases the best way of telling a user where a component of a machine is located is to show a picture with the component highlighted in some way rather than to describe the location textually; for this reason Figure 7.10 is probably better than Figure 7.12. Similarly, the best way to communicate a set of numeric data values (how much each department in an organisation spent last year, for example) is usually via a chart or table, not via words. On the other hand, some types of information seem better communicated textually; for example, the purpose of a component, or a description of special circumstances which forced a department to overspend its budget, is often best expressed in words.

It is difficult to make a precise characterisation of what kind of information is best communicated textually and what kind is best communicated graphically, although in a very rough sense it seems that graphics is often better at communicating concrete 'who', 'what', and 'where' information than abstract 'how' or 'why' information. Graphics is also probably better at communicating a large number of related and structurally similar facts (such as the interdependencies between subtasks) than a large number of diverse facts (such as the type of information found in a secondary-school yearbook).

An interesting point made by Stenning and Oberlander (1995) is that graphical representations sometimes do not make clear what information is essential and what is not. For example, if we use a set of pictures or an animation to show a user how to fix a flat tire on a bicycle, she might not realise that it is not necessary to stand exactly where the person in the picture is standing. If this kind of confusion is undesirable, it may be best to use text instead of (or in addition to) graphics.

The best way of communicating information in documents is undoubtedly to combine text and graphics, using each medium where it is most effective; this indeed is what happens in many human-written documents. Unfortunately, we cannot yet say in precise terms how to do this in an automatic document generation system.

Degree of User Expertise

Another factor in determining whether text or graphics should be used is the ability of the user to decipher the conventions of the form of expression being used. Speakers of a natural language possess a tremendous amount of knowledge of their language, including a vocabulary of tens of thousands of words, plus a very rich set of syntactic, semantic, and pragmatic rules for producing and interpreting sentences made up of these words. This knowledge represents an immense base of shared conventions that make communication possible. The language of graphics, on the other hand, is not so conventionalised. There are, of course, some graphical conventions that are widely shared. The layperson may know the meaning of a few hundred traffic signs and be aware of a few rules of interpretation that are broadly applicable in reading graphical representations (for example, if two objects are linked with an edge, they are related in some fashion). However, graphical conventions are often specific to the needs of particular user groups, and this may make graphical representations more appropriate for experts.

For example, some document users may be a little confused by the graphic in Figure 7.11. It may not be apparent that the inset in the top-left corner encodes an instruction to push the switch. If there is reason to suspect that such confusion may be present, it would be better to describe the action textually, as is done in Figure 7.10. However, for document users who are accustomed to this particular graphical convention, the presentation in Figure 7.11 may be quite adequate. Another example, from Petre (1995), is that experienced engineers use a rich set of conventions to interpret circuit diagrams; for example, bistable flip-flops are usually drawn as two vertically aligned NAND gates. This helps experienced engineers interpret diagrams; an experienced engineer can recognise a bistable flip-flop represented by means of this convention without needing to trace out the interconnection wiring between the two gates. Circuit diagrams are less useful for novices who have not learned these conventions.

In general terms, because the conventions for interpretation of linguistic material are widely shared, they do not need to be spelled out; in the case of graphics, however, the rules of interpretation may need to be specified explicitly. Indeed, Mittal et al. (1998) point out that even for documents which primarily communicate information graphically, it may be useful to have an NLG system generate explanatory text captions for the graphics, especially if the user is not familiar with the graphical presentations used in the document.

The Delivery Medium

Finally, an important real-world influence on the choice of text or graphics in many applications is the limitations of the delivery mechanism or particular characteristics of the user population. For example, it is not possible to use graphical representations if the document is being delivered aurally or via telex, and it may not be desirable to use graphical elements if the document is being delivered on a slow network link. However, text may not be practical if the user population is a worldwide group which has no language in common or consists of small children with a limited knowledge of language. Thus, returning to the examples at the beginning of this section, while in principle Figure 7.10 is best, something like the content of Figure 7.12 should be used if the instructions are delivered by telephone (through a help desk, for example), while Figure 7.11 might be best if the instructions are going to be distributed around the world to people who speak different languages.

From a practical perspective, perhaps one of the simplest and best ways of determining what information to communicate textually and what to communicate graphically is to study documents produced by human experts. If a certain piece of information is traditionally presented using one mode rather than the other, then this may constitute an argument for having a computer document generation system do the same. Of course, the traditional wisdom has to be balanced against the benefits of the opportunities afforded by new technology. In some cases, human-authored documents may not use graphical elements simply because of the expense of creating them by hand.

7.3.3 Commonalities between Text and Graphics

An interesting theoretical issue is how similar automatic text generation is to automatic graphics generation. Are these fundamentally different processes, or are there common underlying principles that apply to all attempts to communicate information to people, regardless of the media used?

Many kinds of similarities have been proposed in the research literature. For example, it has been suggested that text and graphics generation systems could use similar content determination systems (Feiner and McKeown, 1990; Roth and Hefley, 1993; Wahlster et al., 1993). The heart of content determination is determining what information is appropriate and relevant and should therefore be communicated; this is true regardless of whether the information is being communicated by text, speech, a formal language, graphics, animation, or any other means.

Although this hypothesis seems plausible, there is currently insufficient evidence to evaluate it. A few research systems which produce documents that contain both text and graphics have used similar content planning techniques for both the textual and graphical components of the document (Feiner and McKeown, 1990; Wahlster et al., 1993). If we compare systems which generate only graphics with those which generate only text, however, it can be difficult to find similarities other than in very general terms (for example, good advice in both media is to study documents produced by human experts). This may partially be due to the fact that NLG systems and systems which generate graphics are usually used to communicate different kinds of information.

Researchers have also pointed out that some phenomena which have been studied in linguistics seem to have analogues in graphics; some aspects are discussed below.

Conversational Implicature. People make inferences from the way in which a piece of information is communicated, as well as the actual content (Grice, 1975). For example, if someone says *Mrs Jones made a series of sounds approximating the score of Home Sweet Home*, most hearers will assume what Mrs Jones did could not truthfully be described as singing. If this were the case, then the speaker would have simply said *Mrs Jones sang Home Sweet Home*. This phenomenon is called CONVERSATIONAL IMPLICATURE, and has been extensively discussed in the linguistics literature. Marks and Reiter (1990) have suggested that similar inferences occur with graphics. For example, if someone draws a diagram of a computer network with all servers except one vertically aligned, most viewers will assume that there must be something different about the unaligned server.

Sublanguages. Texts frequently must conform to the rules of a particular genre. As discussed above, conventions are very strong in diagram genres as well (Petre, 1995; Reiter, 1995b). There is nothing in principle wrong with drawing a flip-flop with horizontally aligned gates instead of vertically aligned gates, but a diagram drawn in this way will be more difficult for people to understand – especially experts who have already internalised the interpretation conventions.

Structuring. Texts are hierarchically structured into sentences, paragraphs, sections, chapters, and so on. A textual document consisting of a single paragraph with several hundred sentences would not be easy to comprehend. Similarly, complex diagrams with several hundred elements can be difficult to understand, and some experts recommend producing a hierarchically structured set of small diagrams instead of one large diagram (Martin, 1987).

Discourse Relations. André and Rist (1994a) argue that RST-like discourse relations can also be applied to graphics. For instance, Figure 7.13 shows the document plan behind the output shown in Figure 7.10; here, the graphic as a whole is linked by an **Enable** relation to the text, and within the graphic the general image of the modem is linked by a **Provide-Background** relation to the image of the switch.

In summary, researchers have investigated applying a wide variety of ideas developed within linguistics to the domain of graphics. Less work has been done, however, on the application of ideas from graphics generation to NLG.

7.3.4   *Implementing Text and Graphics Integration*

Ideally, a computerised document generation system should be able to generate documents which contain both text and graphics, using each medium to its best advantage. There are different ways in which the textual and graphical components of such systems can be combined, and these different architectures offer different opportunities for media allocation:

Minimal Integration. In a system where there is minimal integration of the textual and graphical generation processes, the overall communicative goal is divided by a human analyst into textual and graphical components, and generators are built

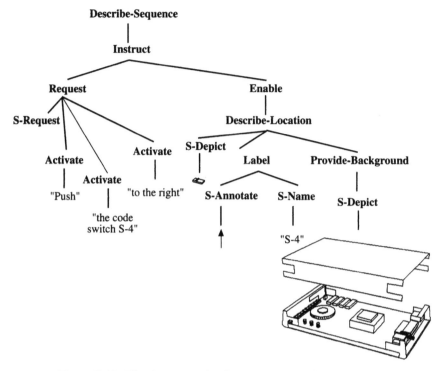

Figure 7.13 The document plan for the output in Figure 7.10. (Courtesy of Elizabeth André.)

for each. There is no operational integration between the text generator and the graphics generator. For example, an analyst might design a multimodal version of WEATHERREPORTER by combining the existing text generator (without changing it in any way) with a graphics generator that produces a graph of temperature and rainfall over the month in question; to all intents and purposes we then simply have two different modalities being used quite independently.

Integrated Content Planning. In a system where content planning is integrated, a common content planner will decide what information needs to be communicated, and then call text and graphics generators to convey the relevant parts of this information. The media allocation is typically carried out using rules such as those discussed above. Once the information has been dispatched to either generator, the text and graphics generators do not interact with each other. For example, a multimodal version of IDAS (see Section 1.3.3) might use graphics to convey all location information (by generating a picture of the machine with appropriate labelled arrows), and text to communicate the specific actions the user is requested to carry out.

Integrated Text and Graphics. A system of this kind integrates the textual and graphical representations of information at a very fine-grained level. For example, the text might include referring expressions that refer to properties of the graphical presentation; see André and Rist (1994b) for a discussion of such a model.

Systems which involve only minimal integration of text and graphics are of course the simplest kind to construct. The other types of integration require changes to the underlying algorithms that might otherwise have been used by the separate components. Just as importantly, it may be necessary to change representations and the domain models and message definitions. For example, the procedure described in Section 4.2 for building domain and message models was based on analysing a corpus of target *texts*; but models built by analysing texts are unlikely to be appropriate for producing graphics. Similarly, the document plan representation described in Section 3.4 is unlikely to be suitable for generating multimodal documents. Because this field is so new, it is difficult to make general comments about how algorithms, representations, and methodologies should be adapted to produce multimodal documents. At this point in time, there is much to be learned simply by studying existing multimodal systems; references to a number of these are provided in Section 7.6.

7.4   Hypertext

So far our discussion has focussed on characteristics of document generation that do not explicitly take account of whether the document will be presented on-line or on paper. When we look specifically at on-line document generation, a number of other opportunities open up. The on-line environment makes it possible to increase the kinds of media used in a document, so that, for example, we can incorporate audio, video, and other kinds of animation. Explorations of what is possible have only barely begun; here, we focus only on one aspect of on-line documents, this being the scope for creating hypertext documents rather than simple linear documents.

7.4.1   Hypertext and Its Uses

Hypertext Defined

A hypertext document is an on-line document that can be read in a nonlinear fashion by virtue of links within the document which allow the reader to jump from one place to another at the click of a mouse. Although the basic idea of hypertext has been around for some time, it is only in recent years with the explosion of interest in the World Wide Web that hypertext has become a part of everyday life for many people. There are other, more complex, forms of hypertext beyond what is found on the World Wide Web; however, we will focus here on hypertext in the World Wide Web context since this is where we expect to see most hypertext applications of NLG technology in the next decade.

A typical hypertext contains mouse-sensitive regions – either linguistic units such as words or phrases, or graphical elements – which the user can click on. The result of clicking on one of these ANCHORS is that the user is transported to somewhere else: either to another document or to somewhere else in the current document. Crucially, the new document may not exist prior to the user's mouse click. The result of clicking can be the invocation of a program whose results are returned for the user to view. It is this capability that Web-based NLG systems capitalise upon.

One of the most straightforward uses of hypertext is to allow ease of access to related documents; this is achieved by means of what we will call REFERENCE LINKS. On the World Wide Web, most hypertext links are probably of this kind; it is precisely this characteristic that gives the World Wide Web its name. Reference links may appear interwoven into the text on a page or may be collected together at a specific location on the page, perhaps along the top or bottom of the displayed material.

A variant of the reference link which is popular in on-line help systems is the GLOSSARY LINK, which pops up a definition of a term or a short explanatory note when clicked. The information viewed as a result of clicking on a glossary link typically does not contain further links.

Hypertext links may also be used to assist in navigating the structure of a complex document. For example, if a document contains more than one screenful of information, it may be useful to initially show the user an outline that lists the document's sections and let the user request which sections to read by clicking on the appropriate section heading. The requested section may exist as a separate document, or it may exist at a specific location within the current document. In some hypertext systems, the outline can be expanded to incorporate the requested section in-line.

Hypertext as Dialogue

If an NLG system produces output which is read on-line, it is usually fairly straightforward to add some hypertext links to this output. Such links can significantly increase the usefulness of the generated text, making it much easier for the user to quickly access related documents. Indeed, in the late 1990s many users expect that on-line documents will contain hypertext links, and may be disappointed by on-line texts which do not contain such links.

As noted above, clicking on a link may not cause display of a preexisting document; instead, it may cause invocation of a program whose results are then displayed on the screen. For example, all of the hypertext links shown in Figure 7.1 cause new invocations of the NLG system which then generates the requested documents: clicking on Crocodile will cause the generation and display of a document about crocodiles, and clicking on Chinese Alligator will cause the generation and display of a document about Chinese alligators.

Sometimes the term DYNAMIC HYPERTEXT is used for NLG systems where the output consists of hypertext nodes that are created dynamically, and hence can be customised according to a user model, the discourse history, and other contextual factors. Dynamic hypertext is a fairly recent development, and our understanding of the best way to use this medium is still evolving.

Within work on NLG, hypertext can be used to support a dialogue between the user and the computer. Under this view, hypertext links are seen not as links to documents, but rather as questions or requests that the user can make, and to which the system will respond. Hypertext allows more limited interaction than the alternative of allowing users to issue natural language queries and requests. However, a reliable hypertextual interface is easier to implement than a natural language query interface; and more important, it makes clear to the user what questions can be dealt with by the system at any given point.

The notion of hypertext as dialogue is present in both IDAS and PEBA. IDAS views every hypertext click as a user request or question. Of all hypertextual NLG systems constructed to date, Moore's (1994) PEA system supports the most complex dialogue-like interactions: for example, the system allows users to ask why a particular piece of information has been communicated, or to request further explanation of a point not understood.

Whether this view of hypertext will gain widespread acceptance remains an open question. The most common metaphor for hypertext on the Web is that of browsing through an information space populated by documents; this has somewhat different connotations from a view of hypertext as a conversation with an information-providing entity. For example, there is the subtle question of what should happen when a user clicks a second time on a link that has been clicked on before. In the conception of hypertext as a device for exploring an information space, clicking on a link should bring up the linked document, and exactly the same document should appear every time the link is clicked. In the conception of hypertext as a conversational medium, clicking on a link for a second time could be construed as asking a question a second time, and there is no reason why the response should be the same on both occasions. Indeed, a helpful system should probably make the second response more detailed, since one reason for asking a question again is because the original response was not understood. The ability to offer a different answer the second time around comes naturally to an NLG system, since typically answers will be generated in a context that includes a dynamically-updated discourse model; however, this may not be what the user expects. This and related issues are discussed in Dale et al. (1999).

7.4.2   Implementing Hypertext-based NLG Systems

Adding hypertextual properties to the documents created by an NLG system impacts on a number of aspects of our architecture.

Document Planning

Hypertext links are essentially about the inclusion of content into a document, even if that content is a mouse click away from the generated document itself. Given this, the document planner should be responsible for specifying the inclusion of hypertext links. There may be some exceptions to this, as we will discuss below: For some links, the document planner may not know that a link is required, since its inclusion may depend on linguistic content only determined at a later stage in the generation process.

To build an NLG system which generates hypertexts, we need, then, to extend the basic document planning mechanism. For example, a rule-based document planner could have rules for adding hypertext links as well as specifying document content; this is what is done in the IDAS system. A plan-based system can reason about what hypertext links might be useful to the user, as is done in PEA (Moore, 1994). A schema-based system can have basic operations for adding links as well as adding clauses; this is what happens in PEBA. In each case, the process of adding a link is treated analogously to that of adding a clause, and similar design decisions need to be made about whether the reasoning involved should be shallow or deep, whether user models should be taken into account, and so on.

Links should be added in a way which makes the hypertext network as a whole comprehensible to the user, so that he or she can develop a good mental model of what information is present in the network and how the network can be navigated. In very general terms, it is often better to have a simple and predictable set of links than a complex and unpredictable set, even if the former requires the user to perform more mouse clicks; and it is important to be wary of adding too many links just because the technology makes it possible. One suggestion made by Reiter et al. (1995) is to regard the network as a QUESTION SPACE which users can traverse. In the IDAS system, each node answers a specific question about a specific entity, and users can move from a node to other questions about the same object, or to questions about related objects (such as subcomponents of the current object). This is a fairly simple navigation model, but it is one that seems quite comprehensible to users.

Another approach to links is to treat them as ways of presenting optional information. If the document planner is unsure about whether or not a piece of information should be included, it can include a link to a node giving this information and include directly in the current node only that information which is known to be important. This approach may have the disadvantage of making the network as a whole less understandable and predictable, but is well suited to a view of hypertext as dialogue, as discussed above; under that view, links to optional information can be seen as natural elaboration questions which a user might want to ask. This model also lessens the burden of choice making on the NLG system; the user can decide what information is relevant and important, instead of the system having to make these decisions (Levine et al., 1991).

Microplanning

The presence of some links may depend on specific lexical content in the generated text. Since, in our architecture, the lexical content is not determined until we reach the microplanning stage, these links can be added only at that point. This is most obvious in the case of glossary links: If a technical term is used, then the microplanner may have the responsibility for adding a link to a glossary item that explains that term. The microplanner may also take responsibility for adding links to descriptions of entities referred to in the text if the content of the link depends on the content of the description.

One important design choice in microplanning in a hypertext environment is the question of how to model discourses for the purpose of generating referring expressions. The generation of referring expressions requires a discourse model which lists those objects that have already been mentioned in the text. In a hypertext system, it is unclear whether the discourse model should include objects mentioned in previously visited nodes. On the one hand, if the user has read the previous nodes, then presumably objects mentioned in these nodes are salient for the user and hence should be represented in the discourse model. However, intuition suggests that users frequently only partially read or skim information presented on-screen, and so it may not be appropriate to automatically add mentioned entities to the discourse model. Of course, in the absence of eye-tracking devices being built into terminals, there is no easy way to determine which parts of a displayed screen a user has read. Given this, it may be best to adopt a cautious strategy and assume that the previous nodes have not been read; this then has the consequence, of course, that subsequent texts may be more redundant than they need to be.

To take a concrete example of this issue, a fairly plausible strategy for referring expression generation would refer to a well-known former Prime Minister of the UK by means of the expression *Prime Minister Margaret Thatcher* for the initial reference and by means of the form *Thatcher* in subsequent references. In a hypertext system, we have to decide whether this means that the expression *Prime Minister Margaret Thatcher* should be used for the first reference to this person in *every* node which refers to her, or whether it means that *Prime Minister Margaret Thatcher* should only be used in the *first* node visited which refers to her. In principle the 'right' answer to this question may depend on how thoroughly the user has read the first node which mentioned Thatcher, but this is information that the NLG system does not have.

Surface Realisation

The realiser's job is a simple one here. If the phrase specification language being used supports hypertext annotations, then the realiser's job is to map these into the appropriate annotations for the hypertext delivery system being used. For the World Wide Web, of course, this will be HTML.

One choice the realiser will have to make is how many words to associate with an anchor (hypertext link). For instance, consider the anchor that appears as Crocodylidae Family in the PEBA output shown in Figure 7.1. This is only one possible anchor of a number that could have been chosen. Other alternatives are Crocodylidae and the Crocodylidea Family. There is no straightforward answer as to which choice is best, although different solutions may carry different connotations.

7.5   Speech Output

So far in this chapter we have considered some of the questions that arise when we look at the generation of what we might call VISIBLE LANGUAGE. We should not forget, of course, that in many contexts the most appropriate means of delivery may be speech; so in this section we turn to the generation of spoken language.

7.5.1   *The Benefits of Speech Output*

There are a number of situations where the delivery of information via speech is to be preferred over delivery via text. Spoken output is especially useful in cases where users are unable or unwilling to read written text on a computer monitor or other display device. This is the case, for example, in telephone-based information systems, such as the special information numbers that people can call to obtain weather forecasts, sports results, or airline scheduling updates. It is also useful in 'eyes-busy' situations where the user cannot look at a display screen because of having to look elsewhere, as might be the case when a doctor is examining a patient or a driver is being provided with route information via a Global Positioning System (GPS) device. Last but not least, spoken output is essential for users who are unable to read because of some disability.

Some users may also prefer spoken output, even if they are able to look at a monitor. For example, people who are not experienced computer users may in some cases feel more comfortable hearing information presented orally, because that is what they are used to. Also, speech may be a natural mode of communication in some computer games, in part because speech can be inflected to indicate emotional states such as excitement.

Software for generating spoken output from text, called SPEECH SYNTHESIS software, has improved significantly in recent years, and there now are a number of packages available both on the market and as free downloadable software from a number of research institutions. Generally speaking, the quality of synthesised speech is such that it is most intelligible in short segments. A single synthesised

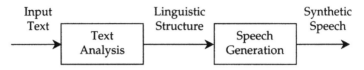

Figure 7.14   The architecture of a text-to-speech system.

sentence is usually much easier to understand than a segment of spoken text several paragraphs in length. As synthesis technology advances, however, the intelligibility of longer speech segments is improving.

Most applications which use speech synthesis to generate spoken output do not currently use NLG techniques. However, as well as improving the appropriateness of what is said, NLG techniques also hold promise for improving the quality of synthesised speech, as we will discuss below; accordingly, there is growing interest among researchers in combining NLG with speech synthesis technology.

7.5.2   Text-to-Speech Systems

To understand the issues here, we first require a basic understanding of how existing text-to-speech (TTS) systems work. Figure 7.14 shows a simple diagram of the component functionality of most TTS systems. The important point to note here is that, before synthesising speech from an input text stream, a TTS system first typically carries out an analysis of the input text. This analysis is required in order to determine some important aspects of the text that have a bearing on how the text should be spoken. The most obvious of these is that different sentence forms have different INTONATION PATTERNS, as is easily demonstrated by comparing how the following two sentences sound when spoken naturally:

(7.6)   a. John can open the door.
         b. Can John open the door?

Here, the second sentence is typically spoken with a rising intonation at the end; this is generally true of polar (*yes/no*) questions. Declarative sentence forms, exemplified by the first sentence above, are typically spoken with a falling intonation at the end – although as we will see below, in reality the situation is more complex than this. In order to speak a sentence appropriately, then, a TTS system must first work out what kind of sentence it is. This is relatively straightforward in the above case, since all it requires is identification of the final punctuation mark; however, there are more complex aspects of linguistic analysis that a TTS system needs to perform.

Text Normalisation

Speaking a text is not just a matter of sending the words in that text to be spoken, one at a time, to a speech-synthesising device: Some textual elements need to be converted into something speakable. So, for example, any expressions involving numbers or special characters are spoken in ways that are not apparent from the linguistic form itself. Such forms have to be NORMALISED, so that, for example, *28/3/98* may be spoken as *the twenty-eighth of March nineteen ninety eight*, and *80kph* may be spoken as *eighty kilometers an hour*. In a TTS system, these phenomena are generally dealt with by means of special-case pronunciation rules.

Homograph Disambiguation

Natural languages contain HOMOGRAPHS: words which are spelled the same but are spoken differently, depending upon their part of speech or their meaning. Compare, for example, the spoken form of the word *lives* in the following two sentences:

(7.7)   a. John lives in Edinburgh.
         b. A cat has nine lives.

A text-to-speech system has to work out which form of the word is intended. This is generally done by carrying out some analysis of the input string in order to assign part-of-speech tags, since in many cases homographs are distinguished by part of speech: Typically the noun and verb instances of a homograph will be pronounced differently. There are cases, however, where the part of speech is the same for both instances, as in the case of words like *bow* in the following pair of sentences:

(7.8)   a. At the end of the performance, John took a bow.
         b. John shot the target with a bow and arrow.

Homograph disambiguation is not entirely distinct from text normalisation: for example, the abbreviation *St.* is ambiguous as to whether it should be pronounced *Street* or *Saint*.

Prosody Assignment

This is the most complicated aspect of generating synthesised speech. Prosody is the term used to cover the pitch, speed, and volume with which syllables, words, phrases, and sentences are spoken. Our example of the two sentence types above is one case where prosody plays a role, but the assignment of prosody is made more complex by the fact that real utterances tend to break down into a number of INTONATION UNITS, each requiring appropriate prosody to be applied. Consider how the following sentences sound when spoken naturally:

(7.9)   a. When I came in from the cold, the spy I saw on the floor was not the
            person I had spoken to on the phone.
         b. John, not a good archer at the best of times, only managed to hit the
            target once – not with *every* shot, which is what he claimed he could do.

Each sentence breaks down into a number of intonation units or intonational
phrases, with the overall pronunciation of the sentence taking on a rhythmic structure. These intonation units can sometimes be identified by looking for punctuation
marks such as commas; but in the general case there may be no such surface clues,
and the intonation may be related to syntactic structure in subtle ways which are
still the subject of ongoing research. This means that for a TTS system to produce
good prosody, it has to carry out quite sophisticated analysis of the text.

The basic point, then, is that TTS systems need some knowledge of the structure
and content of the text to be spoken if they are to do a good job of speaking the text.
Most TTS systems provide some mechanism for augmenting the bare text stream
with additional information that can be used to improve the output quality, either
by overriding the results of analysis the TTS system might perform or by giving
the system information that it would not be able to work out for itself. Figure 7.15
shows some of the annotations provided by SABLE, a recent attempt to provide
a standard language for speech synthesis markup.[4] Each tag here is interpreted
appropriately by the TTS system.

Phenomenon	Example
Emphasis	`The leaders of <EMPH>Denmark</EMPH> and` `<EMPH>India</EMPH> meet on Friday.`
Breaks	`Without style, <BREAK LEVEL="large"> Grace` `and I are in trouble.`

Pitch change	`Without his penguin, <PITCH BASE="-20\%">`
	 `which he left at home,</PITCH> he could not`
	 `enter the restaurant.`

Pronunciation	`<PRON SUB="tomahto">tomato</PRON>`

Special processing	`At <SAYAS MODE="time">2pm</SAYAS> on`
	 `<SAYAS MODE="date" MODETYPE="YM">98/3`
	 `</SAYAS> Mike will send <SAYAS`
	 `MODE="currency">$4000</SAYAS> to <SAYAS`
	 `MODE="net" MODETYPE="email">me@acme.com`
	 `</SAYAS>.`

Figure 7.15   SABLE mark-ups for controlling speech synthesis.

---

[4] All examples here are drawn from the SABLE version 0.1 specification; information about
the SABLE specification can be found at `http://www.cstr.ed.ac.uk/projects/`
`sable.html`.

Concept-to-Speech

As we have seen, text-to-speech systems effectively reverse engineer their input in order to determine information they need to produce appropriate output. The key problem is that, given the current state of the art in natural language analysis, this process provides insufficient knowledge about the sources of constraints on intonation, with the result that it is difficult to determine the appropriate assignment of intonation. Ultimately, syntactic analysis – which itself is at the bounds of current NL analysis capabilities where unrestricted text is concerned – is not sufficient. Intonation is more than a reflection of the surface syntactic structure of the text, and in the final analysis depends on communicative goals underlying the utterance.

Of course, this is information that we can reasonably expect an NLG system to already be capable of providing: an NLG system will know which particular word sense is intended when a homograph is used, it will know what the type and the structure of a sentence is, and, most importantly, it will know why it is using a particular utterance. It makes sense, then, to consider linking an NLG system to a TTS system in such a way that the need for analysis of the input stream by the TTS system is removed. By doing this, we provide an input to the speech synthesis process that is richer than that normally assumed by TTS systems; accordingly, this approach is sometimes referred to as CONCEPT-TO-SPEECH.

To see the benefits of having access to this rich information source, consider the utterance *John washed the dog*. This can be uttered as a response to each of the following questions, but the intonation used in uttering this response will vary depending on the question:

(7.10)   a. What did John wash?
         b. Who washed the dog?

Although the one sentence serves as a response to each of the two questions, in each case the sentence will carry a different stress pattern in order to mark the information that is NEW. In the case of the first question, the noun phrase *the dog* carries this new information whereas in the case of the second question it is the noun phrase *John* that carries the new information. An NLG system, since it has deliberately constructed the sentence in order to satisfy the request for information, will know what information is given in the context and what is new, and can assign appropriate intonation in line with this. Similarly, provided we have an appropriate theory that correlates syntactic structure with prosodic structure, an NLG system will know where the appropriate intonation boundaries should fall in a longer utterance.

7.5.3   *Implementing Concept-to-Speech*

If we want to speech-enable an NLG system in a richer way than simply applying a TTS system to the NLG system's output, there are two general issues we need to address:

- How can the appropriate prosodic and intonational annotations described above be produced?
- How should the content, structure, and style of the text be modified to reflect that fact that it will be spoken instead of read?

We can review how these questions impact on each of the components of our NLG architecture as follows.

Document Planning

First of all, it seems reasonable to suppose that a document generated for spoken presentation may have a different content and structure from a document generated for visual presentation. Speech and writing are very different forms of language, and indeed the kinds of uses to which each are put vary considerably: There are linguistic acts which would make little sense, or seem very odd, if transplanted from one medium to the other. The document planner may therefore need to adopt different strategies for both content determination and document structuring, depending upon the intended output modality. For any given domain of application, what is required here is best determined by a careful empirical analysis of information provision in that domain.

As a simple example, the document planner may need to apply different considerations with regard to the length of the generated output: because speech takes time to utter and cannot be skimmed by the recipient in the way that text can, the document planner may have to limit the size of spoken documents; in contrast, length considerations are probably less of an issue in written text. More speculatively, it may be appropriate to repeat information more often in spoken documents than in written text, because there is no correlate in the spoken form of the scope for rereading provided by the written form.

Some overall characteristics of the spoken output, such as speed of talking and the emotional attitude expressed in the speech, are probably best determined within the document planning component, since these are likely to be based on the system's communicative goals and known characteristics of the user.

One possible impact of length limitations and the difficulty of revisiting already uttered text is that dialogue may be more important in spoken systems than in text-based systems. Dialogue provides a natural way for users to 'home in' on the information they need, or to request that a previous utterance be repeated or clarified.

Microplanning

Since the microplanner is responsible for lexicalisation, it is the appropriate place to include information that will allow the later stages of the process to ensure that words are pronounced properly. In the context of an NLG system, there would seem to be little need for a text normalisation stage. Instead, the microplanner should build lexicogrammatical constructions that are already in a form suitable for speaking. Since the microplanner also determines the overall sentential structures to be used, it should ensure that the phrase specifications constructed clearly indicate the information structural properties of the utterance, so that these can be mapped into appropriate prosodic contours by the realisation process.

From a stylistic perspective, spoken text is clearly different from written text (see Halliday, 1985b, for a detailed discussion of this question). In the context of NLG systems, McKeown et al. (1997) suggest that, among other things, spoken output should be short, syntactically simple, and relatively informal. Further research is needed to better understand how to interpret these criteria, especially as they may conflict. For example, as McKeown et al. point out, brevity may conflict with syntactic simplicity.

Surface Realisation

The function of the realiser is to map distinctions at the level of meaning – here including aspects of information structuring – into prosodic distinctions. The relevant information will almost all have been determined by earlier stages of processing, although where the realiser has some latitude with respect to the choice of syntactic constructions, it also then needs to know enough about prosody to be able to annotate these structures appropriately. For our purposes, it is reasonable to assume that the role of the realiser is to take the information specified in the input phrase specification and to build an output stream that includes mark-up annotations along the lines of that shown in Figure 7.15; some of the information provided here replaces the punctuation symbols that the realiser would insert in the case of written output.

7.6   Further Reading

In this chapter we have covered a very broad range of research issues in a relatively small space, and so we have only been able to scratch the surface of many of the issues involved. We provide here some pointers to the relevant literature for the interested reader who wants to pursue these topics further.

While many papers have been published on the individual topics of typography, hypertext generation, the integration of text and graphics, and speech generation, very little has been published on integrating all these aspects into a general architecture for document generation. Probably the most advanced work on generating rich multimodal documents has been carried out at the DFKI in Saarbrücken and at Columbia University; examples of systems built at these laboratories include COMET (Feiner and McKeown, 1990), WIP (Wahlster et al., 1993), PPP (Rist, André, and Müller, 1997), and MAGIC (McKeown et al., 1997).

Relatively little has been published on typographic issues in NLG, with the work by Hovy and Arens (1991) and Dale (1992b) being two exceptions. There is, however, a rich literature aimed at human writers and document designers on the best use of typefaces, list structures, boxes, and so forth; this literature may suggest rules which can be incorporated into an NLG system. Good starting points are books giving writing advice to students, such as that by Horner (1998). The *Chicago Manual of Style* (University of Chicago Press, 1993) provides an exhaustive description of typographic conventions in English.

There is a very large general literature on computer graphics. A standard introductory textbook to this area is by Foley et al. (1994). Petre (1995) points out some of the problems with graphics and emphasises that graphical representations are often less effective than people believe them to be. Two of the best known systems which generate documents that contain both text and graphics are WIP (Wahlster et al., 1993) and COMET (Feiner and McKeown, 1990). A useful collection edited by Maybury (1993) contains many papers that discuss the integration of text and graphics, including papers by Roth and Hefley (1993) on media choice, and André and Rist (1993) on integrated content determination for multimodal documents. Mittal et al. (1998) present an interesting system which generates explanatory captions for a data graphic.

Because of the popularity of the Web, any reasonable bookstore will probably have numerous books on hypertext, with titles like *The Complete Idiot's Guide to Creating an HTML Web Page* (McFedries, 1997). A good introduction to hypertext from a more academic perspective is the chapter on hypermedia and the Web in Shneiderman's (1998) textbook on user interfaces. A good up-to-date source of recent research papers on hypertext is the annual ACM Hypertext Conference. There is also a growing literature on dynamic hypertext and on how NLG systems can produce documents with this property; Knott et al. (1996) provide a useful review of much of this work. Milosavljevic, Tulloch, and Dale (1996) and Reiter et al. (1995) describe how hypertext is used in the PEBA and IDAS systems, respectively. As with typography, advice aimed at human hypertext authors can suggest rules for an NLG system; in addition to the previously mentioned sources, a useful Web-accessible document on writing effective hypertext is `http://www.ibm.com/ibm/hci/guidelines/guidelines`.

There is a general literature on speech synthesis; one textbook which covers this topic is Dutoit (1997). There are many companies which sell commercial speech-synthesis systems. Microsoft Research currently makes available for free its speech synthesis package; see `http://microsoft.com/iit` for details. Halliday (1985b) argues convincingly for speech and writing being viewed as quite distinct forms of language use. There is relatively little work on combining NLG with speech, since this is a very new area, but two systems which do this are DYD (van Deemter and Odijk, 1997) and MAGIC (McKeown et al., 1997); a recent workshop devoted to this topic is documented by Alter, Finkler, and Pirker (1997). Prevost's work (Prevost, 1996) on integrating intonation with categorial grammar shows how existing linguistic theories can be extended to allow the incorporation of prosody.

Appendix: NLG Systems Mentioned in This Book

In this appendix, we provide a tabular listing of every NLG system that is mentioned in this book. In each case we provide a brief description of what the system does and a pointer to a source in the literature where further information can be found. Systems are listed alphabetically by system name.

System	Description	Sources
ALETHGEN	Helps customer-service representatives write letters.	Coch (1996b)
COMET	Produces multimodal (text and graphics) instructions.	McKeown et al. (1990)
DYD	Generates spoken descriptions of music CDs.	van Deemter and Odijk (1997)
DRAFTER	Helps technical authors write documents in English and French.	Paris et al. (1995)
ECRAN	Generates descriptions of movies, using a model of the user's interests.	Geldof and van de Velde (1997)
EPICURE	Generates recipes.	Dale (1990)
FOG	Produces weather forecasts in French and English.	Goldberg, Driedger, and Kittredge (1994)
FUF	A syntactic realisation system, based on functional unification.	Elhadad (1989)
GRASSIC	An advanced mail-merge system which produces personalised asthma information leaflets.	Osman et al. (1994)
ICICLE	Teaches the syntax of written English to deaf people.	McCoy, Pennington, and Suri (1996)
IDAS	Generates on-line technical documentation from a knowledge base.	Reiter, Mellish, and Levine (1995)
IGEN	A system which allows feedback from later to earlier stages of the pipeline.	Rubinoff (1992)
JAPE	Creates jokes.	Binstead and Ritchie (1997)

(Continued)

System	Description	Sources
KAMP	Generates sophisticated referring expressions.	Appelt (1985)
KNIGHT	Explains complex biological phenomena.	Lester and Porter (1997)
KPML	A syntactic realisation system (the successor to PENMAN), based on systemic grammar.	Bateman (1997)
LFS	Generates summaries of statistical data, in English and French.	Iordanskaja et al. (1992)
MAGIC	Produces multimedia healthcare briefings.	McKeown et al. (1997)
MODELEXPLAINER	Produces textual descriptions of object-oriented software models.	Lavoie, Rambow, and Reiter (1997)
MUMBLE	Syntactic realisation system.	McDonald (1981)
NIGEL	System grammar of English, used in PENMAN and KPML.	Mann (1983)
PEA	A dialogue system which teaches students about a programming language.	Moore (1994)
PEBA	Produces Web pages that describe or compare animals, with embedded hypertext links.	Milosavljevic and Dale (1996)
PENMAN	A syntactic realisation system (the predecessor to KPML), based on systemic grammar.	Matthiessen and Bateman (1991)
PIGLET	Produces personalised explanations of information in a patient's medical record.	Cawsey, Binstead, and Jones (1995)
PLANDOC	Produces reports summarising the effects of simulated changes to a telephone network.	McKeown, Kukich, and Shaw (1994)
PPP	Creates an animated character which explains to a user how to perform various tasks, using a mixture of text, speech, and graphics.	André, Müller, and Rist (1996)
REALPRO	A syntactic realisation system, based on Meaning-Text Theory.	Lavoie and Rambow (1997)
STOP	Generates personalised smoking-cessation letters.	Reiter et al. (1999)
STREAK	Summarises what happened in a basketball game.	Robin and McKeown (1996)
SURGE	The English grammar used with FUF.	Elhadad and Robin (1997)
TEMSIS	Provides environmental information in French and German.	Busemann and Horacek (1998)
TAILOR	Tailors descriptions of objects for different users.	Paris (1988)
TEXT	Generates textual paraphrases of information held in a database.	McKeown (1985)
WIP	Produces multimodal (text and graphics) instructions.	Wahlster et al. (1993)

References

Adorni, G. and M. Zock, editors. 1996. *Trends in Natural Language Generation*. Lecture Notes in Computer Science. Springer, Berlin.

AECMA. 1986. A guide for the preparation of aircraft maintenance documentation in the international aerospace maintenance language. Available from BDC Publishing Services, Slack Lane, Derby, UK.

Allen, James. 1995. *Natural Language Understanding*. Benjamin Cummings, Redwood City, CA, second edition.

Allen, James and C. Raymond Perrault. 1980. Analyzing intention in utterances. *Artificial Intelligence*, 15:143–178.

Alter, Kai, Wolfgang Finkler, and Hannes Pirker, editors. 1997. *Proceedings of the ACL-1997 Workshop on Concept-to-Speech Generation*. Association for Computational Linguistics.

André, E., J. Müller, and T. Rist. 1996. The PPP Persona: A Multipurpose Animated Presentation Agent. In *Advanced Visual Interfaces*. ACM Press, pages 245–247.

André, Elizabeth and Thomas Rist. 1993. The design of illustrated documents as a planning task. In Mark Maybury, editor, *Intelligent Multimedia Interfaces*. AAAI Press.

André, Elizabeth and Thomas Rist. 1994a. Generating coherent presentations employing textual and visual material. *Artificial Intelligence Review*, 9:147–165.

André, Elizabeth and Thomas Rist. 1994b. Referring to world objects with text and pictures. In *Proceedings of the Fifteenth International Conference on Computational Linguistics (COLING-1994)*, pages 530–534.

Appelt, Doug. 1985. *Planning English Referring Expressions*. Cambridge University Press, New York.

Appelt, Douglas E. and Amichai Kronfeld. 1987. A computational model of referring. In *Proceedings of the Tenth International Joint Conference on Artificial Intelligence (IJCAI-87)*, volume 2, pages 640–647, Milan, Italy, August 23–28.

Arnold, D., L. Balkan, R. Lee Humphreys, S. Meijer, and L. Sadler. 1994. *Machine Translation: An Introductory Guide*. NCC Blackwell, Oxford, England.

Baecker, Ronald M. and William A. S. Buxton, editors. 1987. *Readings in Human-Computer Interaction*. Morgan Kaufmann, Los Altos, CA.

Barker, Richard. 1990. *Case Method: Entity-Relationship Modelling*. Addison-Wesley, Reading, MA.

Bateman, John. 1997. Enabling technology for multilingual natural language generation: The KPML development environment. *Natural Language Engineering*, 3:15–55.

Bateman, John, Robert Kasper, Johanna Moore, and Richard Whitney. 1990. A general organization of knowledge for natural language processing: The Penman upper model. Technical report, Information Sciences Institute, Marina del Rey, CA 90292.

Bateman, John, Christian Matthiessen, Keizo Nanri, and Licheng Zeng. 1991. The re-use of linguistic resources across languages in multilingual generation components. In *Proceedings of the 12th International Joint Conference on Artificial Intelligence (IJCAI-89)*, pages 966–971, Sydney, Australia.

Bertin, J. 1983. *Semiology of Graphics: Diagrams, Networks, Maps*. Translated by William Berg. University of Wisconsin Press, Madison.

Binstead, Kim and Graeme Ritchie. 1997. Computational rules for punning riddles. *Humor*, 10:25–76.

Booch, Grady. 1994. *Object-Oriented Analysis and Design with Applications*. Benjamin Cummings, Redwood City, CA, second edition.

Brachman, Ronald and James Schmolze. 1985. An overview of the KL-ONE knowledge representation system. *Cognitive Science*, 9:171–216.

Busemann, Stephan. 1996. Best-first surface realization. In *Proceedings of the Eighth International Workshop on Natural-Language Generation (INLG-1996)*, pages 101–110.

Busemann, Stephan and Helmut Horacek. 1998. A flexible shallow approach to text generation. In *Proceedings of the Ninth International Workshop on Natural Language Generation (INLG-1998)*, pages 238–247.

Carnap, Rudolf. 1947. *Meaning and Necessity*. University of Chicago Press, Chicago.

Cawsey, Alison, Kim Binstead, and Ray Jones. 1995. Personalised explanations for patient education. In *Proceedings of the Fifth European Workshop on Natural Language Generation*, pages 59–74.

Coch, José. 1996a. Evaluating and comparing three text production techniques. In *Proceedings of the Sixteenth International Conference on Computational Linguistics (COLING-1996)*.

Coch, José. 1996b. Overview of AlethGen. In *Proceedings of the Eighth International Workshop on Natural-Language Generation (INLG-1996) (Demonstrations and Posters)*, pages 25–28.

Cohen, Phil, Jerry Morgan, and Martha Pollack, editors. 1990. *Intentions in Communication*. MIT Press, Cambridge, MA.

Collins, Allan and Edward E Smith, editors. 1988. *Readings in Cognitive Science.* Morgan Kaufmann, Los Altos, CA.

Cruse, D. 1986. *Lexical Semantics.* Cambridge University Press, Cambridge.

Crystal, David. 1987. *The Cambridge Encyclopedia of Language.* Cambridge University Press, Cambridge.

Dale, Robert. 1990. Generating recipes: An overview of Epicure. In Dale, Mellish, and Zock (1990), pages 229–255.

Dale, Robert. 1992a. *Generating Referring Expressions: Constructing Descriptions in a Domain of Objects and Processes.* MIT Press, Cambridge, MA.

Dale, Robert. 1992b. Visible language: Multimodal constraints in information presentation. In Robert Dale, Eduard Hovy, Dietmar Rösner, and Oliviero Stock, editors, *Aspects of Automated Natural Language Generation: Proceedings of the Sixth International Natural Language Generation Workshop.* Springer-Verlag, Berlin.

Dale, Robert, Barbara Di Eugenio, and Donia Scott. 1998. Introduction to the special issue on natural language generation. *Computational Linguistics*, 24(3), September.

Dale, Robert, Eduard H. Hovy, Dietmar Rösner, and Oliviero Stock, editors. 1992. *Aspects of Automated Natural Language Generation.* Lecture Notes in Artificial Intelligence, 587. Springer-Verlag, Berlin, April.

Dale, Robert and Chris Mellish. 1998. Towards evaluation in natural language generation. In *Proceedings of the First International Conference on Language Resources and Evaluation*, Granada, Spain, May 28–30.

Dale, Robert, Chris Mellish, and Michael Zock, editors. 1990. *Current Research in Natural Language Generation.* Academic Press, New York.

Dale, Robert, Jon Oberlander, Maria Milosavljevic, and Alistair Knott. 1999. Integrating natural language generation and hypertext to produce dynamic documents. *Interacting with Computers.*

Dale, Robert and Ehud Reiter. 1995. Computational interpretations of the Gricean maxims in the generation of referring expressions. *Cognitive Science*, 19: 233–263.

Dalianis, Hercules and Eduard Hovy. 1996. Aggregation in natural language generation. In Giovanni Adorni and Michael Zock, editors, *Trends in Natural Language Generation: An Artificial Intelligence Perspective.* Springer, Berlin, pages 88–105.

Danlos, Laurence and Fiammetta Namer. 1988. Morphology and cross dependencies in the synthesis of personal pronouns in Romance languages. In *Proceedings of the 12th International Conference on Computational Linguistics (COLING-88)*, volume 1, pages 139–141.

Davey, Anthony C. 1979. *Discourse Production.* Edinburgh University Press, Edinburgh, Scotland.

Dix, Alan. 1993. *Human-Computer Interaction*. Prentice-Hall, Englewood Cliffs, NJ.

Dixon, Peter. 1982. Plans and written directions for complex tasks. *Journal of Verbal Learning and Verbal Behavior*, 21:70–84.

Dutoit, Thierry. 1997. *An Introduction to Text-to-Speech Synthesis*. Kluwer, Dordrecht, The Netherlands.

Earley, Jay. 1970. An efficient context-free parsing algorithm. *Communications of the ACM*, 13:94–102.

Elhadad, Michael. 1989. FUF: The universal unifier user manual. Technical report, Department of Computer Science, Columbia University, New York.

Elhadad, Michael, Kathleen McKeown, and Jacques Robin. 1997. Floating constraints in lexical choice. *Computational Linguistics*, 23:195–239.

Elhadad, Michael and Jacques Robin. 1997. SURGE: A comprehensive plug-in syntactic realisation component for text generation. Technical report, Computer Science Dept, Ben-Gurion University, Beer Sheva, Israel.

Fauconnier, Gilles. 1985. *Mental Spaces*. MIT Press, Cambridge, MA.

Feiner, Steve and Kathleen McKeown. 1990. Coordinating text and graphics in explanation generation. In *Proceedings of the 8th National Conference on Artificial Intelligence (AAAI-1990)*, volume 1, pages 442–449.

Foley, James, Andries van Dam, Steven Feiner, John Hughes, and Richard Philips. 1994. *Introduction to Computer Graphics*. Addison-Wesley, Reading, MA.

Forsythe, Diana. 1995. Using ethnography in the design of an explanation system. *Expert Systems with Applications*, 8(4):403–417.

Frege, Gottlob. 1977. On sense and reference. In Peter Geach and Max Black, editors, *Translations from the Philosophical Writings of Gottlob Frege*. Blackwell, Oxford, 3rd edition, pages 56–78.

Gazdar, Gerald and Chris Mellish. 1989. *Natural Language Processing in Lisp: An Introduction to Computational Linguistics*. Addison-Wesley, Wokingham, England.

Geldof, Sabine and Walter van de Velde. 1997. An architecture for template based (hyper) text generation. In *Proceedings of the Sixth European Workshop on Natural Language Generation*, pages 28–37, Duisberg, Germany.

Goldberg, Eli, Norbert Driedger, and Richard Kittredge. 1994. Using natural-language processing to produce weather forecasts. *IEEE Expert*, 9(2):45–53.

Goldman, Neil M. 1975. Conceptual generation. In Roger C. Schank and Christopher K. Riesbeck, editors, *Conceptual Information Processing*. American Elsevier, New York.

Grice, H. Paul. 1975. Logic and conversation. In P. Cole and J. Morgan, editors, *Syntax and Semantics: Vol 3, Speech Acts*. Academic Press, New York, pages 43–58.

Grosz, Barbara, Karen Sparck Jones, and Bonnie Webber, editors. 1986. *Readings in Natural Language Processing*. Morgan Kaufmann, Los Altos, CA.

Grosz, Barbara and Candace Sidner. 1986. Attention, intention, and the structure of discourse. *Computational Linguistics*, 12:175–206.

Halliday, Michael A. K. 1985a. *An Introduction to Functional Grammar*. Edward Arnold, London.

Halliday, Michael A. K. 1985b. *Spoken and Written Language*. Deakin University Press, Geelung, Victoria, Australia.

Horacek, Helmut. 1997. An algorithm for generating referential descriptions with flexible interfaces. In *Proceedings of 35th Annual Meeting of the Association for Computational Linguistics (ACL-97)*, pages 206–213.

Horacek, Helmut and Michael Zock, editors. 1993. *New Concepts in Natural Language Generation: Planning, Realization, and Systems*. Pinter Publishers, New York.

Horner, Winifred. 1998. *Harbrace College Handbook*. Holt Rinehart and Winston, New York, thirteenth edition.

Hovy, Eduard. 1988. Planning coherent multisentential text. In *Proceedings of the 26th Annual Meeting of the Association for Computational Linguistics (ACL-88)*, pages 163–169.

Hovy, Eduard H. 1990. Pragmatics and natural language generation. *Artificial Intelligence*, 43(2):153–197, May.

Hovy, Eduard H. 1993. Automated discourse generation using discourse structure relations. *Artificial Intelligence*, 63(1–2):341–385.

Hovy, Eduard H. and Yigal Arens. 1991. Automatic generation of formatted text. In *Proceedings of the Ninth National Conference on Artificial Intelligence (AAAI-91)*, pages 92–97, July 14–19.

Hutchins, William. 1986. *Machine Translation: Past, Present, and Future*. Ellis Horwood, Chichester.

Inui, Kentaro, Takenobu Tokunaga, and Hozumi Tanaka. 1992. Text revision: A model and its implementation. In R. Dale et al., editors, *Aspects of Automated Natural Language Generation: Proceedings of the Sixth International Natural Language Generation Workshop*. Springer-Verlag, Berlin, pages 215–230.

Iordanskaja, Lidija, Myunghee Kim, Richard Kittredge, Benoit Lavoie, and Alian Polguère. 1992. Generation of extended bilingual statistical reports. In *Proceedings of the 14th International Conference on Computational Linguistics (COLING-1992)*, volume 3, pages 1019–1023.

Kasper, Robert. 1989. A flexible interface for linking applications to Penman's sentence generator. In *Proceedings of the 1989 DARPA Speech and Natural Language Workshop*, pages 153–158, Philadelphia.

Kay, Martin. 1979. Functional grammar. In *Proceedings of the Fifth Meeting of the Berkeley Linguistics Society*, pages 142–158, Berkeley, CA, 17–19 February.

Kay, Martin, Jean Mark Gawron, and Peter Norvig. 1994. *Verbmobil: A Translation System for Face-to-Face Dialog*. CSLI/University of Chicago Press, Stanford, CA/Chicago.

Kempen, Gerard, editor. 1987. *Natural Language Generation: New Results in Artificial Intelligence, Psychology and Linguistics.* NATO ASI Series–135. Martinus Nijhoff Publishers, Boston.

Kempen, Gerard. 1989. Language generation systems. In I. S. Batori, W. Lenders, and W. Putschke, editors, *Computational Linguistics: An International Handbook on Computer Oriented Language Research and Applications.* de Gruyter, Berlin, pages 471–480.

Kittredge, Richard, Tanya Korelsky, and Owen Rambow. 1991. On the need for domain communication language. *Computational Intelligence,* 7(4):305–314.

Knott, Alistair. 1996. A Data-Driven Methodology for Motivating a Set of Coherence Relations. Unpublished Ph.D. thesis, University of Edinburgh, Edinburgh.

Knott, Alistair, Chris Mellish, Jon Oberlander, and Mick O'Donnell. 1996. Sources of flexibility in dynamic hypertext generation. In *Proceedings of the Eighth International Workshop on Natural-Language Generation (INLG-1996),* pages 151–160.

Kukich, Karen, Rebecca Passoneau, Kathy McKeown, Dragomir Radev, Vasileios Hatzivassiloglou, and Hongyang Jing. 1997. Software re-use and evolution in text generation applications. In *Proceedings of the ACL-1997 Workshop on From Research to Commercial Applications: Making NLP Work in Practice,* pages 13–21.

Lamport, Leslie. 1994. *LaTeX: A Document Preparation System.* Addison-Wesley, Reading, MA, second edition.

Lavoie, Benoit and Owen Rambow. 1997. A fast and portable realizer for text generation. In *Proceedings of the Fifth Conference on Applied Natural-Language Processing (ANLP-1997),* pages 265–268.

Lavoie, Benoit, Owen Rambow, and Ehud Reiter. 1997. Customizable descriptions of object-oriented models. In *Proceedings of the Fifth Conference on Applied Natural-Language Processing (ANLP-1997),* pages 253–256.

Lenat, Doug. 1995. CYC: A large-scale investment in knowledge infrastructure. *Communications of the ACM,* 38(11).

Lester, James and Bruce Porter. 1997. Developing and empirically evaluating robust explanation generators: The KNIGHT experiments. *Computational Linguistics,* 23(1):65–101.

Levelt, Willem. 1989. *Speaking: From Intention to Articulation.* MIT Press, Cambridge, MA.

Levine, John, Alison Cawsey, Chris Mellish, Lawrence Poynter, Ehud Reiter, Paul Tyson, and John Walker. 1991. IDAS: Combining hypertext and natural language generation. In *Proceedings of the Third European Workshop on Natural Language Generation,* pages 55–62, Innsbruck, Austria.

Levine, John and Chris Mellish. 1995. The IDAS user trials: Quantitative evaluation of an applied natural language generation system. In *Proceedings of the Fifth European Workshop on Natural Language Generation,* pages 75–93, Leiden, The Netherlands.

Lyons, John. 1977. *Semantics*. Cambridge University Press, Cambridge.

Mackinlay, J. 1986. Automating the design of graphical presentations of relational information. *ACM Transactions on Graphics*, 5:110–141.

Maier, Elizabeth and Eduard Hovy. 1993. Organising discourse structure relations using metafunctions. In Helmut Horacek and Michael Zock, editors, *New Concepts in Natural Language Generation*. Pinter, pages 69–86.

Mann, William. 1982. The Anatomy of a Systemic Choice. Technical report ISI/RR-82-104, Information Sciences Institute, Marina del Ray, CA.

Mann, William and Sandra A. Thompson. 1987. Rhetorical Structure Theory: A Theory of Text Organisation. Technical report ISI/RS-87-190, Information Sciences Institute, Marina del Ray, CA.

Mann, William and Sandra Thompson. 1988. Rhetorical structure theory: Towards a functional theory of text organisation. *Text*, 3:243–281.

Mann, William C. 1983. An overview of the NIGEL text generation grammar. In *Proceedings of the 21st Annual Meeting of the ACL*, pages 79–84, Massachusetts Institute of Technology, Cambridge, MA, June 15–17.

Mann, William C. 1987. What is special about natural language generation research? In *Proceedings of the Third Conference on Theoretical Issues in Natural Language Processing (TINLAP-3)*, pages 206–210, New Mexico State University, Las Cruces, New Mexico, January 7–9. See also Wilks (1989).

Mann, William C. and James A. Moore. 1981. Computer generation of multiparagraph English text. *American Journal of Computational Linguistics*, 7(1): 17–29.

Marcu, Daniel. 1997. From local to global coherence: A bottom-up approach to text planning. In *Proceedings of Fourteenth National Conference on Artificial Intelligence (AAAI-1997)*, pages 629–635.

Marks, Joseph and Ehud Reiter. 1990. Avoiding unwanted conversational implicatures in text and graphics. In *Proceedings of the Eighth National Conference on Artificial Intelligence (AAAI-1990)*, pages 450–456.

Martin, James. 1987. *Recommended Diagramming Standards for Analysts and Programmers*. Prentice-Hall, Englewood Cliffs, NJ.

Matthiessen, Christian and John A. Bateman. 1991. *Text Generation and Systemic-Functional Linguistics: Experiences from English and Japanese*. Francis Pinter Publishers, London.

Maybury, Mark, editor. 1993. *Intelligent Multimedia Interfaces*. AAAI Press.

McCoy, Kathleen, Christopher Pennington, and Linda Suri. 1996. Considering the effects of second language learning on generation. In *Proceedings of the Eighth International Workshop on Natural-Language Generation (INLG-1996)*, pages 71–80.

McDonald, David. 1999. Natural language generation. In Robert Dale, Hermann Moisl, and Harold Somers, editors, *A Handbook of Natural Language Processing Techniques*. Marcel Dekker, New York.

McDonald, David D. 1981. MUMBLE: A flexible system for language production.

In *Proceedings of the Seventh International Joint Conference on Artificial Intelligence (IJCAI-81)*, Vol. 2, page 1062, University of British Columbia, Vancouver, BC, August 24–28.

McDonald, David D. 1992. Natural language generation. In Stuart C. Shapiro, editor, *Encyclopedia of Artificial Intelligence*. John Wiley and Sons, New York, 2nd edition, pages 983–997.

McDonald, David D. and Leonard Bolc. 1988. *Natural Language Generation Systems*. Springer-Verlag, New York.

McFedries, Paul. 1997. *The Complete Idiot's Guide to Creating an HTML Web Page*. Que Press, Indianapolis, IN.

McKeown, Kathleen. 1985. *Text Generation*. Cambridge University Press, Cambridge.

McKeown, Kathleen, Karen Kukich, and James Shaw. 1994. Practical issues in automatic document generation. In *Proceedings of the Fourth Conference on Applied Natural-Language Processing (ANLP-1994)*, pages 7–14.

McKeown, Kathleen, Shimei Pan, James Shaw, Desmond Jordon, and Barry Allen. 1997. Language generation for multimedia healthcare briefings. In *Proceedings of the Fifth Conference on Applied Natural-Language Processing (ANLP-1997)*, pages 277–282.

McKeown, Kathleen R., Michael Elhadad, Yumiko Fukumoto, Jong Lim, Christine Lombardi, Jacques Robin, and Frank A. Smadja. 1990. Natural language generation in COMET. In Dale, Mellish, and Zock (1990), pages 103–139.

Mel'čuk, Igor. 1988. *Dependency Syntax: Theory and Practice*. State University of New York Press, Albany, NY.

Mellish, Chris. 1991. Approaches to realization in natural language generation. In E. Klein and F. Veltman, editors, *Natural Language and Speech, Symposium Proceedings*, pages 95–116. Springer-Verlag, Berlin.

Meteer, Marie. 1991. Bridging the generation gap between text planning and linguistic realization. *Computational Intelligence*, 7(4):296–304, November.

Milosavljevic, Maria. 1997. Content selection in comparison generation. In *Proceedings of the 6th European Workshop on Natural Language Generation*, pages 72–81, 24–26 March 1997.

Milosavljevic, Maria and Robert Dale. 1996. Strategies for comparison in encyclopedia descriptions. In *Proceedings of the Eighth International Workshop on Natural-Language Generation (INLG-1996)*, pages 161–170.

Milosavljevic, Maria, Adrian Tulloch, and Robert Dale. 1996. Text generation in a dynamic hypertext environment. In *Proceedings of the 19th Australasian Computer Science Conference*, pages 417–426, Melbourne, Australia, 31 January–2 February.

Mittal, Vibhu, Johanna Moore, Giuseppe Carenini, and Steven Roth. 1998. Describing complex charts in natural language: A caption generation system. *Computational Linguistics*, 24(3):431–467.

Moore, Johanna. 1994. *Participating in Explanatory Dialogues*. MIT Press, Cambridge, MA.

Moore, Johanna and Cecile Paris. 1993. Planning text for advisory dialogues. *Computational Linguistics*, 19:651–694.

Nogier, Jean-François and Michael Zock. 1991. Lexical choice as pattern matching. In T. Nagle, J. Nagle, L. Gerholz, and P. Elklund, editors, *Current directions in conceptual structures research*. Springer, Berlin.

Nunberg, Geoffrey. 1990. *The Linguistics of Punctuation*. Number 18 in CSLI Lecture Notes. University of Chicago Press, Chicago.

Osman, Liesl, Mona Abdalla, James Beattie, Susan Ross, Ian Russell, James Friend, Joseph Legge, and Graham Douglas. 1994. Reducing hospital admission through computer supported education for asthma patients. *British Medical Journal*, 308:568–571.

Paris, Cecile. 1988. Tailoring object descriptions to the user's level of expertise. *Computational Linguistics*, 14(3):64–78.

Paris, Cecile, Keith Vander Linden, Marcus Fischer, Anthony Hartley, Lyn Pemberton, Richard Power, and Donia Scott. 1995. A support tool for writing multilingual instructions. In *Proceedings of the Fourteenth International Joint Conference on Artificial Intelligence (IJCAI-1995)*, pages 1398–1404.

Paris, Cécile L., William R. Swartout, and William C. Mann, editors. 1991. *Natural Language Generation in Artificial Intelligence and Computational Linguistics*. Kluwer Academic Publishers, Boston.

Pattabhiraman, T. and Nick Cercone. 1991. Introduction to the special issue on natural language generation. *Computational Intelligence*, 7(4), November.

Pereira, Fernando and David Warren. 1980. Definite clause grammars for language analysis. *Artificial Intelligence*, 13:231–278.

Petre, Marian. 1995. Why looking isn't always seeing: Readership skills and graphical programming. *Communications of the ACM*, 38(6):33–44.

Pinker, Stephen. 1994. *The Language Instinct*. Lane, London.

Polanyi, Livia. 1988. A formal model of the structure of discourse. *Journal of Pragmatics*, 12:601–638.

Pollard, Carl and Ivan Sag. 1994. *Head Driven Phrase Structure Grammar*. University of Chicago Press, Chicago.

Pressman, Roger, editor. 1997. *Software Engineering: A Practitioner's Approach (Fourth Edition)*. McGraw-Hill, New York.

Prevost, Scott. 1996. An information structural approach to spoken language generation. In *Proceedings of the 34th Annual Meeting of the Association for Computational Linguistics*, Santa Cruz, May 28–30.

Quirk, Randolph. 1985. *A Comprehensive Grammar of the English Language*. Longman, Harlow.

Rambow, Owen and Tanya Korelsky. 1992. Applied text generation. In *Proceedings of the Third ACL Conference on Applied Natural Language Processing*, pages 40–47, Trento, Italy.

Reichman, Rachel. 1985. *Getting Computers to Talk Like You and Me*. MIT Press, Cambridge, MA.

Reiter, Ehud. 1990. The computational complexity of avoiding conversational implicatures. In *Proceedings of the 28th Annual Meeting of the ACL*, pages 97–104, University of Pittsburgh, Pittsburgh, PA, June 6–9.

Reiter, Ehud. 1991. A new model of lexical choice for nouns. *Computational Intelligence*, 7(4):240–251.

Reiter, Ehud. 1994. Has a consensus NL Generation architecture appeared, and is it psycholinguistically plausible? In *Proceedings of the Seventh International Workshop on Natural Language Generation (INLGW-1994)*, pages 163–170.

Reiter, Ehud. 1995a. NLG vs. templates. In *Proceedings of the Fifth European Workshop on Natural Language Generation*, pages 95–105, Leiden, The Netherlands.

Reiter, Ehud. 1995b. Sublanguages in text and graphics. In John Lee, editor, *Proceedings of the First International Workshop on Intelligence and Multimodality in Multimedia Interfaces (IMMI-1995)*, HCRC, University of Edinburgh, Edinburgh, Scotland.

Reiter, Ehud, Alison Cawsey, Liesl Osman, and Yvonne Roff. 1997. Knowledge acquisition for content selection. In *Proceedings of the Sixth European Workshop on Natural Language Generation*, pages 117–126, Duisberg, Germany.

Reiter, Ehud and Chris Mellish. 1993. Optimizing the costs and benefits of natural language generation. In *Proceedings of the Thirteenth International Joint Conference on Artificial Intelligence (IJCAI-1993)*, pages 1164–1169.

Reiter, Ehud, Chris Mellish, and John Levine. 1995. Automatic generation of technical documentation. *Applied Artificial Intelligence*, 9(3):259–287.

Reiter, Ehud and Liesl Osman. 1997. Tailored patient information: Some issues and questions. In *Proceedings of the ACL-1997 Workshop on From Research to Commercial Applications: Making NLP Work in Practice*, pages 29–34, Madrid, Spain.

Reiter, Ehud, Roma Robertson, and Liesl Osman. 1999. Types of knowledge required to personalise smoking cessation letters. In Werner Horn et al. (Eds.), *Proceedings of the Joint European Conference on Artificial Intelligence in Medicine and Medical Decision Making (AIMDM'99)*, pages 389–399, Springer-Verlag, Berlin.

Rist, Thomas, Elizabeth André, and Jochen Müller. 1997. Adding animated presentation agents to the interface. In *Proceedings of the 1997 International Conference on Intelligent User Interfaces*, pages 79–86.

Ritchie, Graeme, Graham Russell, Alan Black, and Stephen Pulman. 1992. *Computational Morphology: Practical Mechanisms for the English Lexicon*. MIT Press, Cambridge, MA.

Robin, Jacques and Kathleen McKeown. 1996. Empirically designing and evaluating a new revision-based model for summary generation. *Artificial Intelligence*, 85:135–179.

Roth, Steven and William Hefley. 1993. Intelligent multimedia presentation systems: Research and principles. In Mark Maybury, editor, *Intelligent Multimedia Interfaces*. AAAI Press, pages 13–58.

Rubinoff, Robert. 1992. Integrating text planning and linguistic choice by annotating linguistic structures. In R. Dale et al., editors, *Aspects of Automated Natural Language Generation: Proceedings of the Sixth International Natural Language Generation Workshop*. Springer-Verlag, pages 45–56.

Russell, Stuart and Peter Norvig. 1995. *Artificial Intelligence: A Modern Approach*. Prentice-Hall, Englewood Cliffs, NJ.

Scott, A. Carlisle, Jan Clayton, and Elizabeth Gibson. 1991. *A Practical Guide to Knowledge Acquisition*. Addison-Wesley, Reading, MA.

Scott, Donia R. and Clarisse Sieckenius de Souza. 1990. Getting the message across in RST-based text generation. In Dale, Mellish, and Zock (1990), pages 47–73.

Seligmann, Doree and Steven Feiner. 1991. Automated generation of intent-based 3D illustrations. *Computer Graphics*, 25:123–132.

Shaw, James. 1998a. Clause aggregation using linguistic knowledge. In *Proceedings of the Ninth International Workshop on Natural Language Generation (INLG-1998)*, pages 138–147.

Shaw, James. 1998b. Segregatory coordination and ellipsis in text generation. In *Proceedings of 36th Annual Meeting of the Association for Computational Linguistics and the 17th International Conference on Computational Linguistics (COLING-ACL '98)*, pages 1220–1226.

Shieber, Stuart, Gertjan van Noord, Fernando Pereira, and Robert Moore. 1990. Semantic-head-driven generation. *Computational Linguistics*, 16:30–42.

Shieber, Stuart M. 1988. A uniform architecture for parsing and generation. In *Proceedings of the 12th International Conference on Computational Linguistics (COLING-88)*, volume 1, pages 614–619, Budapest, August 22–27.

Shneiderman, Ben. 1998. *Designing the User Interface: Strategies for Effective Human-Computer Interaction*. Addison-Wesley, Reading, MA, third edition.

Smith, Edward and Douglas Medin. 1981. *Categories and Concepts*. Harvard University Press, Cambridge, MA.

Sonnenschein, Susan. 1985. The development of referential communication skills: Some situations in which speakers give redundant messages. *Journal of Psycholinguistic Research*, 14:489–508.

Springer, Stephen, Paul Buta, and Thomas Wolf. 1991. Automatic letter composition for customer service. In Reid Smith and Carlisle Scott, editors, *Innovative Applications of Artificial Intelligence 3 (Proceedings of CAIA-1991)*. AAAI Press.

Stede, Manfred. 1996. Lexical options in multilingual generation from a knowledge base. In Giovanni Adorni and Michael Zock, editors, *Trends in Natural Language Generation: An Artificial Intelligence Perspective*. Springer, Berlin, pages 222–237.

Stenning, Keith and Jon Oberlander. 1995. A cognitive theory of graphical and linguistic reasoning: Logic and implementation. *Cognitive Science*, 19:97–140.

Sugiyama, Kozo, Shojiro Tagawa, and Mitsuhiko Toda. 1981. Methods for visual understanding of hierarchical system structures. *IEEE Transactions on Systems, Man, and Cybernetics*, SMC-11(2):109–125.

Teich, Elke. 1998. *Systemic Functional Grammar in Natural Language Generation: Linguistic Description and Computational Representation*. Cassell Academic Publishers, London.

Thompson, Henry. 1977. Strategy and tactics: A model for language production. In *Papers from the 13th Regional Meeting of the Chicago Linguistics Society*, Chicago.

Tufte, Edward. 1983. *The Visual Display of Quantitative Information*. Graphics Press, Cheshire, CT.

Tufte, Edward. 1990. *Envisioning Information*. Graphics Press, Cheshire, CT.

University of Chicago Press. 1993. *The Chicago Manual of Style*. University of Chicago Press, fourteenth edition.

Uschold, Mike and Michael Gruniger. 1996. Ontologies: Principles, methods, and applications. *Knowledge Engineering Review*, 11(2).

van Deemter, Kees and Jan Odijk. 1997. Context modeling and the generation of spoken discourse. *Speech Communication*, 21:101–121.

van Noord, Gertjan. 1990. An overview of head-driven bottom-up generation. In Robert Dale, Chris Mellish, and Michael Zock, editors, *Current Research in Natural Language Generation*. Academic Press, New York, pages 141–165.

Vander Linden, Keith and James Martin. 1995. Expressing rhetorical relations in instructional texts: A case study of the purpose relation. *Computational Linguistics*, 21(1):29–57.

Wahlster, Wolfgang, Elisabeth André, Wolfgang Finkler, Hans-Jürgen Profitlich, and Thomas Rist. 1993. Plan-based integration of natural language and graphics generation. *Artificial Intelligence*, 63:387–427.

Wanner, Leo and Eduard Hovy. 1996. The HealthDoc sentence planner. In *Proceedings of the Eighth International Workshop on Natural-Language Generation (INLG-1996)*, pages 1–10.

White, Michael. 1995. Presenting punctuation. In *Proceedings of the Fifth European Workshop on Natural Language Generation*, pages 107–125.

Wilks, Yorick, editor. 1989. *Theoretical Issues in Natural Language Processing (TINLAP-3)*. Lawrence Erlbaum Associates, Hillsdale, NJ.

Winograd, Terry. 1983. *Language as a Cognitive Process*, volume 1. Addison Wesley, Reading, MA.

Yeh, Ching-Long and Chris Mellish. 1997. An empirical study on the generation of anaphora in Chinese. *Computational Linguistics*, 23(1):169–190.

Zock, Michael and Gérard Sabah, editors. 1988a. *Advances in Natural Language Generation: An Interdisciplinary Perspective*, volume 1. Ablex Publishing Corporation, Norwood, NJ.

Zock, Michael and Gérard Sabah, editors. 1988b. *Advances in Natural Language Generation: An Interdisciplinary Perspective*, volume 2. Ablex Publishing Corporation, Norwood, NJ.

Index

abstract syntactic structure, 69, 75, 120–2,
134, 137, 168–9
  as realiser input, 173, 191, 193
aggregation, 14–15, 49, 56–7, 93, 132–44,
157–8
  architectural issues, 65, 74–5, 116,
  156–7
  hypotactic, *see* embedding, syntactic
  and lexicalisation, 129, 139
  and typography, 206–7
ALETHGEN, 5–6, 38, 191, 229
ambiguity, 147, 148, 151, 196
anaphor, *see* referring expressions
architecture
  document planner, 110–12
  microplanner, 122–4
  non-pipeline, 76–7, 115, 122, 157
  pipeline, 59–60, 72, 76–7, 78, 111, 123
  two-stage, 75, 115–16
artificial intelligence, 2, 21, 86, 100–1
attentional state, 148
attribute-value matrix (AVM), 61
authoring aid, 5, 6, 34–5

Bulgarian, 172

canned text, 68–9, 75, 135–6, 137, 169,
193–4
category
  content determination, 100–1
  syntactic, 127–8, 180
champion, 39

choice
  aggregation, 140–2
  lexical, 52–5, 57, 126–9
  of a realiser, 192–4, 197
  syntactic, 52, 227
choosers, 177–8
classes, *see* concepts
clause, 176
  embedded, 139–40, 142
  relative, 139, 142, 157
clinical trial, 17, 39
collocation, 131
comparisons, 96
complexity
  computational, 153
  syntactic, 140–1
computer aided software engineering, 6,
14–15
concepts, 61, 86–8, 144, 174
concept-to-speech, 225–7
conciseness, 128, 140–1, *see also*
constraint, size or length
condition-action, 141
conjunction
  shared participants, 136
  shared structure, 137–9
  simple, 133–6
connectives, *see* conjunction
consistency, 29, 36, 90, 128
constituent, textual, 33–5
constraint
  satisfaction, 77, 101, 108

www.ingramcontent.com/pod-product-compliance
Ingram Content Group UK Ltd.
Pitfield, Milton Keynes, MK11 3LW, UK
UKHW040704180125
453697UK00010B/397

9 780521 024518